DAMN DUTCH

Pennsylvania Germans
at Gettysburg

DAMN DUTCH

Pennsylvania Germans at Gettysburg

David L. Valuska and Christian B. Keller

With contributions by
Scott Hartwig and Martin Oefele

Foreword by Don Yoder

STACKPOLE
BOOKS

Originally published in hardcover by Stackpole Books, copyright ©2004

Published 2010 in paperback by
STACKPOLE BOOKS
5067 Ritter Road
Mechanicsburg, PA 17055
www.stackpolebooks.com

Printed in the United States of America

10 9 8 7 6 5 4 3 2 1

FIRST PAPERBACK EDITION

Cover design by Wendy Reynolds

Cover: The 93rd P.V.I., from the Robert Diem Collection, U.S. Army Military History Institute

ISBN-13: 978-0-8117-0674-2 (paperback)
ISBN-10: 0-8117-0674-5 (paperback)

Library of Congress Cataloging-in-Publication Data

Valuska, David L., 1938–
    Damn Dutch : Pennsylvania Germans at Gettysburg / David L. Valuska and Christian B. Keller
        p. cm.
    Includes bibliographical references and index.
    ISBN 0-8117-0074-7
    1. Gettysburg, Battle of, Gettysburg, Pa., 1863. 2. Pennsylvania—History—Civil War, 1861–1865—Participation, German American. 3. United States—History—Civil War, 1861–1865—Participation, German American.
4. Pennsylvania—History—Civil War, 1861–1865—Regimental histories.
5. United States—History—Civil War, 1861–1865—Regimental histories.
6. Pennsylvania Dutch—History. I. Keller, Christian B. II. Title.
E475.53 .V235 2010
97307'349–dc22
                                2003014343

Contents

Maps

FOREWORD

Don Yoder

This book neatly traces the participation in and reaction to the Civil War on the part of Pennsylvania's "Germans"—both the Pennsylvania Dutch of the seventeenth, eighteenth, and early nineteenth century migrations and the later emigrants from German-speaking Central Europe who arrived in the nineteenth century, the so-called German-Americans. These two groups were not the same, despite their common German ethnic origins, their use of the German language, and in some cases their denominational adherence.

They did not always get along in America. The Pennsylvania Dutch were more adjusted to the overarching American culture; the German-Americans—especially the political refugees from the failed revolutions of 1830 and 1848—were often still linked emotionally to the German *Vaterland* and preferred to settle in "Little Germanies," very often in major cities like Philadelphia, Cincinnati, Louisville, Cleveland, St. Louis, Chicago, and Milwaukee. There were, of course, rural German-Americans too, but most of them settled in the Midwest, while the solid agricultural base of the Pennsylvania Dutch was in Pennsylvania, but with significant daughter colonies in the South, Ontario, the Midwest, and the Plains States.

The Civil War, America's first modern war, with all its military innovations and social tragedies, had profound social and psychological effects on both groups. Judging from the Pennsylvania county histories, most of the able men in every township of the Dutch Country in Eastern, Central, and Western Pennsylvania were taken into the army—and many never returned.

The women of the area were often left with small children and without adequate male help on their farms.

For the Pennsylvania Dutch, this radical uprooting of the men and their constant contacts with Anglo-American soldiers and Southerners helped to shape up their own ethnic consciousness, the sense of who they were as Americans as distinct from other American groups. And by being thrown together with the German-Americans during the war, the Dutchmen became aware of the social and cultural gulf that separated the two groups, which gave powerful impetus to the development of a separate, independent Pennsylvania Dutch consciousness.

The authors deftly examine the Pennsylvania regiments that included German-Americans and those with large Pennsylvania Dutch components—an ethnographic analysis never before available.

The battle of Gettysburg, the turning point of the war, is the central theme of the book, and the story of its preliminaries, the battle itself, and its results are told through fascinating local sources—diaries of Dutch farm wives who describe the incursions of the Southern forces, official missives of ministers and newspaper editors, and letters sent home by common soldiers in blue uniform—a rich vein of personal testimony on the whole human tragedy of war.

My compliments to David L. Valuska, Christian B. Keller, and their collaborators for a valuable, original, and absorbing book. It will take its place on the shelves of Pennsylvania history, American ethnic studies, and analyses of the German-Americans and the Pennsylvania Dutch—and above all, it will be welcomed across the country by students of the Civil War.

Roughwood
Devon, Pennsylvania

ACKNOWLEDGMENTS

In the course of researching and writing this book, we have jointly and individually incurred many debts. We are grateful to all who assisted us in the preparation and completion of this study, which is the culmination of more than twenty years between us of thought, research, rumination, and reflection. Most particularly, we would like to express our thanks to the countless archivists and librarians who helped us: Richard Sommers of the Military History Institute, Carlisle Barracks, Pennsylvania; Michael Musick of the National Archives, Washington, D.C.; the research staff of the Pennsylvania German Cultural Heritage Center at Kutztown University; and the staff of the library of the German Society of Pennsylvania, Philadelphia.

Don Yoder, Robert Kline, Troy Boyer, Roland Paul, Dave Fooks, and William Donner provided encouragement and support, and without their constructive criticism and input, the story of the Pennsylvania Dutch soldiers would not have been told accurately. Gary W. Gallagher, Mark E. Neely Jr., Carol Reardon, William Pencak, Joerg Nagler, Wolfgang Hochbruck, and Andrea Mehrlaender all provided expert counsel, camaraderie, and unique insights into the lives of German-American soldiers. We are also indebted to the members of the various Pennsylvania Dutch Grundsow Lodges and Fersommlings and to the students in our ethnic and Civil War courses in both the United States and Germany.

Kutztown University provided a sabbatical leave, and grants provided by the German Historical Institute, Washington, D.C., and the Friends of the National Parks at Gettysburg were critical in supplying much-needed financial assistance during the research phases of the book. A year of teaching and researching in Germany, awarded by C.I.E.S. and the Fulbright Commission, allowed Chris to spend countless pleasant hours discussing the intricacies of German-American history with good friends and colleagues.

Our two contributors, Martin Oefele, formerly of the American Studies Department at the University of Munich, and Scott Hartwig, chief historian of Gettysburg National Military Park, were delightful to work with. Their patience and forbearance throughout this process were much appreciated. We also wish to thank Mary Henry of the Pennsylvania German Cultural Heritage Center for her administrative and translational support. Thanks also to Kyle Weaver and Amy Cooper at Stackpole Books for their support and encouragement.

Without the love, patience, and understanding of our wives, Deborah E. B. Keller and Charlotte N. Valuska, this book would not exist. David's children Andrea and Joanne and his grandchildren Elizabeth, Charlotte, and David G., and Chris's mother, Patricia, were sources of joy and emotional comfort.

To all those who have gone unmentioned here but who helped us in innumerable ways, we extend our heartfelt thanks.

INTRODUCTION

Christian B. Keller and David L. Valuska

In her landmark work *Foreigners in the Union Army and Navy,* Ella Lonn claims that in 1860 the German-born population of the United States numbered 1,301,136 citizens, and of these, 138,244 resided in Pennsylvania.[1] In addition to these foreign-born residents, Pennsylvania was home to hundreds of thousands of people of remoter German ancestry who retained German folkways and spoke a dialect combining German and English. Commonly referred to as the "Pennsylvania Dutch" (or "Dutch," for short), these individuals were also ethnically German and, along with the German-born inhabitants and their immediate offspring—called "German-Americans" in this book—composed a large portion of Pennsylvania's population on the eve of the Civil War. Some historians have estimated that the total German-speaking population in Civil War-era Pennsylvania was approximately one-third of the state's citizenry.[2] If one also considered the number of Pennsylvanians of German ethnicity who no longer spoke German in the 1860s, that proportion would certainly be higher. Clearly, the Germans in Pennsylvania were demographically important.

It is not just their sheer numbers, however, that make the Keystone State's Germans a worthy subject of historical inquiry. Their experiences also demonstrate the power that ethnic identity had on both ethnic and nonethnic Americans during the Civil War. Indeed, during the campaign and battle of Gettysburg, ethnic consciousness permeated the daily lives of civilians and soldiers and played a major role in directing their behavior.

The battle of Gettysburg was not won because of the Pennsylvania Germans. But their role in the battle was significant, and as the following chapters show, Pennsylvania Dutch and German-American troops participated in many of the critical actions taken on the battlefield during those three bloody days. In certain instances, their regiments saved the Union's fortunes, but the same could be said of the regiments of other states and other ethnicities. The Pennsylvania Germans of both varieties were not the only Germans in the North during the conflict, and they were certainly not the only ethnic Americans. Their experiences at Gettysburg, however, were representative of both groups.

Books about the American Civil War number in the thousands. Very few, however, deal with ethnic minorities, who collectively composed a large percentage of the Union armies. Of that small number of books, even fewer specifically examine the Germans, who may have been neglected by historians because of the language of many of the primary sources and the comparatively stronger scholarly interest in the Irish. The handful of works that have examined the Germans in the war—such as those by Lonn, William Burton, and Wilhelm Kaufmann—are outdated, filiopietistic, or based primarily on secondary sources. A small number of regimental histories and an excellent biography of Franz Sigel have appeared in recent years, but they are handicapped by their necessarily restricted scope, and none deals with Germans from Pennsylvania.[3]

This book provides a unique perspective on Pennsylvania's German-speaking peoples in the middle nineteenth century and combines traditional military history with social and ethnic history. By relying on many of the primary German-language and dialect sources passed over by previous scholars, and by examining the state with perhaps the largest ethnically German population in 1860, we hope to raise several important questions about ethnic identity and, specifically, its role in the American Civil War: How did temporal differences among German immigrants affect their behavior during the conflict? How did the Germans interpret the war through their ethnic lenses? How did religious denomination become an important ethnic identifier? How well did the German regiments fight at Gettysburg, and what was their significance in the Union victory? How was the Americanization process affected (if at all) by the Pennsylvania Germans' participation at Gettysburg? The answers to these historical questions are important not only in a corrective sense, shedding light on our understanding of the role of ethnic Germans in the war, but also in an

instructive sense, presenting concepts that might be useful to those interested in ethnicity in the nineteenth-century United States, the evolution of
ethnic identity, or the behavior of modern ethnic groups during a time
of national crisis.

One of the primary problems confronting historians working with
minority groups is how to identify persons in their subject group. This
study faced the same problem, and although use of the German language
was the primary identifier, other clues in the sources helped single out
those acceptable for use. Nonethnic sources, such as English-language
newspapers, were essential in providing legitimacy and context, but they
had to be carefully evaluated when used as the primary source for a given
subject. The role of the church and the use of church records as ethnic
signposts presented another problematic issue, along with the perennial
question of who spoke for the mass of the people. For example, newspaper
editors were certainly leaders in their communities, but were they in touch
with the sentiments of the majority of their readers?

The following chapters draw on a variety of sources. Collections of
letters or firsthand accounts (such as diaries and memoirs) from soldiers in
both the German-American and Pennsylvania Dutch regiments proved
critical. Many of these letters exist as manuscripts in various archives
throughout Pennsylvania, and several were published in the German-
language newspapers. We have translated material from these sources where
appropriate. Letter collections from non-Germans provided context to the
German accounts, and published memoirs and diaries from Pennsylvania
Dutch civilians were essential in analyzing the reaction to the Confederate
invasion in the summer of 1863. Many of the non-German accounts were
taken from published secondary sources.

The regimental Day, Order, Letter, and Record Books of the primary
German-American regiments, located at the National Archives, proved
useful in examining their battlefield performance. German-language newspapers published in Pittsburgh, Philadelphia, Allentown, Reading, and
Skippackville were also important primary sources. They contained many
of the more vivid soldiers' letters and editorial responses to the Eleventh
Corps' performance on the first day at Gettysburg. Thirteen of the most
influential English-language newspapers were the major tools in analyzing
Anglo-American reactions to the German troops' performance, which in
turn influenced the response of the German-American editors. The *Official
Records of the Union and Confederate Armies* was useful for officers' postaction

reports, and countless secondary sources contained firsthand accounts, provided historiographical background, or left clues for further research.[4]

Retention of the German language was the most critical factor when
examining the authors or subjects of source materials. Hence, determining
the identity of Pennsylvania's German-Americans was not particularly difficult. These people all spoke German as their first language, so nearly all
records left by them, such as letters, diaries, memoirs, and regimental
descriptive books, were written in German.[5] Additionally, their major newspapers, published in Philadelphia and Pittsburgh, were written in German
and served the German speakers of these cities. As mentioned earlier, the
rubric "German-American" represents not only German immigrants born
in Europe but also their children and grandchildren, with language again
being the primary identifier. Little distinction is made between original
immigrants and their descendants in this book, since, as many ethnic scholars have argued, the urban neighborhoods were home to several generations of German speakers. If the children and grandchildren left records in
German, we considered them part of the immigrant German community.

Another method of identifying German-American soldiers involved
distinguishing the ethnically German regiments from the nonethnic ones.
Kaufmann, Lonn, and Burton agree that certain infantry regiments, partic-
ularly the 27th, 73d, 74th, 75th, and 98th Pennsylvania, were ethnically
German and were recruited from the urban German neighborhoods of
Philadelphia and Pittsburgh. After checking their claims against the official
regimental records in the National Archives and the Pennsylvania State
Archives, it became evident that these regiments were unquestionably German in character and composition, though some had higher percentages of
Germans than others. In general, the litmus test used to identify a German
regiment was whether the Regimental Order Book was written at some
point in German (reasoning that a non-German regiment would not record
its daily and monthly orders in a foreign language). Hence, the regimental
books and papers of these units were key source materials.[6]

The Pennsylvania Dutch were more challenging to identify. Although
the preferred method of communication among them was the Pennsylvanisch Deitsch dialect, this was considered a spoken language, and no official records were ever kept in this dialect during the Civil War. Further,
newspapers and most church records were printed in High German, making it difficult to distinguish the Dutch from the German-Americans based
only on language differences in these sources. Additionally, many Dutch

soldiers and civilians, more familiar with written English than with written German, wrote their letters and diaries in English—which they could muddle through better than the High German they heard only in church or read only in newspapers. As many scholars have argued, some Pennsylvania Dutch were more anglicized than others by the 1860s; some had become English speakers and subscribed to English-language newspapers. Yet most of these people still retained strong German folkways and traditions and remained members of the major German religious denominations. Thus, were they actually ethnic Germans?

We argue that they were, making them eligible for inclusion in our analysis. Since determination of their German ethnicity could not be completely verified by checking their surnames—a practice many genealogists and even some historians have condoned in the past—background information that comments on their ethnicity, such as religious denomination, is included if available. Frequently, letters from Pennsylvania Dutch people written in English betrayed their German background simply by their spelling (*Gott* versus *God,* for example, or *spelt* instead of *spelled*), by the use of peculiarly German idioms, or by frequent references to religious philosophies well known as belonging to German denominations. These details are highlighted throughout the chapters, when possible, to reinforce the legitimacy of a source's inclusion in the analysis. The Pennsylvania Dutch newspapers, though linguistically almost identical to their urban German counterparts, can be easily identified by their place of publication. A paper published in Reading, for instance, the county seat of primarily Dutch Berks County, would have been read mainly by Pennsylvania Dutch and not by German-Americans.

Two critical questions need to be answered at this point. First, does religious denomination equate with or compose a large part of ethnic identity? Nora Helen Faires, Steven Nolt, and a host of other authors have argued that religion often became the defining characteristic of American ethnic groups. Faires explains that "the Church played a greater role for many ethnic groups than it did in the society the immigrants left. Religious values are readily transferable cultural ideas. Hence the first institution established in many immigrant communities was the church. The failure to reestablish other social institutions often caused the church to take on some of the functions which these other institutions had performed in the old society." The church defined a large part of the ethnic identity for many ethnic groups in the nineteenth century, particularly those that may have

shed other, more obvious ethnic traits, such as native language. In some
ethnic groups, the "parish house became a social center, supplanting the
village square as the place where friends gathered to socialize." This was particularly true for many of the German sectarians, who were prohibited from
unnecessary contact with "outsiders" and viewed their religious doctrines
as rules that governed their daily lives. Robert P. Swierenga adds that "while
a few immigrants were secularists, for the vast majority religion and ethnicity were so closely intertwined as to be indistinguishable." Religion was
undoubtedly a key component of ethnicity for both types of Pennsylvania
Germans. Hence official religious records, such as minutes from synodic
meetings and letters between religious leaders, are included as evidence in
some chapters. In the case of nonofficial source materials written in English,
if a plausible connection could be made to a German religious denomination, the author was categorized as ethnically German.[7]

The second question involves the reliability of newspaper editorials as
representations of a public consensus. Regardless of their specific field, historians have struggled with this problem since newspapers became an
acceptable source for research. William Joyce, a specialist on the nineteenth-
century Irish-American press, has argued that editors of major urban newspapers were an "immigrant elite" who played a critical role in how others
of their ethnic group interpreted "native culture, American culture, and the
immigrant's relation to both." The editors, although not necessarily of the
same socioeconomic class as the bulk of their readers, nonetheless provided
leadership that both guided and responded to the attitudes and needs of the
ethnic groups living where their papers circulated. One of the primary
roles of the editors was defining "the process of [ethnic] adjustment to
American society," so the editorials of the major newspapers focused on
issues of interest to the specific ethnic group. In the case of the Irish-
American press, Joyce explains that "the handful of powerful editors and
publishers dominating the Irish-American press had a critical influence on
the transformation of the social identity of Irish immigrants."[8]

Historians examining the German-language press in the United States,
many of whom specialized in the radical German labor movement, concur
with Joyce's observations. Renate Kiesewetter, for example, writing about
Chicago's German-language labor newspapers, concludes that "an editor
who wrote the daily editorial could play a considerable role in shaping
political opinion." Ken Fones-Wolf and Elliott Shore, in their study of
Philadelphia's Gilded Age German-language press, maintain that the edi-

tors could not ignore the opinions of their readers and had to write editorials reflective of their subscribers' beliefs: "The German-language press was not able to simply overwhelm its working-class clientele with the ethnic elite's perspectives. Instead, it played a far more vital role among the German-American working class when it recognized the political and cultural demands of immigrant wage earners." The practices of editors of the Pennsylvania German-language newspapers during the Civil War could not have differed substantially from those of other ethnic and German editors; thus, this study implicitly accepts the notion that their editorials more or less represented the opinions of their readers.[9]

We believe the following chapters stand well enough on their own without prior explanation; however, we tried to follow a rough chronological format for the book. We also included what may at first glance appear to be simply a rehash of well-worn battle history, but this information is necessary to better place the experiences of Pennsylvania's Germans in their proper context.

CHAPTER 1

Diverse German Immigrants and Ethnic Identity on the Eve of the Civil War

Christian B. Keller

More than three decades ago, noted Pennsylvania historian Philip S. Klein identified three major historical questions encountered by scholars researching the Pennsylvania Germans: who they were, exactly; why so little had been written about them; and how much they had acculturated into mainstream American society. This book, by examining ethnic Germans in Pennsylvania during the Civil War, deals with the same questions in light of the battle of Gettysburg. This chapter begins by explaining the differences between the two major German-speaking populations of the state, how they conceived of themselves and others, and what condition their communities were in on the eve of war.[1]

In 1860, Germans in Pennsylvania—both the Pennsylvania Dutch and the German-Americans—were "ethnic Americans" by most historical standards. What exactly defines an ethnic American, however, has been exhaustively debated and increasingly refined over the last half century. Historians John Higham and Oscar Handlin and sociologist Milton Gordon provided much of the modern theoretical basis in the 1950s and early 1960s with their substantiation of the traditional "melting-pot" theory of immigration, which argued that the European ethnics of the nineteenth century essentially merged into the greater American society after only two or three generations in the United States. Constant exposure to and interaction with the "core culture," the melting-pot theorists argued, inevitably forced immigrants into the American mold, a positive result that produced social harmony for both ethnics and nonethnics alike. But only a few years after the melting-pot explanation of ethnic America had seemingly settled the question, a contrary perspective called "cultural pluralism" gained favor, which valued diversity in society and regarded the melting pot as a false and harmful ideal. To a degree, this approach was influenced by the social upheavals of the 1960s and early 1970s, but it became the foundation for the "new ethnicity," which celebrated the survival of ethnicity in the modern United States.[2]

The new ethnicity, championed by scholars such as Nathan Glazer and Daniel Moynihan, argued that ethnic Americans could be both ethnics and Americans simultaneously, as they had been throughout the nineteenth century. This school of thought, and the works drawn from it, provided the first scholarly treatments of "ethnic identity," a difficult term to define, but critical for a discussion about Pennsylvania Germans. Most scholars agree that the formation of ethnic identity is an exceedingly complex process that begins when an immigrant "steps off the boat" and is strengthened or weakened depending on whether the original immigrant and his or her offspring live among others like them—in ethnic neighborhoods, for instance—or choose to live outside the confines of these communities. Language, religion, and fraternal and professional associations all contribute significantly to building personal identity and produce an ethnic consciousness in both individuals and groups. Ethnic identity and the rate of assimilation are thus closely intertwined and influence each other. Recent studies also suggest that ethnic identity changes among the generations, allowing a resurgence of ethnic traits in younger generations that were spurned by older ones, or that one's ethnic identity may be the result of "invented" traditions or cultural mores adopted over time to replace the older, original ones lost long ago.[3]

Don Yoder has written extensively on nearly every aspect of the Pennsylvania Germans and is regarded as one of the foremost experts in the field. In particular, he is interested in the development and preservation of ethnicity among the Pennsylvania Dutch. His explanation of ethnic identity not only distills many of the arguments of the aforementioned scholars into a tight description but also is subject specific and particularly useful to a book about Pennsylvania Germans in the Civil War. According to Yoder:

> Ethnic consciousness, or ethnic identity, is an attitude toward one-self and one's cultural world, which is shaped in individuals and eventually in groups through contact with other self-conscious

groups of human beings with whom one comes into regular contact. Although a sense of group identification exists in most ethnic groups, it varies from individual to individual, from mildly passive consciousness of one's ethnic roots to the ardent ethnicity of activist leaders who want to "do something" to defend, protect, and advance the group and its culture.

This definition applies to both Pennsylvania Dutch and German-Americans, since both groups possessed their own separate ethnic identities during the period of the Civil War—while still remaining ethnically German, in opposition to the rest of the Pennsylvania population.[4]

Deciding which groups to include under the blanket heading of "Pennsylvania German" was even more critical to Klein than was defining ethnic identity, and this problem strikes at the heart of this book. As Marianne Wokeck has explained, Germans immigrated to Penn's colony in multiple "waves" before the Revolutionary War and continued coming in the nineteenth century. Although certain German principalities and states, such as the Rhenish Palatinate or Baden, contributed a majority of immigrants in some of these migrations, there was no political entity known as "Germany" until Bismarck's unification in 1871, and thus no real sense of unity among the German immigrants. Even after the failed revolutions of 1848–49, Germans who came to Pennsylvania referred to themselves as Württembergers, Swabians, Prussians, Bavarians, Palatines, or Badeners. Kathleen Conzen's observation about German immigration to the United States in general applies equally well to Pennsylvania: "Quite simply, the German immigration was too lengthy, numerous, and diverse to support a single cohesive identity or to be described in terms of any single basic set of behavior patterns." Only in the middle nineteenth century, after several years—or generations—spent in America, during which time the immigrants from various German states intermingled, would they begin collectively to call themselves "Germans" or "German-Americans" to differentiate themselves from other Americans. Additionally, Yoder has argued that the descendants of immigrants from the colonial period never really thought of themselves as Germans but as "Pennsylvanians with a difference." Thus, they developed an ethnic identity that was neither German nor American, but a curious amalgam of the two. Religious, partisan, and class disparities joined temporal differences among the immigration waves to create a highly divided German community in the Keystone State in the nineteenth century.[5]

Clearly, then, the Pennsylvania Germans were not a monolithic ethnic group on the eve of the Civil War. Descendants of colonial immigrants, recent refugees from the economic and political chaos of post-1848 Germany, and thousands of others who arrived in between all called Pennsylvania home, and they were further fractured along religious and political lines. Despite this cacophony of backgrounds, belief systems, and dialects, however, there was one overarching, undeniable delineation that separated one major body of Pennsylvania's ethnic Germans from the other: time. Historians of Pennsylvania and most German-American scholars generally recognize the existence, broadly constructed, of two different German populations in the state during the nineteenth century, separated by the relative amount of time each group had spent there. The older and more acculturated population—popularly termed the "Pennsylvania Dutch"— was hardly a unified ethnic bloc, composed as it was of competing religious denominations and individuals at varying stages of Americanization, but it possessed other commonalities that strongly distinguished it from the recently arrived German immigrants, who composed the other group.[6]

The Pennsylvania Dutch in the 1860s were nearly all descendants of eighteenth-century German immigrants who had fled their European homes to escape economic hardship, war, and religious persecution. Attracted by William Penn's promise of religious toleration and cheap land, they arrived in increasingly large numbers in a series of loosely defined "waves" from the 1680s until approximately 1810. These colonial and later revolutionary-era German immigrants arrived with varying degrees of wealth at their disposal, but the overwhelming majority quickly moved beyond Philadelphia and its environs to settle in a broad arc of land about fifty miles north and west of the city, composing most of the later counties of Berks, Lancaster, York, Lehigh, Northampton, Lebanon, and Schuylkill and large segments of Montgomery and Bucks Counties. After the best limestone-rich soil in these counties was taken, German newcomers and the offspring of the original immigrants spread farther west, competing with the Scots-Irish in Cumberland, Dauphin, Franklin, Adams, Northumberland, Snyder, and Centre Counties. By 1860, the descendants of the first German immigrants occupied much of the best agricultural land in Pennsylvania and composed a large minority within the greater Anglo-American population, estimated by some historians to be as high as 600,000 persons, or almost a third of the Keystone State's population.[7]

The Pennsylvania Dutch lived primarily on family farms passed down through the generations. Towns such as Reading, Lancaster, and Allentown originally developed not as sites of independent manufacture and business but as centers of trade, government, and education whose existence depended on the constant patronage of and interaction with the rural populace. High German was considered the language of law, science, politics, and religion, so the Dutch printed their newspapers in a traditional Gothic German script, and nearly all the denominations conducted their church services in High German. At home or among friends, however, they communicated in Pennsylvanisch Deitsch, a dialect of German similar to that spoken in the Rhineland-Pfalz region of the old country, with choice admixtures of English.[8] These people retained not only Germanic languages but also distinctive German folkways and cultural traditions, which similarly defined their ethnic identity and were passed down like the family farms from generation to generation. Germanic architectural styles, such as arched cellar windows, central chimneys, and gabled roofs on houses and barns; agricultural techniques, such as the copious use of manure as fertilizer, the planting of orchards on every farm, and the fastidious care and supervision of livestock (as opposed to non-German husbandry practices, which allowed animals to roam freely); and religious practices, such as the strict reliance on the Bible as both a spiritual and an educational guide, characterized many Pennsylvania Dutch families. Importantly, the younger generations, raised among these many German traditions, rarely broke with them as they aged. According to Frederic Klees, "there was never the break between the first and second generations that there was among later immigrants"; their culture was "not sloughed off in any violent effort to prove themselves Americans." Walter Kollmorgen likened the major components of Dutch German ethnicity to a triangular foundation that never cracked:

> The Pennsylvania German farmer sensed correctly that his cultural patterns rested on a foundation of language, religion, and agrarian mores. A weakening or the disappearance of any one of these supporting buttresses, he felt, meant a loss of unity in the family and parish, the encroachment of other religions and other ways of life, and perhaps even the abandonment of the ancestral home.[9]

Hence, the Pennsylvania Dutch "[saw] no reason to change," perceiving change—or at least rapid and major alterations to the status quo—to be a threat to their way of life. This belief was expressed politically and socially throughout the nineteenth century, particularly in response to the Civil War, but also on earlier, less momentous occasions. A good example was Dutch resistance to the public school movement in Pennsylvania. Some historians have argued that Dutch parents were not against education per se; rather, they feared that teaching English to their children would harm the retention and use of both High German and Pennsylvanisch Deitsch, which in turn "would disrupt a cherished way of life." In contrast, as several scholars have shown, the Dutch were willing to adopt certain elements of the greater Anglo-American population that they found useful—such as the introduction of Sunday schools in the German churches to assist in the religious instruction of their children, or use of the English language to conduct business and politics with English speakers—as long as the assimilation process occurred on their own terms. The key element here was which society initiated the acculturation process. If it was thrust on the Dutch from the outside, such as the public school agitation or the attempts of Yankee Congregational and Presbyterian missionaries to "convert" the "heathen Germans" in the eighteenth and early nineteenth centuries, the intrusion was resisted. If the Dutch themselves decided to adopt a non-German habit or tradition, it was accepted as complementary to their already extant Weltanschauung.[10]

By the middle of the nineteenth century, the Pennsylvania Dutch thus possessed an ethnic identity with a "well-defined culture and social system" that was separate from the dominant Anglo-Saxon one but was no longer purely German. According to Henry Bradshaw Fearon, who traveled among them in the antebellum period, they were viewed by their English-speaking neighbors as "excellent practical farmers, very industrious, very mercenary, and very ignorant." Another traveler commented that their "ignorance and superstitions" were negative qualities but claimed that they had nonetheless become "a very opulent community." The Dutch, in turn, viewed their non-German neighbors somewhat suspiciously, satisfied to do business with them but fearful of too much cultural interaction. As one historian put it, the Dutch had become a compact, "more or less permanent, differentiated subcultural entity" within the broader Pennsylvania population. Ethnic historians have recently attempted to explain this "hybridization" phenomenon. Eric Hobsbawm, Terence Ranger, and Kathleen Conzen, among others, argue that "traditional" societies, such as ethnic communities that have been separated from their original homeland, may actually "reinvent" lost customs or adopt new ones from the dominant culture to preserve the remnants of their original ethnic identity. Although the Pennsylvania Dutch could collectively trace direct paths back to their German ancestry, the fact that they selectively borrowed certain customs from their Anglo-American neighbors over time supports the belief that they had created a hybrid ethnic identity by the time of the Civil War.[11]

They were conservative both politically and socially, and life as the nineteenth century Pennsylvania Dutch knew it existed only on their farms and in the counties in which they lived—"the rest of the world hardly existed" for them, according to one author. Distrustful of strangers and imported customs, the Dutch particularly disliked New Englanders, not only because of memories of the unwanted evangelists but also because of the numerous itinerant peddlers from farther north who plied the back roads of Pennsylvania selling cheap jewelry and other gewgaws. Most Dutch farmers considered the peddlers a nuisance and the purchase of their wares an unnecessary extravagance; the term "Yankee" actually became a synonym for "cheat." As a result of the various Dutch communities' collective negative experience of things emanating from New England, it is no surprise they also responded poorly to political parties associated with the region, although their immediate reasons for doing so were often rooted in local problems.[12]

The Federalist party, at first well received by the Dutch, quickly became perceived as a league between the New England elite and their corresponding numbers in Pennsylvania: the landed Scots-Irish, Quakers, and English officeholders. These people, considered former Tories, had consistently united since the Revolution to keep the Germans out of higher local government. The sparking point that ignited extralegal conflict between the groups was the first national direct tax, imposed by the Federalists to pay for an impending war with France in 1798, and the Fries rebellion, which broke out in protest of it. The Federalists aroused the ire of the Pennsylvania Dutch by taxing property based on the number of windows in houses (which smacked of a similar tax some had paid in Europe), by appointing their traditional Anglo-American rivals as the tax collectors, and by responding to the rebellion with strong-arm tactics, which appeared to many to be prejudicial. As Kenneth Keller explains, "the tax caused irritation in the [German counties], but the most galling aspect of it was that those who were to collect it were members of a despised cultural minority that had opposed independence and monopolized local offices." The instiga-

tors of the Fries rebellion, centered in heavily German Northampton
County, were ultimately pardoned by President John Adams after he realized the exceptionally bad press the entire affair was receiving, but the damage had been done. The emerging Democratic-Republican party
immediately capitalized on the Federalists' errors. Historian William T. Parsons describes the result:

> Although enclaves of Federalist Germans remained in Bucks,
> Montgomery, and Northampton Counties, the bulk of the Penn-
> sylvania Dutch flocked to the Democratic-Republican standard.
> Some were converted from Federalist principles by the ill-advised
> measures against the Fries Rebellion, but others were pleased that
> the Democratic-Republicans ran German candidates.[13]

The Pennsylvania Dutch would find the transition from Jefferson's
party to the Democrats of the antebellum period an easy and logical move.
As the nineteenth century unfolded, they would become staunch support-
ers of Democratic candidates on the local, state, and national levels. The
Democratic ideal of the yeoman farmer was attractive to them, as were the
Democrats' decentralizing policies toward the national government and
campaigns against privilege. Several Pennsylvania governors in the early
antebellum period were ethnically Dutch, including Simon Snyder, Joseph
Hiester, and John Andrew Melchior Schulze. Andrew Jackson's presidential
victory in 1828 was hailed as a personal triumph by many in the Dutch
counties, and despite Jackson's overreliance on Martin Van Buren and the
New York State Democrats, Pennsylvania Dutch lawmakers remained loyal
to their new leader. Jackson was imbued with almost demigod status by
rank-and-file Dutch Democrats long after he left office. Even after the Civil
War, one housewife explained her husband's behavior to a visitor by saying,
"Don't get offended at anything he says; he is a good man, if he is old and
still votes for Jackson. . . . He can't get Old Hickory out of his head." Not
surprisingly, when the impulse for social reform swept New England and
much of the rest of the country in the 1830s and 1840s, the great majority of
Pennsylvania Dutch remained firmly rooted with the Democrats, shunned
both the Whigs and the various third parties, and refused to be reformed.
The spell of Jackson was far too strong to break, and social reformers, particularly abolitionists, reminded them of the meddling outsiders of their
parents' and grandparents' generations, boding only disruption in the course

of daily life.[14]

Interestingly, the Dutch had already fought a round against the abolitionists. One historian maintains that Pennsylvania Dutch Lutheran and German Reformed assemblymen—nearly all of them nonslaveholders—had voted against the abolition of slavery in the Federal period. They did this not because they thought slavery was an inherent good but because of fears that "a radical alteration in the status of large numbers of Pennsylvania Negroes would compound [the Germans'] already difficult adjustment" within the greater Anglo-American population. Although the nativist Know-Nothing movement of the 1850s helped galvanize Dutch loyalty to the Democrats—who professed to be the party of the immigrant—the Dutch, unlike the immigrant Germans, were only slightly concerned. They knew full well that the newer European immigrants (particularly the Catholics among them), and not themselves, were the primary targets. It was the rise of the Republicans—with their perceived New England bias and their promises of major changes in the fabric of American life—that bothered the Pennsylvania Dutch the most.[15]

It is important to note that the modern stereotype of the Pennsylvania Dutchman—dressed in black clothing, wearing a broad-brimmed hat, and sporting a long, dark beard—is not only an inaccurate description of the modern Pennsylvania Dutch but an even more erroneous image of the Dutch of nineteenth-century Pennsylvania. Although Old Order Amish and conservative Mennonites were an important subgroup within the Pennsylvanisch-speaking population, they were, as Theron Schlabach explains, "a minority within a minority." The majority of the Pennsylvania Dutch in the 1860s were Lutherans and German Reformed, as they had been since the 1750s. German Baptist Brethren (frequently called Dunkers), Schwenkfelders, and a few German Methodists composed another major segment of the Dutch population.[16]

At first glance, it may appear that the denominational differences among the Dutch would have hindered a sense of ethnic unity, especially considering the temporal disparities in their arrival in the Keystone State. Unquestionably, the great diversity among the German churches was a major reason—if not the primary reason—why the Pennsylvania Dutch never succeeded in unifying as an ethnic or political bloc. By 1860, about a third of the German Reformed and Lutheran congregations had converted to English-language services, and they struggled with their traditional, German-language brethren for control of their regional districts (synods or classes). More critically, Yoder explains that the great division between the "sectarian" churches (Amish, Mennonite, and most Dunker congregations) and the "church" Germans (Lutheran and German Reformed) "formed an almost unbridgeable chasm down the very middle of Pennsylvania German society." The theological backgrounds of these two major groups were inherently different, their approaches to the world around them (and thus to Americanizing influences) were different, and their political allegiances were frequently different. However, the church Germans far outnumbered their sectarian counterparts and, with the exception of Franklin, Montgomery, and Lancaster Counties, controlled the German-language partisan press and hence the direction of Dutch voting. Yoder also observes that by the mid-nineteenth century, rigid barriers between denominations within each of the primary religious groups (sectarian and church) had subsided, allowing many Pennsylvania Dutch to speak confidently in ethnic terms of "unser Satt Leit—'our kind of people.'" The Lutherans and German Reformed were particularly successful at bridging their differences, and as long as they spoke the same language, they often shared church buildings, parochial schools, and even pastors.[17]

Of all the Pennsylvania Dutch, the sectarians were the most unassimilated into American society in 1860. The Mennonites, Amish, and Dunkers shared the Pennsylvanisch Deitsch dialect, a Germanic heritage, and a strong agricultural tradition with their Lutheran and Reformed neighbors, but the three sects shared another characteristic that set them even further apart from the greater American population: religious separatism. All three groups preached varying degrees of isolation from the corrupting influences of the world around them, which translated into practical measures that effectively separated them—or at least shielded them—from the society in which they lived. As Roger Sappington explains for the Dunkers, "during the nineteenth century Brethren in many respects separated themselves from the society in which they lived, because they believed to do so was to choose the Christian way of life. Perhaps their approach should be described as nonconformity, since the Brethren were convinced a Christian should be different from a non-Christian." Active political participation (beyond exercising the franchise and holding minor local offices), membership in fraternal societies, support of the military (including the draft), and tolerance for human suffering and cruelty (including slavery) were all prohibited by the principal tenets of the sectarian churches. Of course, "the Brethren were human and subject to human weaknesses, such as . . . participating in political activities," Sappington continues, but "these activities were considered

1791 St. John's Union Church. Kutztown Union Church (Lutheran-Reformed) in a Civil War era photo. Churches such as this one dominated the Pennsylvania Dutch countryside. DAVID L. VALUSKA COLLECTION

weaknesses" and were strongly frowned on by church elders.[18]

Not surprisingly, the sectarians became pacifists during the war and conscientiously objected to the draft. Although a few members of the sectarian churches served as soldiers, the vast majority did not and struggled to uphold their religious scruples.

Although the newer German immigrants were sometimes absorbed into the Pennsylvania Dutch farming communities and settled in small numbers in the Dutch towns to take advantage of business and employment opportunities, the vast majority of the German-Americans settled in or immediately next to the major cities, particularly Philadelphia and Pittsburgh. Living there in ethnic neighborhoods, or "Little Germanies," many found employment in the mills and factories, worked as day laborers, or set up small businesses such as breweries, butcher shops, or dry goods stores. A few worked white-collar jobs. These people spoke a dialect of modern High German dissimilar to Pennsylvanisch Deitsch and arrived with considerably less capital at their disposal than the longer-established Pennsylvania Dutch, although some of those who came in the 1830s and early 1840s had managed to achieve prosperity by the time of the Civil War. The majority of the German-Americans, however, were refugees from the chaos of post-1848 Germany. Fleeing the economic and political instability created by the failure of the democratic revolution, many of the newer arrivals came to Pittsburgh and Philadelphia imbued with at least some indignation at the defeat of the liberalizing impulse in Europe, and a few were actual political emigrés. Despite the fact that the urban-dwelling German leadership was divided, as Walter Kamphoefner explains, between "Dreissiger" and "Forty-eighters" (1830s-era and post-1848 political emigrés), time of arrival in America apparently had little effect on German-American unity. Many early chroniclers of the nineteenth-century German immigration tended to overemphasize the differences between the two groups, highlighting their squabbles instead of their general consensus of opinion. Recent scholarship now argues that the supposed great divide between the "Greys" (the 1830s emigrés) and the "Greens" (the Forty-eighters) was not much of a division at all, especially on the eve of the Civil War, when Dreissiger and Forty-eighter generally united behind the Republican party.[19]

The major divisions among the German-Americans were created by religious differences (Protestant versus Catholic) and competing loyalties among immigrants from different German states; for example, former Prussians associated socially and politically with former Prussians, and former Badeners stuck with former southern Germans. Bruce Levine has also claimed that class conflict further splintered the immigrant Germans throughout the United States, although it appears that this was less of a problem in Pittsburgh than in New York and the midwestern cities. Several historians have linked immigrant religious affiliation with partisan support and concluded, in the now famous "ethnocultural thesis," that conservative Protestants such as Lutherans allied with Catholics by typically voting Democratic, whereas pietists and "reformed" denominations usually supported the Republicans in the 1856 and 1860 elections. The jury is still out on the ethnocultural thesis, but the fine scholarship of the 1970s and early 1980s, strongly based on hard, empirical evidence, is convincing. Thus, the old theory that the Germans completely rallied to the Republican banner during the 1860 election seems less likely.[20]

Despite all the divisions among the German-Americans of Pennsylvania, there were centripetal forces at work in the antebellum period that drew them together. Most important of these was the establishment and growth of what some scholars have called a sense of "Deutschtum." Political, religious, provincial, and class differences aside, urban-dwelling Germans throughout the United States quickly realized that they had one great similarity: They were all German speakers in a predominantly English-speaking land and shared a recent common ancestry in that part of Europe where German was spoken. Stan Nadel has argued that it was precisely the multitude of differences among the immigrant German community that "provided the mechanism for integrating such a large and diverse group of people into a community by drawing each of its members into a complex web of conflicting loyalties." Because of their many "crosscutting loyalties," most immigrant Germans, rather than professing undivided loyalty to one single group—which, by necessity, would estrange them from others they also valued—directed their loyalty "to the whole expressed by a combination of all of them—the German-American community of Kleindeutschland." This overall sense of belonging to a greater German community strongly contributed to the rise of the ethnically German neighborhoods in Philadelphia and Pittsburgh, replete with countless German societies and organizations, such as the turnvereins. Although these clubs sometimes engendered old regional divisions, as Lesley Kawaguchi has shown, they also fostered a sense of belonging to the greater Deutschtum within the urban neighborhoods.[21]

A recent theory also argues that the creation of a sense of Deutschtum in America, albeit isolated in each urban enclave, ironically created more unity among recent German immigrants nationwide than had existed back in pre-Bismarckian Germany. Hence, Pennsylvania's German-Americans would find common cause with those from New York, Milwaukee, Cincinnati, and other cities with major German populations in the Civil War era. This sense of ethnic community across state lines, although not developed politically to any great degree, linked urban-dwelling Germans in the North both psychologically and culturally and guaranteed a more or less common German-American reaction to any event that brought either public praise or calumny on Germans, regardless of geography.[22]

Nativism provided the other major unifier among Pennsylvania's German-Americans in 1860. The Keystone State had been one of the birthplaces of the Know-Nothing or American party of the 1850s, which openly professed its disdain for foreigners and pursued a political agenda that, among other goals, would stifle immigration and stiffen naturalization laws. Supplanted and substantially absorbed by the Republican party, the Know-Nothing movement nonetheless died hard in Pennsylvania, and Germans in the state were probably more conscious of nativist prejudices than were those in most other states of the Union. Know-Nothings lamented the growing political and cultural influence of the Irish and German immigrants, whom they frequently lumped together as "papists" and blamed for everything from street brawls to intemperance. Nativists particularly disliked the refugees of the 1848 revolution, believing that their primary purpose in the United States was not political asylum but agitation for a separate German state in North America, a more "Germanized" American culture, or embroilment of the country in German and European political problems. Indeed, as Ray Billington argues, some of the German radicals did entertain such plans and created several revolutionary German societies, including two in Pennsylvania.[23]

Radical dreams of a more German United States quickly subsided, yet their residue sparked fear and resentment among many Anglo-Americans, who deserted particularly the Whig party but also the Democrats to join the Know-Nothings. Cleary, fear of radical Germans was not the primary reason the nativists did so well in Pennsylvania; local issues, temperance, anti Catholicism, and disgust with corruption within the traditional parties also attracted voters. But the Know-Nothings "controlled nearly 120,000 votes in Pennsylvania, approximately one-third of the total" in 1854, and they remained strong there and in neighboring Maryland long after the party had collapsed elsewhere. That fact was certainly not lost on immigrant Germans.[24]

Dale Knobel concludes that nativist beliefs and nationalism among Anglo-Americans were frequently linked. Thus, blaming the country's troubles on foreigners, particularly Irish and Germans, was considered an "American" thing to do for many nonethnics in the 1850s and 1860s. Although the Republican party managed to subsume its Know-Nothing roots in the 1860 election to a large degree, the majority of German voters in Philadelphia remained Democratic and voted against Lincoln out of a lingering fear of nativism. Events in the Civil War would prove their fears justified, as the anti-foreigner prejudice was only temporarily hidden from view and returned with a vengeance, particularly after the battle of Chancellorsville. German-Americans in Pennsylvania fully realized the potential threat that nativism posed to their liberties as Americans and thus took comfort in associating with other German speakers, regardless of previous differences.[25]

Clearly, Pennsylvania's German-Americans were both divided and unified in 1860, just as their Dutch neighbors were in the rural counties. That was about the only similarity between the two groups, however. The great disparity between these two major German populations in practically every aspect of life made it unlikely that they would react similarly to the demands and exigencies of the Civil War. As Yoder has pointed out, the two conflicting worlds of the Pennsylvania Germans had already begun to clash by the 1850s and would continue to grate in the postwar period. The German-Americans generally regarded the Pennsylvania Dutch as culturally inferior, bastardized American-German hybrids who spoke, in the words of one observer, "a gibberish speech" and "whose thickheaded peasant arrogance everywhere opposes in the most nauseous manner every attempt at education beyond reading and writing, Bible and catechism." The Pennsylvania Dutch called the immigrant Germans "Europeans," "Germany-Germans," or "Deitschlenner" and refused to interact with the newcomers, considering their leaders to be idealistic dreamers with no practical attributes and the rank and file to be ignorant foreigners who allowed themselves to be led around by the nose. The urban world of "Gemütlichkeit," of beer gardens, voluntary societies, and turnvereins, held no appeal for the rural-dwelling Dutch, who felt no bond with the German-Americans and no pressing need to travel to the large cities where they lived.[26]

The only regular contact the two populations appear to have had in 1860 was in the realm of religion, in which German-born and –trained ministers still occasionally presided over Dutch congregations. Even here, however, the two groups clashed, especially over the use of High German in worship. By 1860, the Pennsylvania Lutherans had split into two wings. The smaller one espoused the use of English, adopted a liberalized theology, and founded its own seminary at Gettysburg; the other wing, composed of both German-American and conservative Pennsylvania Dutch congregations, retained the German language and a strict adherence to the unaltered Augsburg Confession.[27]

CHAPTER 2

German-Americans and the War up to Gettysburg

Martin Oefele

Apart from its importance as the first total or "modern" war, the Civil War had another momentous meaning for all Americans—native born as well as immigrants. "The war completed the ruin of organized nativism by absorbing xenophobes and immigrants in a common cause," historian John Higham noted in 1963. "Now the foreigner had a new prestige; he was a comrade-at-arms. The clash that alienated sections reconciled their component nationalities." Although the conflict over the Union certainly did not eliminate nativism—and may have even drawn some ethnic groups, such as the Germans, closer together—the common cause that both Anglo-Americans and immigrants fought for in the Northern army and on the home front instilled notions of mutual respect. Foreign-born soldiers defended their new country, and native Americans were forced to acknowledge the participation of immigrants in the struggle to preserve the American Republic. This chapter outlines the role of German-American soldiers and regiments in the first two years of the war, highlighting their interactions with Anglo-Americans. At the same time, it provides a short summary of military events during that period, with a focus on the eastern theater of operations.[1]

On July 21, 1861, three months after Confederate batteries had fired on Fort Sumter and President Lincoln had called for 75,000 volunteers, the two main field armies in the East met for the first time in battle. There had been minor clashes in Missouri in May and June, but both sides expected the decisive battle of the still infant Civil War to take place at Bull Run

Creek in Virginia. The troops and their commanders were equally inexperienced, and except for a few veterans of the Mexican and Seminole wars, most participants did not know what lay in store for them. Numerous spectators who rode out from Washington in their carriages mirrored the general sentiment that the armed conflict would be but a matter of days—if not hours.

In May, Major General Irvin McDowell's Federal army had taken Arlington Heights in northern Virginia with a view to moving against Richmond. By mid-July, the Union forces set out to cut railroad lines at Manassas Junction, the first step on their way to the Confederate capital. On the south bank of Bull Run Creek, Confederate troops under General Pierre G. T. Beauregard had taken up positions, while General Joseph E. Johnston moved another force east from the Shenandoah Valley. Few had predicted a long and bloody struggle between the hostile parties, but the ensuing battle suddenly proved them right. On July 21, the Union troops executed a masterful flanking movement and pushed back the enemy, but by the end of the day, they had been pushed back themselves and retreated in utter confusion. The first major land battle had been fought and lost by a stunned North, while Southerners celebrated their hero General Thomas "Stonewall" Jackson and rejoiced in the successful defense of Virginia's "sacred" soil. Both sides quickly realized that the war would not be short and that the optimistic enlistment terms of three months were likely to be expanded. Additionally, both Southerners and Northerners suddenly came face-to-face with the horrors of war, as the combined losses of 3,600 dead and wounded destroyed the romantic illusions that many young recruits had harbored about the conflict. It would take arduous drill, strict discipline, and much more bloody fighting to end the conflict.[2]

As early as First Manassas, the army that was to fight the Union's war in the East had established its ethnic and social makeup, which would prevail throughout the next four years. American farmers and city boys who had never been away from home before would serve alongside immigrants from Ireland, the German states, Scandinavia, and the rest of Europe. African-Americans, who had offered their services to the U.S. Army at the first call for volunteers, could not enter the ranks because the federal government—as well as the white society at large—perceived the conflict as a "white man's war" solely for the preservation of the Union. It would take another year before military and civil authorities started to accept black soldiers. German-Americans and other foreign-born soldiers, however, served in the

Union army from the very beginning. When the need for companies and regiments arose in the early days of the war, the German population of the Northern cities responded quickly. Soldiers and officers trained and tested in Europe knew how to organize military units and drew on the large numbers of immigrants who had already joined the paramilitary turnverein organizations. These clubs were among the first to mobilize in the spring of 1861, providing Lincoln with several well-drilled and fully equipped ethnically German companies. From the nuclei of these companies, immigrant regiments were rapidly created and paraded through the streets of the Northern cities, frequently sporting German uniforms and battle flags. The 7th New York "Steuben" Infantry under Colonel Georg von Schack, for example, carried the black, red, and gold colors of the 1848 revolution, along with the national American colors. Often led by well-known veteran officers, these units proudly recalled German military traditions and received much attention from the German-American population.[3]

It was the largely ethnic First Brigade of General Dixon Miles's Fifth Division under Colonel Louis (Ludwig) Blenker that stood its ground during the first battle of Manassas and covered the Federal retreat to the capital. Born in Rhenish Bavaria, Blenker was one of the European Forty-eighters who had fled their home countries after the abortive uprisings in 1848 and 1849. Early in the war, he enthusiastically supported the desire of many immigrants to form a consolidated ethnic command under German officers. Although his brigade had not seen active fighting at Manassas, the thoroughly drilled regiments had covered the overall Union retreat and then withdrew in good order, models of steadiness and discipline amidst the chaos of the Union disaster. Undoubtedly impressed by his brigade's performance, Blenker aspired for a larger command and wrote to Secretary of War Simon Cameron shortly after the battle: "In consequence of numerous letters, requests, offers, and petitions sent to me from all parts of the Union, especially from the States of New York, New Jersey, and Pennsylvania, by men of position and influence, I have the conviction that I can raise in the shortest delay a second whole German brigade, consisting of officers and partly of men who have seen service and actual war abroad, and to organize in this way a German division."[4]

This petition clearly reflected the ongoing ethnic recruitment patterns in the northeastern cities, where immigrants of local influence gathered men to create companies and then propelled themselves into leading positions as these units' officers. German social and singing clubs, workers' unions, and

Brigadier General Louis Blenker, commander of the famed "German Division."
MASSACHUSETTS COMMANDERY MILITARY ORDER OF THE LOYAL LEGION AND THE U.S. ARMY MILITARY HISTORY INSTITUTE

societies composed of former citizens of specific German states all provided companies to be placed under Federal—and, if possible, ethnic—command. Eager to maintain a firm grip on both German ethnic identity and the enlistment process, Blenker labored to fuse these scattered units into one mass before they blended in with the greater Federal army. Complaining in August 1861 that too many ethnic regiments were organizing at the same time, the newly appointed brigadier general told Major General George McClellan that "instead of finishing and completing ten or twelve full regiments, we have twenty-five or thirty skeletons, and every so-called colonel has a personal interest that his men do not join another organization to complete it, fearing he would lose his pretended and cherished colonel-ship." To remedy this situation, Blenker suggested that he be allowed to send

officers to New York and Philadelphia "to collect and unite all these muti-
lated and scattered companies and regiments" under his own command.
Blenker finally got what he wanted and had all the new ethnic regiments
from New York and Pennsylvania transferred to his "German" brigade during the summer of 1861.[5]

Immigrant recruits signed up for the Union army out of various motivations. For some, the military promised adventure and travel in their new
home country; others saw military service as a civil duty in a democratic
society. As Sergeant Albert Krause from Prussia told his family in 1862, "I
am marching into battle with courage and desire. The [United] States have
adopted me, I have been able to earn a living, and now, when the country is
in peril, I should not defend it with flesh and blood?!" The degree to which
patriotism as an enlistment motive surpassed the desire for adventure and
monetary reward among the Germans and other immigrants is not clear.
Certainly, many foreign-born Union soldiers joined the army for economic
reasons rather than because of an idealistic devotion to the cause. The rapidly developing American economy had seen a drastic increase of indus-
trialized labor in the decades before the war that had put scores of skilled
craftsmen out of work. Strongly concentrated in these professions, German-
Americans were also hit hard by major financial panics (1854 and 1857–58)
that forced many unemployed to flee the eastern cities and search for new
possibilities. For these jobless immigrants, the army provided at least temporary financial relief. After First Manassas, when it became clear that the war
would not be a matter of weeks, Congress appropriated funds for enlistment
bounties. Thus, the prospect of steady pay plus immediate cash in hand
provided important enticements to enlist. Another incentive for immigrants—and Anglo-Americans as well—to join the army was the influence
of friends and relatives who had already enlisted. Civil War military units
were formed, to a large extent, at the local level, and in many cases, several
family or community members went off to war together under the command of officers they had known for some time. In his study of the motivations of Germans in the Union army, Wolfgang Helbich concludes that
probably only 10 percent of them joined the army out of idealistic reasons.
Conversely, William Burton credits immigrants with a higher level of patriotism and suggests that "there was little difference between the ethnic and
the non-ethnic volunteer" in terms of motivation.[6]

Whatever their initial motivations, for the majority of both immigrants
and native born, emancipation of the slaves was not their goal. Hartmut Keil

points out that before the war, immigrants' main concern had been the purchase of farmland and its cultivation. "It was often out of self-interest," Keil notes, "that immigrants were opposed to slavery, that they adhered to the Jeffersonian notion of the yeoman farmer as the pillar of a democratic society." If Germans took up arms against the institution of slavery, it was usually because they wanted, like most Yankee soldiers, to prevent its further expansion and to protect their own economic freedom. Idealism, however, was not completely unknown among German recruits. Many Forty-eighters—mostly from Germany and Hungary—linked the Civil War to their own past and turned it into another chance to fight for democracy and republicanism against what they perceived as an oppressive, aristocratic Southern society. Several of them had been politically active before the war, and some even publicly argued against slavery; Carl Schurz, for instance, became the most prominent ethnic politician of his time. Another revolutionary veteran and a former lieutenant in the Prussian artillery, Fritz Anneke, urged his fellow immigrants to do their part in the Americans' "Second Fight for Freedom," as he called it.[7]

In addition to the various idealistic and more mundane motivations to join the Union army, immigrants recognized that participation in the war was their route to full recognition as American citizens. Germans and other foreign-born soldiers expected their sacrifice for the Union to elevate their status in postwar society. "Germanness" as an expression of a distinct ethnicity had not matured prior to the war. Instead, immigrants from the various German states and regions frequently adhered to their separate regional identities. This impression is sustained by the fact that the great majority of immigrant recruits did not list Germany or Prussia when asked for their national origin; instead, they named their respective kingdoms, dukedoms, or provinces. An ethnic German consciousness did not completely solidify among immigrants from German-speaking Europe until they had the opportunity to unite behind a cause that combined their ethnic distinctiveness and their loyalty to the Union.[8]

Eventually, some 200,000 soldiers of direct German descent served in the Union army, about one-fifth of them in predominantly ethnic units. Many German immigrants felt that they could contribute substantially to the Northern war effort. As Blenker indicated in his letter to Cameron, a high percentage of them had served in the German armies or in the revolutionary forces and possessed military know-how and a sense of discipline that the Anglo-Americans often lacked. Due to their previous military training in

Major General August V. Kautz. MASSACHUSETTS COMMANDERY MILITARY ORDER OF THE LOYAL LEGION AND THE U.S. ARMY MILITARY HISTORY INSTITUTE

the old country and in the turnvereine, more experienced German officers and soldiers tended to look down on the raw Anglo-American recruits, who often lacked the most basic formal drill and discipline. German-born West Point graduate August Valentin Kautz combined the professional view of an educated officer and a somewhat conceited European perspective in his observations of the new Federal volunteer army. Arriving in Washington from his distant frontier post on the Pacific coast shortly after the disaster of First Manassas, Kautz was shocked when he encountered the newly formed army. "About eighty recruits were turned over to me to be organized into Company B [6th U.S. Cavalry]. Not one of them has an idea of duty or discipline," the officer confided in his private journal. Ethnic war narratives abound with such mocking reference to the American volunteers' alleged lowliness. Whether real or not, the immigrants' self-professed professional superiority often led to serious conflicts with Anglo-American comrades, as well as intensified hatred by their enemies.[9]

It cannot be ascertained whether more ethnic clashes were caused by American nativism, as immigrants claimed, or by German haughtiness regarding their professional and cultural supremacy. In Missouri and other regions along the border, especially, opposition to Germans as the most prominent group of nonslaveholding immigrants had long simmered and then erupted during the bloody fight over popular sovereignty in the Kansas Territory. After the election of Abraham Lincoln in 1860, German immigrants were quick to point out that their political counterweight had secured Lincoln's victory and saved heavily secessionist Missouri for the Union. Indeed, as the German *Westliche Post* from St. Louis reported in May, "all the hate around here is directed against the 'Dutch' who soon will be able to enjoy the blessings of the 'mob-law.'" The fact that several exiled immigrants had actively campaigned for Lincoln increased the visibility of their ethnic political influence and soon led to a firm entrenchment of the "myth of 1860"[10] among immigrants and hostile Southerners alike. Carl Schurz, for example, did little to dispel the exaggerated notion that midwestern Germans had unanimously cast their votes for the Republican candidate. Together with other ethnic politicians, he shrewdly played his cards to assure the government of the indispensable German loyalty.[11]

This notion intensified when pro-Southern Missouri governor Claiborne Jackson pledged in 1861 that he would do everything to keep Missouri "by her sister slave-holding States." Jackson refused to provide volunteers to the federal government and threatened to take over the city's arsenal with his militia and force the state into secession. In response, the local Union commander, Captain Nathaniel Lyon of the 2d U.S. Infantry, temporarily mustered in four loyal regiments, resorting to the readily trained pool of German turners and other immigrants. One of their leaders was Franz Sigel, a former revolutionary hero from Baden, who actively recruited two regiments and was elected commander of the 3d Missouri Volunteers. Other Forty-eighters came from the surrounding states to join these prestigious outfits, including Adolf Dengler and Friedrich Hecker, who left their homes in Belleville, across the border in Illinois, to enter Sigel's regiment. On May 10, Lyon's troops overwhelmed and captured the Missourians at Camp Jackson, an action that strengthened the loyalist German self-consciousness. The resulting unrest between large parts of the city's American population and the ethnic troops irrevocably forged the German-American conception of having "rescued" Missouri.[12]

For weeks, the St. Louis German press celebrated the victory and praised the ongoing "people's revolution." The *Westliche Post* had already compared the emerging conflict with the European triumph over Napoleon, whose "dwindling powers" had sunk "into the dust" at Leipzig. With the assistance of their foreign-born comrades, Americans now were called on to defend their young nation:

> The current revolution of the people is greater and far more momentous than the one of 1776. In its victory rest all hopes of the free people in America and the whole world. . . . Following our victory—and we *shall*, we *must* be victorious—the triumphant shout of the liberated European nations will echo over the ocean and greet us as their saviours and brothers. . . . Thus . . . everyone to the sacred fight for the restoration of freedom, of the republic, of humanity's unshakeable rock of hope.[13]

Subsequent events in Missouri soon led to the emergence of Franz Sigel as the tragic hero of the German-American population. When the German regiments under his command failed in the battle of Wilson's Creek, ethnic soldiers—at least in the western theater of operations—could no longer point to their military reputation and instead rallied behind their idol, who in the eyes of many had turned into a scapegoat for Union defeat. Major General Henry Halleck, chief of staff of the Union armies, decided to replace Sigel, and the indignant officer resigned his commission. German-Americans all over the Union rose in protest against such seemingly unfair treatment, and Halleck immediately offered to reinstate Sigel. Sharing the ethnic outrage of numerous other German newspapers, the Davenport *Demokrat* demanded a complete reversal in Union appointment policies and commented harshly that "if Sigel were made head of the army, he would bring the war to a speedy end." Back in command by January, thanks to what Stephen Engle calls Lincoln's "tactful handling of the affair," Sigel partly redeemed German honor in the battle of Pea Ridge on the Missouri-Arkansas border in March 1862. Sigel's troops, composed of two primarily ethnic divisions under Peter Joseph Osterhaus and Hungarian Alexander Asboth, and two Anglo-American divisions under Brigadier General Samuel R. Curtis beat back a superior Confederate force led by General Earl Van Dorn that was trying to invade Missouri. Yet Sigel's quarrels with Halleck and the military establishment never abated.[14]

Meanwhile, President Lincoln had bestowed military command in the East on a promising thirty-four-year-old general. George B. McClellan was probably the best thing that could have happened to the Northern army after the humiliation of First Manassas. Relieving McDowell the day after the battle, McClellan possessed the full confidence of the government and the traumatized public alike. "Little Mac," as he soon became known among his adoring troops, immediately took to reorganizing his forces, now called the Army of the Potomac. Lincoln had authorized the recruitment of up to a million three-year men, and McClellan was to mold them into a functioning army. With a distinct sense of professionalism, the general introduced formal drill, laid out tidy and hygienic camps, and succeeded in boosting morale among the troops through parades and grand reviews.[15]

Benefiting from McClellan's organizational talent were Louis Blenker and the eastern German regiments. In October, the Union high commander authorized the consolidation of all ethnic regiments and complied with the German officer's wish that they "be known as Blenker's division." By February 1862, this division consisted of three brigades under Brigadier Generals Julius Stahel and Heinrich Bohlen and Colonel Adolph von Steinwehr, totaling 10,117 men. Stahel's brigade comprised Blenker's own regiment, the 8th New York "1st German Rifles" Infantry, the multiethnic 39th New York "Garibaldi Guard," the 45th New York "5th German Rifles," and the first German regiment from Pennsylvania, the 27th Infantry. Under Steinwehr's command stood the 29th New York "Astor Rifles" or "1st German Infantry," the 54th and 68th New York "2d German Rifles" Infantries, and the predominantly German 73d Pennsylvania. Probably the most German brigade was Bohlen's, made up of the 58th New York "Polish Legion" Regiment and the 35th and 40th Pennsylvania Infantries. The Polish Legion, despite its name, included a large number of Prussians, in addition to ethnic Poles and other nationalities; the 35th Pennsylvania, later renamed the 74th, was raised almost exclusively from the German population of Pittsburgh. The 40th (later renamed the 75th), as Christian Keller shows, was recruited completely from Philadelphia's Germans and included a large number of men who had served in Europe. In addition, two unbrigaded New York regiments served under Blenker—the 4th Cavalry and the 41st "DeKalb" or "Yager" Regiment. Stationed at Hunter's Chapel near Fairfax Court House until March 1862, the regiments perfected their already renowned formal drill and were instrumental in fortifying the capital's western approaches.[16]

The rapid growth of the volunteer army and the resulting need for more officers led to the inevitable appointment of less-qualified men to high-ranking positions, often according to their political loyalty and standing. By commissioning inexperienced Carl Schurz to brigadier general in the spring of 1862, for example, Lincoln catered to the immigrant's influence among his fellow countrymen. August Kautz, a captain in the 6th U.S. Cavalry since July, was appalled by this frantic commissioning of incompetent men. Contemplating the resulting damage to the army, Kautz later wrote in his memoirs:

> What forcibly impressed me with astonishment, was the rush for promotion. Officers, who had failed to do themselves credit as Commanders of Companies, were Colonels of Regiments and demanding to be made Brigadier Generals. They did not seem to reflect upon the responsibility they were seeking, as though the war was going to be a holiday affair and the care of thousands of human lives was a task of easy execution; as though nothing was required to make a man a General except the shoulder strap that indicated rank. When I reflect upon what it cost the country in blood and treasure before these Holiday Heros [sic] found their proper position, I am astonished that no precautions are taken by our legislature to guard against such experience in the future.[17]

Aware that officers in the volunteer regiments were promoted faster than in the regulars, Kautz refused to enlist in the former out of fear of losing his professional integrity. Unfortunately for the German-American image in American society, other immigrants were less shy when it came to self-estimation and claiming what they saw as their just desserts. Pointing to their (sometimes purely imaginary) importance to the Union army because of their prior military education, some immigrants loudly demanded officers' commissions and often blamed nativist prejudice if they did not receive commands.[18]

In several instances, German officers harmed the cause of their compatriots by accentuating their supposedly superior ethnic differences. For example, by generously permitting the consumption of alcohol in their units, regimental commanders often collided with American standards of temperance. And in December 1861, when Confederate cavalry raiders broke through the Federal picket line at Annandale, Virginia, an Anglo-

American officer indirectly blamed the German sentries of the 45th New York for the incident, because "a very free use of liquor" was tolerated in their ranks. Exaggerated tidiness in the German camps and the preferred use of German as the command language also provoked bad feelings among Anglo-American comrades. As commander of the Army of the Potomac's German division, Louis Blenker ostentatiously insisted that all official correspondence in his command be conducted in German.[19]

If German high-handedness alienated Americans, charges of nativist discrimination further soured interethnic relations. It is true that Blenker, together with many European officers, had to bear the skepticism of West Pointers who did not easily accept outsiders promoted in their stead. Yet the Germans never realized a fundamental distinction of the American military system that stemmed from the revolutionary experience and the founding principles of the United States. Traditionally suspicious toward army officers as possible agents of monarchical suppression, Americans had never learned to appreciate the value of professionally trained soldiers. Consequently, officers educated at the U.S. Military Academy had established an elitist group consciousness that in some cases survived even Southern secession. Considering the rampant nativism among the general population in the decades preceding the Civil War, prejudice among Anglo-American army officers against newcomers from foreign countries was not surprising. European professionals, for their part, sometimes could not understand why their experience and training were perceived to be of little use in the face of a full-scale war. In Sigel's case, as in many others, this sense of personal importance was combined with a lofty character, which often infuriated Anglo-Americans.[20]

All during the fall and winter of 1861, the Northern population eagerly looked forward to the coming spring offensive that, according to McClellan's promises, would conquer Richmond and the South. The "young Napoleon" devised a three-pronged attack to end the war. While the Army of the Potomac struck at the Confederate capital, another Federal army would push into Kentucky and Tennessee and occupy the Mississippi Valley, thus cutting off the trans-Mississippi Confederate states. In addition, the Union navy would blockade the entire coast from North Carolina to Texas and clear the Mississippi River, destroying the formidable defenses along its banks. This strategy essentially followed the Anaconda Plan formulated by General in Chief Winfield Scott, but it was credited to McClellan after he replaced Scott in November. Now, Little Mac was both general in chief and commanding general of the largest army ever assembled in North America, and everybody expected him to march it south. Yet McClellan had grown unexpectedly hesitant, unsure of the preparedness and strength of his army, and repeatedy postponed his advance. Only after General Joseph E. Johnston, commanding the chief Southern army in Virginia, had fallen back behind the Rappahannock River did McClellan decide to act. In March 1862, he transported his entire army by water all the way down Chesapeake Bay to establish a spearhead at the southeastern tip of the Virginia peninsula, below Richmond. Desperate for action, Lincoln approved the plan, but not before significantly reducing McClellan's sphere of command and replacing him with Henry Halleck as general in chief. On April 4, a full eight months after First Manassas, the Army of the Potomac finally moved out of Fortress Monroe and up the peninsula. Out of a misguided concern about Confederate numbers that did not exist, however, McClellan refused to attack Johnston's understrength defenders and dug in at Yorktown, only a few miles from his point of departure. After the Southerners had finally abandoned their positions and slipped away on May 3, the Army of the Potomac followed cautiously and arrived a few miles outside of Richmond. There, Johnston waited, reinforced with fresh divisions from farther south and determined to hold the city at all costs.[21]

In the meantime, Major General Ulysses S. Grant's western campaign had suffered a severe setback when a Confederate army under General Albert Sidney Johnston surprised his forces near Shiloh on April 6. Several part-ethnic regiments participated in that battle, among them the 45th, 57th, and 58th Illinois Infantries. The 43d Illinois, nicknamed the "Körner Infantry," was composed mainly of German-Americans from Belleville. Its commander, Colonel Julius Raith, fell mortally wounded and was "mourned by his friends and adopted country," according to Major General John A. McClernand. Leading the German 32d Indiana Infantry was Forty-eighter August Willich. "Papa" Willich, as he was called by his adoring men, was a former artillery officer in the Prussian army, a devoted Marxist, and one of the truly charismatic and successful German regimental leaders. Part of Major General Don Carlos Buell's army that reinforced Grant that evening, the 32d Indiana repulsed the charging Confederates in a picture-book manner on the second day and won the respect of Anglo-American soldiers and generals alike. The combined losses of the murderous two-day battle amounted to 20,000 dead and wounded and awakened both the

North and the South to the reality of a truly bloody war. Though the Confederates retreated after the second day's fighting, the Union thrust down the Tennessee River Valley was temporarily checked at Shiloh. At the time, the tragedy of that battle shrouded the fact that Grant had emerged as one of the Union's most competent military leaders. Following Admiral David G. Farragut's capture of New Orleans later that spring, Grant would eventually take the formidable river fort of Vicksburg and regain Union control of the Mississippi Valley. Still, in early April, such important victories did not seem imminent. More ominously for the Union, the threat of British diplomatic recognition of the Confederacy appeared more likely than ever.[22]

Back East, Northern prospects also declined. Stonewall Jackson demonstrated his military acumen in the Shenandoah Valley and amazed friend and foe alike. In March, while McClellan still hesitated to move, Lincoln decided to transfer Blenker's division from the Army of the Potomac west to Major General John C. Frémont's Mountain Department, located in western Virginia. The three German brigades left their camps on March 10 and embarked on what was to become an arduous nine-week march across the Virginia mountains. From Hunter's Chapel, the men marched some thirty miles to Warrenton. Meanwhile, Jackson attacked Federal troops under Nathaniel Banks at Kernstown on March 23, alarming Lincoln so much that he ordered Banks to remain in the valley. Although beaten by the Unionists' superior numbers, the Southerners prevented Banks from reinforcing McClellan on the peninsula. Convinced that Jackson had an immense army at hand, Lincoln was determined to hunt him down, and Blenker received orders to rendezvous with Frémont in the town of Romney, situated on the South Fork of the Potomac.[23]

Even though the troops were unprepared for a march that would ultimately cross three mountain ranges, the German division set out on April 4 toward Salem and proceeded across the Blue Ridge Mountains to Winchester. Plodding along soggy roads in adverse weather, the undersupplied regiments lacked everything from shoes and overcoats to dependable firearms and ambulances. On their way, the soldiers did not encounter great hospitality by Unionist Virginians. Instead, as Blenker later reported, "Not one person, man, woman, or child, dared to avow such a sentiment publicly, while they gave us to understand quite palpably that their sympathy was with their State against the North, and with the Confederate Army against ours." Still, the general found it worth noting that "only the colored

people seemed to be joyful at our coming." Probably to evade the accusations of marauding brought against his troops on their march, Blenker did
not include in his report the numerous fights with bushwhackers along the
way or the acts of plundering his men were forced to engage in to survive.
Supplied with the little available equipment in Winchester, the division
rested two weeks and finally arrived, exhausted and depleted by disease,
in Romney in early May. From there, however, the weary Germans were
soon ordered south to assist Frémont's divisions under Brigadier Generals
Robert H. Milroy and Robert Cumming Schenck in the fight against
Stonewall Jackson and his phantom-like "foot cavalry." By May 11, the division had reached Franklin, where Frémont had gathered his forces. As Frémont later recalled, out of the division's nominal strength of 10,000 men,
barely 7,000 remained fit for service after their arduous march. "The condition of the men," the general reported, "was not such as could have been
desired. They were worn and exhausted by hardships scarcely credible, and in
spite of efforts by myself and others to supply their wants, a large proportion
were without articles of first necessity for service in the field. Of shoes, blan-
kets, and overcoats there was especially great need."[24]

During all of May, Jackson successfully hampered Union efforts to
transfer troops east. Marching nearly 400 miles in one month with some
17,000 men, the Confederate general engaged all three Federal armies in the
Shenandoah Valley and beat them successively in several battles. Although
Jackson held Banks's army in check and damaged it severely at Front Royal
and Winchester, Frémont was ordered to cross the Shenandoah River, march
north, and attack Jackson from the rear. At the same time, Lincoln dispatched
a division under General James Shields west from Manassas. Too slow for the
elusive, hard-marching Confederates, the Union troops failed to trap Jackson, who had suddenly turned south and made for Port Republic, where he
intended to swing east and join General Robert E. Lee in front of Richmond. Finally on June 8, Frémont's advance guard encountered one of
Jackson's divisions under General Richard Ewell before it could cross the
Shenandoah. Meeting the enemy at Cross Keys, the German division was
about to receive its baptism of fire.[25]

Julius Stahel's First Brigade formed the Federal front line. The formerly
unbrigaded 41st New York Infantry had been assigned to his brigade, as
had Battery C of the West Virginia Light Artillery under Captain Frank
Buell and the 2d New York Light Artillery, with Captain Louis Schirmer
commanding. Leading a poorly coordinated first attack, the 8th New York

The Cross Keys Battlefield in 1912. MASSACHUSETTS COMMANDERY MILITARY ORDER OF THE
LOYAL LEGION AND THE U.S. ARMY MILITARY HISTORY INSTITUTE

suffered badly and was unable to contribute substantially to the ensuing
battle. The Confederates then charged into Stahel's left flank, which was
protected by Buell's and Schirmer's batteries. Together with a detachment of
the Pennsylvania Bucktails, the 27th Pennsylvania under Lieutenant Colonel
Adolf Buschbeck fended off several assaults by two Southern regiments,
one of which had actually outflanked them. In a rare show of respect for
their "Dutch" enemies, several Confederate soldiers and officers would testify to the Germans' bravery that day. The advance of a third Southern regiment, however, turned the tide against the Federals. The survivors of the
decimated 8th New York were further reduced while desperately trying to
cover their comrades' retreat. In all, the 1st German Rifles lost 220 dead,
wounded, and missing that day and earned the questionable distinction of
having one of the worst regimental casualty rates.[26]

Heinrich Bohlen's Third Brigade had been placed behind Stahel and
was thrown into action when Stahel's line broke under the renewed Confederate assaults. Colonel Eugen Kozlay's 54th New York Infantry had been
transferred to Bohlen's command, along with two batteries of light artillery
under Captains Michael Wiedrich and Hubert Dilger. The German troops

concentrated around these guns, awaiting the enemy. Confederate General Isaac Trimble, in charge of that side of the field, intended to swing around the Federal left flank, but his men ran into devastating fire from Wiedrich's and Dilger's guns. Standing its ground, the 54th New York contributed to checking the enemy's attack. Colonel Franz Mahler, meanwhile, kept his 75th Pennsylvania Infantry under cover, for which he was later charged with cowardice by Blenker. The Confederates rallied and renewed their efforts, threatening to dislodge Bohlen's defenders. They probably would have failed again, were it not for some petty quarreling about superiority among the German artillery officers. Wiedrich, who ranked below Schirmer, later reported that he "had received orders from General Blenker a few days before that all orders from Captain Schirmer should be obeyed." Schirmer had already hauled his battery to the rear and now told Wiedrich to do the same, although Bohlen had ordered Wiedrich "to stay and keep up the fire." The artillery officer thus removed his guns from the field, "against the protest of General Bohlen." The pullout of the batteries signaled the withdrawal of the infantry. Retreating in good order, the 54th New York and Colonel Alexander von Schimmelfennig's 74th Pennsylvania halted after a short distance and checked the enemy pursuit. Brigadier General Adolph von Steinwehr's brigade, now including the 13th Battery, New York Light Artillery, had remained in the rear during the battle, forming Blenker's reserve. Struck down by sickness, Steinwehr was absent, and Colonel Johann Koltes led the brigade, which ended up retreating without having an opportunity to participate.[27]

Having escaped Frémont's army, Jackson crossed over the Shenandoah and, after a brief battle at Port Republic, retired east to Richmond. There, Confederate President Jefferson Davis had ordered Joseph E. Johnston to attack McClellan and relieve the capital. On May 31, the Southerners drove back Union forces at the battle of Seven Pines, but Johnston was wounded and was replaced by the little-known Robert E. Lee. The new commanding general of the main Southern army, now called the Army of Northern Virginia, was not content to await McClellan's next move and had already prepared for a counteroffensive. Much valuable information for this operation was provided by Major General Jeb Stuart's daring cavalry raid around the entire Union army. The Southern troopers rode 100 miles in four days, during which time they defeated Union pickets in several skirmishes, captured soldiers and supplies, and delivered the information Lee needed about his enemy's positions and strength. Not expecting McClellan to go for an all-out assault against Richmond, Lee decided in June to completely remove the Federal threat from the Confederate capital and prevent a merging of McClellan's divided forces. Although defeated at Mechanicsville on June 26, the Confederate commander succeeded in forcing McClellan to shift his base of supplies southward, away from Richmond. Over the following five days, Lee drove back a superior Union army and its timid commander all the way to Harrison's Landing. The number of Confederate casualties, however, had reached stunning levels. The Seven Days' Battles had cost the South more than 20,000 men dead, wounded, and missing out of some 90,000 effectives; McClellan lost nearly 10,000 dead and wounded and 6,000 captured out of his slightly more numerous force.[28]

Following the humiliating Valley campaign, Lincoln reorganized Union forces in Virginia in June and consolidated Frémont's, Banks's, and McDowell's commands into the Army of Virginia under Major General John Pope. One of the Union officers profiting most from this step was Franz Sigel, who replaced Frémont and could finally secure the position he and his German admirers had so long desired. Although Sigel had not shown much diplomatic talent in his personal quarrels with military officials, his successes in St. Louis and at Pea Ridge had earned him some professional respect in Washington. More important, his fellow German immigrants held him in high esteem and critically scrutinized the way he was being treated by his superiors. Thus, Secretary of War Edwin Stanton had called Sigel to Washington in May 1862 to entrust him with a new military command because, as his biographer points out, "Sigel was viewed by Union officials as a political card to keep the German-American populace interested in the successful prosecution of the war." The immigrant was given command of an army corps to be formed in the Shenandoah Valley that would eventually develop into the largely German Eleventh Corps of the Army of the Potomac. This corps consisted of three divisions under Brigadier Generals Schenck, Steinwehr, and the newly appointed Carl Schurz. After Blenker had laid down his command following various quarrels over his troops' conduct, Sigel broke up his division and dispersed its brigades over the three remaining divisions. Schenck's First Division comprised Stahel's brigade and an Anglo-American brigade of Ohio regiments under Colonel Nathaniel McLean, as well as Wiedrich's and Buell's batteries and three more artillery units. Steinwehr's division consisted of his old brigade, now under Koltes's command. Schurz's division included a mixed German and Anglo-American brigade under Bohlen and the remainder of Bohlen's old brigade, now under the command

Colonel Henry Bohlen and staff of the 75th Pennsylvania in an early 1862 photo, before Bohlen's promotion to general. He is seated at left, Francis Mahler to the right. ROBERT DIEM COLLECTION, U.S. ARMY MILITARY HISTORY INSTITUTE

of Colonel Wladimir Krzyzanowski. When General Bohlen was killed at the batle of Freeman's Ford on August 22, Schimmelfennig took his place. A fourth, predominantly Anglo-American, brigade was led by General Robert Milroy. As part of Pope's new army, Sigel's corps operated in the lower valley until Pope decided to concentrate his forces south of Washington. Ever suspicious of nativist discrimination, Sigel complained about Pope's neglect of his corps and recalled the earlier fate of the German division under Blenker.[29]

Dissatisfied with an administration that, in his opinion, had failed to support him properly and at odds with General in Chief Halleck, McClellan refused to cooperate with Pope's Army of Virginia and removed his army from the Virginia peninsula at a glacial pace. Pope had estranged many of the eastern officers by the demeaning arrogance he displayed toward the Army of the Potomac and his inflated vow that "success and glory are in the advance, disaster and shame lurk in the rear." The self-confident general from the West, however, could not produce any results against his Southern counterparts either. After the indecisive battle of Cedar Mountain, north of Gordonsville, on August 9, Pope tried to position his army for a strike against Lee while waiting for reinforcements that had been ordered from McClellan's army. Lee, however, suddenly divided his forces and sent Jackson on a forced march around the Union right flank to destroy Pope's supply base at Manassas Junction. Pope hurried north, vainly hoping that he might be able to annihilate Jackson before Lee arrived with the rest of the Confederate army. But Lee and his other chief lieutenant, General James Longstreet, moved too fast; meanwhile, McClellan, now south of Washington in Alexandria, defied orders to support Pope and did nothing. Misjudging Confederate troop movements, Pope expected Jackson to withdraw in the face of the superior Union force he was gathering. Jackson's troops, however, were preparing for action along an unfinished railroad track that provided ample cover.[30]

Without a clear picture of his own army's positions, Pope gave Sigel the premature order to attack early on August 29 at the Warrenton Turnpike on the west side of Bull Run creek. Without backup—although Pope had promised to send it—Sigel's three divisions, along with Milroy's troops, attacked Jackson in the morning. Once again, the troops of the former German division faced Stonewall's veterans. Schurz's division found Jackson's left flank and soon was completely engaged. According to Wilhelm Kaufmann, it was Schimmelfennig's brigade that struck the Confederates most successfully and pushed Jackson's famed "Stonewall Brigade" beyond Cushing's Farm. Unable to break the enemy's lines, however, Schimmelfennig fell back and had to remain in action for several more hours against heavy counterattacks. Sigel falsely believed that he had been victorious when he regrouped his force after the fighting ended about sundown. But Longstreet had arrived to reinforce Jackson, and Union Major General Fitz John Porter, out of disgust for Pope, remained inactive and never engaged his Federal troops. Not surprisingly, McClellan ignored the developing situation altogether. Consequently, when the fighting resumed the next morning, Pope's troops had to take on the combined forces of Jackson and Longstreet. Even though Sigel's men bravely attacked again, Confederate resistance proved too strong, and finally Longstreet's fresh troops threw the Yankees back in a massive counterattack. Covering the Union retreat along the Warrenton Pike, Sigel's regiments deployed on Chinn Ridge and stubbornly withstood the enemy's blows, enduring heavy losses. After the Confederates had taken Henry House Hill late in the afternoon, the beaten Army of Virginia retreated

over the Bull Run to Centreville. Sigel's corps had stood in its first major
battle and suffered heavy casualties. Among them was Colonel Johann
Koltes (former commander of the 73d Pennsylvania), who was killed on
the second day while leading his brigade against an enemy battery. Although
"nearly decimated," lauded Sigel, Koltes's brigade had "succeeded in protecting our center and preventing the turning of our flank" during that
action. Sigel himself suffered several wounds during the fight. Captain
Dilger had once again proved his ability as a highly capable artillery officer,
and several other officers received commendations for their brave conduct.
Colonel Mahler, who earlier had been charged with cowardice by Blenker,
led his 75th Pennsylvania with skill and valor.[31]

Yet "this unfortunate battle," as Kaufmann calls it, did nothing to
advance interethnic relations in the Union army. Although Sigel's troops had
probably done the best they could under the circumstances, the general did
not receive the public appreciation that German-Americans demanded.
Instead, critics focused on the unsuccessful attacks of his corps, which were,
admittedly, poorly coordinated. Evidence suggests that at least one Anglo-
American officer—General Phil Kearny—out of disrespect for Sigel's
foreign command, refused to fully support his efforts in the battle. Carl
Schurz, doubtless a much more competent politician than military analyst,
managed to alienate Anglo-American officers when he claimed in his official report that he "found Major-General McDowell with his staff, and
around him troops of several different corps and of all arms, in full retreat."[32]

The Federal casualties caused by Pope's ill-starred campaign amounted
to about 17,000 killed, wounded, and missing. Once again, serious incompetence among the Union leaders combined with Confederate boldness
to produce Northern defeat, and the debacle only added to the ethnic and
political tensions within the Army of the Potomac. Second Manassas also
sealed Pope's fate as commander in Virginia. The luckless general was sent
to Minnesota to fight rebellious Sioux Indians and spent the following
months quarreling about the "studious, unscrupulous, and vindictive publications" against him that were ruining his "reputation as a soldier, and in
some respects my character as a man." Indeed, as Lincoln correctly suspected, McClellan had deliberately withheld troops from Pope because he
had expected—and probably wanted—his rival to fail. Still, the president
saw no other choice than to entrust McClellan with command of the
Army of the Potomac, relying on his professional skills and exceptional
rapport with the troops. The Army of Virginia was dissolved, and Sigel's

corps was assigned to the Army of the Potomac as the Eleventh Army Corps. The German-American troops in the newly created corps spent the following months in garrison at Fairfax Court House, guarding Washington's western approaches and hence avoided the coming campaign.[33]

Following his success at Manassas, Robert E. Lee decided to carry the war into the North with the hope of winning another victory, this time on enemy soil. A Confederate victory in Maryland or Pennsylvania, he figured, could clinch political recognition of the Confederacy in Europe, compel Lincoln to open peace negotiations, and, at the very least, temporarily relieve Virginia from the logistical burdens of supporting his army. On September 3, the Army of Northern Virginia, only about 50,000 strong, headed north with the state capital of Harrisburg, Pennsylvania, as its target. Crossing the Potomac River, Lee once again divided his troops and ordered three columns to take Harpers Ferry and open a supply route into the Shenandoah Valley. Even though he miraculously obtained a copy of Lee's plans revealing that the Army of Northern Virginia had split into four separate forces, McClellan did not use this invaluable advantage wisely and failed to intercept and destroy the enemy's columns piecemeal. Lee, discovering the imminent danger, immediately gave orders to concentrate the scattered pieces of his army at Sharpsburg on Antietam Creek. Finally, McClellan caught up to Lee and prepared to do battle. On September 17, Brigadier General Joseph Hooker's division attacked Stonewall Jackson's men hidden in a cornfield along the Hagerstown Pike and initially drove them back. The Confederates under General John Bell Hood then counterattacked fiercely, but Federal reinforcements managed to check them, suffering severe casualties. After four hours of cruel carnage, both sides had lost 8,000 dead and wounded. The brigades holding Lee's center, formidably positioned along a sunken road, beat back six assaults before the Union attackers finally broke through. In the final part of the battle, Major General Ambrose E. Burnside attempted to roll up Lee's right flank by crossing a bridge over the Antietam and pressing toward Sharpsburg. But when General A. P. Hill's division arrived and assailed the Federal troops, Burnside had to fall back to his old position behind the creek.[34]

The several ethnic regiments participating in the battle of Antietam were assigned to different Anglo-American divisions, and there were no primarily ethnic brigades. German-American General Max Weber, formerly commanding the 20th New York "Turner" Regiment, led a mixed brigade that lost one-third of its strength. The German turners, now under the

Swedish Colonel Ernst von Vegesack, took part in the murderous attacks against the Confederate center and received wholehearted praise by their brigade commander. The regiment, wrote Colonel William Irvin, "was exposed to the heaviest fire in line, which it bore with unyielding courage and returned at every opportunity. The firmness of this regiment deserves very great praise. Colonel Von Vegesack was under fire with his men constantly, and his calm courage ga[v]e an admirable example to them. Each of their stand of colors is rent by the balls and shells of the enemy, and their killed and wounded is 145. This regiment was under my own eye in going into action and frequently during the battle, and I take pleasure in strongly testifying to its bravery and good conduct." The 7th New York "Steuben" Infantry, led by Captain Carl Brestel, took out an enemy battery under heavy losses, capturing three colors and adding to its already strong fighting reputation.[35]

When the bloodiest day in American history ended, no significant ground had been gained by either side. Lee had lost one-quarter of his army, and the two armies combined had suffered 23,000 casualties. Still, the Union could count the battle as a tactical victory because it had forced Lee to abandon his invasion and turn back, and this ultimately allowed Lincoln to issue the Emancipation Proclamation. Once more in a position to pursue and shatter the Army of Northern Virginia, however, McClellan merely regrouped his forces and remained on his side of the creek. Over the next weeks, the lethargic Union movements allowed Lee to maneuver Longstreet between Richmond and the Army of the Potomac and entrench his army around Fredericksburg, about halfway between Richmond and Washington. President Lincoln at last removed McClellan for good and replaced him with Burnside, who commenced a winter campaign against Fredericksburg. After a massive artillery bombardment that did little damage except to civilian property, the Federal army crossed the Rappahannock River on December 12. Burnside planned a grand assault against the rebels for the following day. From their formidable positions, however, the Confederates were able to repulse fourteen disjointed—and again uncoordinated—brigade- and division-level attacks. Burnside was forced to retreat over the river and ultimately went into winter quarters. Lee had again proved his ability to choose the right ground for a battle and to withstand greater enemy numbers, losing fewer than 5,000 men against Burnside's almost 13,000 casualties. Lee's good track record in dealing with numerically superior enemies would be further enhanced when the spring campaign of 1863 commenced. Sigel's Eleventh Corps was spared participation in the Fredericksburg fiasco. Ordered to march toward Fredericksburg too late, the troops came within earshot of the raging battle but could not come to Burnside's rescue. Together with the remaining army, they finally went into winter quarters.[36]

Major General "Fighting" Joe Hooker succeeded Burnside as commander of the Army of the Potomac on January 26, 1863. Confident of success, he devised a bold strategy that called for a second maneuver across the Rappahannock at Fredericksburg while the bulk of the army crossed the river to the northwest, flanked the Army of Northern Virginia, and struck it from the rear. On April 30, Hooker reached Chancellorsville with 70,000 Union troops. The Federal soldiers, including the Germans of the Eleventh Corps, had psychologically recovered from the defeats of the previous year and were eager for a fight. Unfortunately for the ethnic soldiers' spirit, just weeks earlier, Franz Sigel, indignant over what he perceived as Washington's neglect of his troops, had resigned as corps commander and been replaced by Major General Oliver O. Howard. Howard was a West Point–trained, evangelizing New Englander who spoke no German, knew little about the cultural values of his German troops, and cared more about their souls' salvation than their morale.[37]

Outnumbered almost two to one, Robert E. Lee left only a fraction of his army at Fredericksburg to divert Hooker's attention and fool him about the Southerners' strategy. Moving his main force toward Chancellorsville, Lee again divided his army on May 2 and sent Jackson with some 28,000 men on a forced march around the Federals' right flank. Hooker, in his hubris, ignored frantic reports about the movement from both his cavalry scouts and German observers in the Eleventh corps, who correctly surmised that their corps would receive the intial brunt of the Confederate attack. A few German officers, including Schimmelfennig, realized the imminent danger and independently tried to align their troops for the coming blow, but neither Hooker nor Howard ordered a general alarm. The Eleventh Corps had been isolated when Major General Daniel Sickles took two divisions of his corps and left his position to pursue Jackson, believing him to be in retreat. Hooker then detached Brigadier General Francis C. Barlow's brigade of Howard's corps to Sickles, reducing the Eleventh's effective strength from 11,500 to some 8,500 men (of whom some 4,600 were "German or of foreign lineage," as Lonn puts it). In addition to Hooker's complete failure to interpret the intelligence at hand, Howard's decision to position his weakened corps facing south on the unprotected Federal right flank was responsible for the disaster that followed.[38]

Jackson's veterans executed a virtual surprise attack against their foes when they struck Brigadier General Charles Devens's First Division along the Turnpike Road at about 4:30 in the afternoon. "Guns were stacked" at the moment of the attack, "and soldiers were dispersed, reading newspapers, playing cards or preparing supper." Suddenly rabbits and deer scampered through the Union camps, flushed out of the brush by the advancing Confederate line. Colonel Leopold von Gilsa's brigade received the initial blow. His 153d Pennsylvania (composed mainly of Pennsylvania Dutch troops) and the 54th New York could offer only token resistance before they had to fall back, suffering heavy losses. Two regiments of McLean's Ohio brigade soon joined the retreating defenders. The remnants of Devens's division, von Gilsa's 41st and 45th New York, and McLean's 55th and 107th Ohio and 17th Connecticut Infantries simply had to run before the Confederate onslaught. Meeting with Schurz's Third Division positioned behind Devens, the fleeing troops of the First Division soon became entangled with their own comrades, preventing them from forming effectively for battle. Although Schurz had, according to his and Schimmelfennig's postaction reports, regrouped his forces facing west toward the actual thrust of Jackson's attack, he could not prevent the ensuing rout. Brigade formations temporarily dissolved as those units able to breast the enemy advance tried to rally and hold their ground, such as the 58th New York Polish Legion and the 82d Illinois Infantry under famous Forty-eighter Friedrich Hecker. Hecker was wounded during the fight, as was Colonel Wilhelm Heinrich Jacobs as he led the 26th Wisconsin in a valiant stand that cost the regiment dearly.[39]

After the first line of defense had broken, Schimmelfennig's brigade finally succeeded in establishing a somewhat stable second line. Meanwhile, the men of brigade commander Lieutenant Colonel Buschbeck of von Steinwehr's Second Division opened fire on the advancing enemy from behind some shallow breastworks. Aided skillfully by Captain Dilger, who had only one cannon at his disposal, Buschbeck's 27th and 73d Pennsylvania, the 29th and (nonethnic) 157th New York, and remnants of units from other brigades held this defensive position against overwhelming numbers for about half an hour. Acknowledging Buschbeck's achievement in saving much of the Eleventh Corps' artillery and baggage trains, General Howard later recommended Buschbeck for promotion to brigadier general.

During the battle, Howard stated, "Colonel Buschbeck gained respect and encomium from all. More than any other officer, he, with his brigade, checked the pursuing enemy." Dilger, he continued, should receive the brevet rank of lieutenant colonel. "He handled his battery as well as a man could and receives my highest commendation." When the fighting ebbed, the troops under Buschbeck's command retreated in good order toward Chancellorsville.[40]

Flushed with success, the Confederates soon faced a tragedy. Reconnoitering for a night attack that might very well have dealt Hooker's army a mortal blow, General Stonewall Jackson was mistakenly shot by his own men. The general was brought to a field hospital, where his left arm was amputated. Jackson subsequently contracted pneumonia and died eight days later. Lee had, in his own words, lost his right arm and would never again enjoy the services of so talented a lieutenant. General Jeb Stuart, now leading Jackson's troops, staged another attack on May 3 and threw back the Federals even farther. The Eleventh Corps had meanwhile been placed in a less exposed position, but some regiments still saw action and acquitted themselves well. Although wounded himself, General Hooker refused to relinquish command during the battle and seemed incapable of recovering both his nerve and his command ability. Acknowledging defeat, the Unionists retreated over the Rappahannock on May 6. The Union army's 17,000 casualties out of an aggregate strength of some 134,000 were proportionately less damaging than the 13,000 men (out of 61,000) the Confederates lost, but Lee had stopped another Federal offensive in its tracks, accomplishing perhaps his most brilliant victory.[41]

Ella Lonn has rightly observed that the "name and the reputation of the German divisions of Schurz and Von Steinwehr are indissolubly linked with the fate of the Eleventh Corps at Chancellorsville." In the depressed atmosphere following this bloody engagement, the retreat of the Eleventh Corps' German regiments on May 2 was derisively dubbed the "flight of the 'Flying Dutchmen'" by the Anglo-American press. Summarily lumping together the whole corps as ethnic scapegoats, the *New York Times* insisted that the troops, "without waiting for a single volley from the rebels, disgracefully abandoned their positions." The failure of the German officers to rally their men, the *New York Herald* wrote, had caused the ethnic regiments to flee "from the field in panic, nearly effecting the total demoralization of the entire army." The fact that only slightly more than half the troops exposed to the surprise attack had been immigrants was not

A post-war artist's rendition of the "stampede" of the Eleventh Corps at Chancellorsville.

initially acknowledged and therefore did nothing to alleviate the plight of
the Germans. Probably because he was among the best-known German
commanders, General Schurz bore the brunt of the unfair criticism, even
though his division had actually been led and fought reasonably well. Two
weeks after the battle, Schurz complained to Secretary of War Edwin Stanton that because of such degrading reports, his "officers, as well as men,
have had and still have to suffer . . . much abuse and insult at the hands of
the rest of the army." Due to these unfair accusations, for some time after
the battle Schurz wanted to leave the Army of the Potomac. However, he
changed his mind when he realized that such a decision would harm the
ethnic cause in the Union military, arguing, "If we go now, will it not have
the appearance as if we were shaken off by the Army of the Potomac? Would
it not to a certainty confirm the slanders circulated about me? Would it
not seem as if I voluntarily accepted the responsibility for the disaster of
May 2?" Unfortunately, at Gettysburg two months later, Schurz's luck did
not improve, and once more his "Dutch" troops came under scrutiny for
their perceived below-average performance. Whereas German-American
public opinion about Schurz as an inexperienced officer had been split

before Chancellorsville, the ethnic ranks closed in his defense when nativist attacks against his division and German troops in general did not subside.[42]

As Herman Hattaway has noted, "The most significant of all puzzles concerning the Civil War are the questions of loyalty, tenacity, and will." Answers to all three questions would be necessary to explain why German soldiers—and the ethnic regiments of the Eleventh Corps in particular— continued to fight for the Union after Chancellorsville. One would have expected the number of desertions among these troops to rise dramatically in the face of such blatant nativism and prejudice on the part of the Anglo-American majority. Although the questions of ethnic loyalty, tenacity, and will to carry on with the Northern war effort still lack much research, one explanation is that the "myth of 1860," already extant during the conflict, tied the German element to the abstract ideal of the Union after the battle of Chancellorsville. Defiance of unfounded prejudice and nativist ridicule may have also strengthened the immigrants' conviction that the German population had contributed significantly to the Union cause. Many doubt-lessly believed that their suffering would pay off once Anglo-American public opinion recognized this contribution. To a degree, that would hap-pen in the aftermath of Gettysburg, but even there, the specter of nativism cast its ugly shadow.[43]

CHAPTER 3

The Pennsylvania Dutch
as First Defenders

David L. Valuska

The Pennsylvania Dutch in the mid-nineteenth century were a composite ethnic group comprising German-speaking people who had immigrated to America from 1683 through the early 1800s. They came from a variety of geographic areas: western and southern Germany, eastern France, Switzerland, Austria, Belgium, and Holland. The greatest concentration of German immigrants emanated from the areas of the Rhine, Palatinate (Pfalz), Baden, Hessen, Darmstadt, Nassau, Hanau-Lichtenberg, Württemberg, Alsace-Lorraine (in present-day France), Tyrol (in Austria), and several cantons in Switzerland. Over the next 100 years, these German immigrants made accommodations with the predominant English culture and, to a certain degree, they assimilated. They did not, however, give up their language, religion, or folk customs, and as time passed, they became protective of their ways and lifestyles. Living in insular settlements of similar people allowed the development of a culture unique to these German-speaking immigrants.[1]

Steven M. Nolt, in his recent work *Foreigners in Their Own Land,* provides excellent insight into the process of ethnicization-as-Americanization that the Pennsylvania Dutch experienced. The German immigrants established ethnic communities that strengthened their traditional values. These ethnic communities shared a common set of evolved Pennsylvania German folkways and material culture. By dress and lifestyle, the Pennsylvania Dutch were easily discernible as such. Religion was a critical part of their cultural identity, with the Lutheran and German Reformed Churches acting as ethnic magnets, pulling the people into a community of commonly held beliefs reflecting a shared ethnic heritage. Language, both the Pennsylvania Dutch dialect and High German, was a central mark of identity and cultural cohesion, as well as a vital tool of communication.[2] While maintaining many of their ethnic mores, material culture, and folkways, the Pennsylvania Dutch were also going through a slow process of Americanization.

The early immigrants referred to themselves as Pennsilfaanisch Deitsch (Pennsylvania German); hence, they soon became known to their English-speaking neighbors as the Pennsylvania Dutch.[3] Some misconceptions must be put to rest: The Pennsylvania Dutch did not come from Holland, and the majority of Pennsylvania Dutch are Lutheran or Reformed, with a distinct minority being Amish or Mennonite. The terms "Pennsylvania Dutch" and "Pennsylvania German" are often used interchangeably, but for the purposes of this study, the group is referred to as the Pennsylvania Dutch.

When the Southern states seceded in the winter of 1860–61, many Pennsylvania Dutch wanted to take a wait-and-see attitude, because they felt that this was a Republican problem. A close reading of the Pennsylvania German–language newspapers of Reading, Lancaster, and Allentown underscores the political struggle taking place within the strongly Democratic Pennsylvania Dutch areas. Much of the reluctance to take a stand was based on party affiliation and loyalty, and only after Fort Sumter was attacked on April 12, 1861, did a solid consensus supporting the Union emerge. A reading of the Lancaster *Volksfreund und Beobachter, Berks County Demokrat, Reading Adler, Lecha Allentown Patriot,* and *Bauern Freund* clearly demonstrates the division among the eastern Pennsylvania Dutch. The *Volksfreund und Beobachter* and *Lecha Allentown Patriot* supported the Republican party: the *Bauern Freund, Adler,* and *Demokrat,* all favored the Democrats.[4] A reading of these papers during the earlier period from November 1860 through March 1861 clearly indicates party bias as well. The Pennsylvania Dutch Republicans and the Democrats blamed each other for the nation's turmoil. It was not until the firing on Fort Sumter that a greater sense of unity became apparent.[5]

A shock wave swept the North—the flag had been fired on. Many Pennsylvania Dutch were outraged that the Southern states had begun a civil war, but just as many could not support a Republican-prosecuted war against the seceded states. These Dutchmen adhered to the states' rights tenets of the Democratic party, and this antiwar attitude among the Dutch led to the creation of the "copperhead" movement in eastern Pennsylvania.

Many Pennsylvania Dutch refused to enlist in the army and encouraged their friends to do likewise.[6]

However, there was also a strong love for the Union that compelled thousands of Pennsylvania Dutch to enlist. Some of the first to go were men of the Pennsylvania militia dubbed the "First Defenders." These First Defenders were volunteers from militia units from Berks, Schuylkill, Mifflin, and Lehigh Counties who rushed, within days of the firing on Fort Sumter, to defend the nation's capital. Among the First Defenders were units with solid Pennsylvania Dutch contingencies: the Allen Rifles of Allentown, Ringgold Artillery of Reading, National Light Infantry and Washington Artillery of Pottsville, and Logan Rifles of Lewistown.[7] These units were a microcosm of the larger society, with a mixture of Pennsylvania Dutch and their non–German neighbors.

In the early years of the war, quite a few regiments contained a strong contingent of Pennsylvania Dutch.[8] A look at more than 200 regimental records indicates that the following regiments had large concentrations of Pennsylvania Dutch recruits among the Pennsylvania Volunteer Infantry: 30th, 32d, 36th, 46th, 47th, 48th, 50th, 68th, 77th, 79th, 87th, 88th, 93d, 96th, 122d, 128th, 129th, 130th, 147th, 148th, 151st, 153d, 165th, 166th, 167th, 173d, 176th, 178th, 194th, 195th, and 209th.[9] The Dutch preferred to enlist along with their "English" neighbors and thus fought in integrated units.[10]

From 1861 through June 1863, the Pennsylvania Dutch units fought bravely and were conspicuous on all the major battlefields from the peninsula campaign through Chancellorsville. At the battle of Chancellorsville, May 4–5, 1863, it was the 153d Pennsylvania Infantry that took the first assault of Lieutenant General Thomas "Stonewall" Jackson's corps on the Federal right flank.[11]

Following the Confederate victory at Chancellorsville, General Robert E. Lee, commander of the Army of Northern Virginia, asked for and received permission to invade the North for a second time. His first attempt at invasion had met with failure after the bloody one-day battle of Antietam in September 1862. In the summer of 1863, Lee's army began its march up through the Shenandoah Valley and into Maryland; these movements would eventually lead to the three-day battle at Gettysburg, Pennsylvania.

Northerners, and particularly Pennsylvanians, were in a state of high anxiety. The Keystone State's wartime governor, Andrew Curtin, issued a call for emergency troops to enlist for the duration to augment the Army

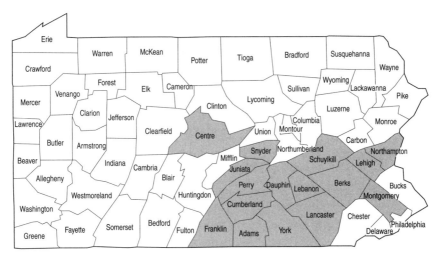

The Pennsylvania "Deutsch" counties

of the Potomac. It would take some time before recruits could be mustered in, and the Pennsylvania Dutch were not sure that the Confederate threat was real. By mid-June 1863, however, it had become apparent to most that it was. By the middle of June, the Army of Northern Virginia was approaching Winchester, Virginia.

As the rebels advanced, they were confronted by a division of the Union army's Eighth Corps commanded by Major General Robert H. Milroy. Lee sent Major General Richard Ewell's Second Corps down the Shenandoah with orders to capture Winchester—and dispose of Milroy. Milroy believed that he was facing an inferior enemy and sent out scouting parties to determine the strength of the rebel advance. One of the first units to encounter the advancing Southerners was the 87th Pennsylvania Volunteer Infantry, drawn primarily from York and Adams Counties. George Hays, a citizen of York, Pennsylvania, had been given permission to recruit a regiment and had made his appeal to the local men. The 87th was made up of a mixture of Pennsylvania Dutch soldiers and their English, Irish, and Scotch neighbors. The Pennsylvania Dutch, however, constituted more than 65 percent of the men in the ranks of the 87th Pennsylvania.[12]

On Friday, June 12, 1863, the 87th Pennsylvania, the 13th Pennsylvania Volunteer Cavalry, and Battery L of the 5th U.S. Artillery were sent on a reconnaissance to determine the enemy's strength. This force, under the command of Colonel John Schall, left Winchester and rode south along the

Valley Turnpike. As they approached Middletown, they were challenged by the Confederate 1st Maryland Cavalry Battalion under the command of Captain W. I. Raisin. Here, the two forces began to skirmish, and Colonel James A. Galligher, commander of the 13th Pennsylvania Cavalry, devised a plan to ambush Raisin's Confederates.[13]

Galligher sent word to Colonel Schall and the 87th that he would feign a retreat, hoping that the Confederates would fall for the old "wounded bird" trick. In the meantime, Schall should set up the infantry and artillery out of sight, thus luring the Confederate cavalry into a trap. The plan worked beautifully, and Captain Raisin's men charged after the retreating rebels. If the Federals had not been overly anxious, the surprise would have been greater, but as it was, the Maryland troopers received a bloody nose for all their bravery. The Confederates had more than fifty men killed or wounded and thirty-seven captured.[14] The 87th Pennsylvania was ordered to fall back to Winchester, where the Pennsylvania Dutchmen contested the advance of the rebels and found themselves engaged in fighting in and around the fortification guarding the city. Early on the morning of June 15, the regiment was ordered to retreat toward Martinsburg.

As the Federals retreated, the Confederates advanced through Winchester and began pursuing them. Southern infantry struck the retreating Yankees at Stephenson's Depot, three miles north of Winchester. Milroy stopped to give battle, and he positioned the 87th, under Colonel William G. Ely, on the right flank in an effort to slow the enemy. His other brigade, under Colonel Andrew T. McReynolds, was to hold the left flank. In McReynolds's command was the 67th Pennsylvania Volunteer Infantry led by Colonel J. F. Staunton. This was a mixed regiment containing a sizable number of Pennsylvania Dutch as well as other ethnic groups.[15]

McReynolds ordered his men to safety behind a stone fence. The colonel then rode off to find the remaining regiment in his brigade. While he was gone, the men of the 67th broke ranks to get water from the farmyard of J. Easter, and all military organization collapsed. Colonel Staunton had committed a great error by allowing his men to become so disorganized.

Choosing a propitious moment, the Confederates launched a vicious attack, routing McReynolds's brigade and sending the Unionists running for safety. The 67th was already in a state of disorder, and the regiment broke. By the end of the brief encounter, 17 men were killed, 38 were wounded, and 791 were captured or missing. Only 117 men escaped the disaster,[16] and they fled to Harpers Ferry, Virginia. In his official report, General Milroy stated that the 67th Pennsylvania had been "principally captured."[17]

On the evening of June 15, as the men of the 67th were being routed, the men of the 87th were marching toward Martinsburg. Soon they heard gunfire and were ordered into a line of battle. Colonel Ely formed up on the right of Colonel McReynolds's brigade and ordered his men to advance into a thicket of woods. Suddenly, they were overwhelmed by enemy fire, as well as by friendly fire that poured into their ranks from the rear. The 87th fought off the enemy for about twenty minutes and then, finding themselves flanked, retreated in confusion. Colonel Schall reported, "My command became scattered, some going to the right and some to the left. . . . I have no order as to our destination." Schall retreated to Harpers Ferry with 180 men, while his lieutenant colonel retreated to Hancock, Maryland, with about 280 men. They had 240 captured, and more than 100 were missing.[18]

The Pennsylvania Dutch soldiers of the 67th and 87th were not well led at the division level. General Milroy's actions were questioned, and he was placed under arrest. A court of inquiry was conducted concerning his handling of the troops at Winchester, and Milroy was found guilty of faulty judgment. In the final analysis, however, President Abraham Lincoln felt that no court-martial was warranted.[19] The Pennsylvania Dutch soldiers had paid a heavy price for the incompetence of the high command.

By late June 1863, the Army of Northern Virginia had crossed the Potomac River and was encroaching into Maryland and Pennsylvania. Toward the end of the month, the Confederate forces had concentrated in and around Chambersburg, York, and Gettysburg. One of the major objectives of the Confederates was Pennsylvania's capital city, Harrisburg. Lieutenant General Richard Ewell, commanding the Confederate Second Corps, was ordered to advance to the Susquehanna River and, if possible, to capture Harrisburg. As Ewell's men advanced, he detached Major General Jubal Early's division to capture the important bridge crossing at Wrightsville, Pennsylvania.

To meet the impending emergency, the federal government created two new military departments: the Department of the Monongahela and the Department of the Susquehanna. Major General Darius N. Couch was ordered to Harrisburg to command the latter, and Major General William T. H. Brooks was sent to Pittsburgh to command the former.[20] Couch's assignment was to organize the troops and to prepare defensive works to protect the state and the city. To meet General Couch's need for manpower, Governor Curtin issued a call for 60,000 troops on June 12, 1863. The governor stated that "to prevent serious raids by the enemy, it is deemed

Captain James A. Stohk,
Co. A, 87th Pennsylvania,
pictured in the officer's
uniform of the Ellsworth's
Zouaves, York, Pennsylvania.
He and other Pennsylvania
Dutch members of the 87th
were originally outfitted in
colorful zouave uniforms.
ROGER HUNT COLLECTION,
U.S. ARMY MILITARY HISTORY
INSTITUTE

necessary to call upon the citizens of Pennsylvania, to furnish promptly all men necessary to organize an army corps of volunteer infantry, cavalry, and artillery, to be designated the Army Corps of the Susquehanna."[21]

The Pennsylvania Dutch did not readily respond to the call. As a matter of fact, there was a paucity of new recruits. Milroy's defeat in the Shenandoah Valley had put a damper on patriotism, and men coming home from the war spoke of the hardships. Another reason for the lukewarm volunteering was that many Pennsylvanians did not believe the threat to be real. In addition, the call was made at a critical time for the care and gathering of crops. Finally, there was a strong copperhead sentiment in the Dutch counties, and many were reluctant to fight in a Republican war—a war that had intruded upon their private way of life and that they perceived might already be lost.[22]

As Couch began preparing for a Confederate invasion, he called for troops to man the defenses. Most of the soldiers directed to him were the men recently called up by Curtin, and they were dubbed the "emergencies." Many had enlisted as individuals rather than by company. They would report to rendezvous points in several major cities, and from there they were sent to Camp Curtin in Harrisburg. These men had agreed to serve for definite periods, such as 30, 90, or 120 days; for most, it was 90 days. Many Pennsylvania Dutch were reluctant to enlist for a regular term in the army and viewed the 90 days in the state militia (as opposed to three years in the army) as a preferable alternative. The service records of these emergency units are checkered, as a brief look at two of the units demonstrates.

On June 18, the 26th Militia was mustered into service at Camp Curtin. This group consisted of 743 officers and men coming mainly from the central part of the state. There was a sizable percentage of Pennsylvania Dutch in their ranks, including, most notably, Private Samuel Pennypacker, later governor of Pennsylvania. There was also a company made up of students from Pennsylvania College in Gettysburg. Most of the men lacked military training, and many did not even know how to handle a weapon.[23]

The men were assembled at Camp Curtin, where they were issued uniforms and accoutrements. While there, the men also chose their officers, and William Jennings was elected colonel. After only two days at Camp Curtin, the 26th was put on a train destined for Gettysburg via Hanover Junction. On the way to Gettysburg, the train hit a cow, and the men were halted six miles from their destination. That night they dined on hardtack and recently butchered beef.[24]

The recruits of the 26th had received virtually no formal military training, and their colonel squandered what precious little time he had to drill them. The men often sat idle. On June 26, the regiment marched into Gettysburg and was fed a breakfast of pie, sandwiches, and coffee by the citizens of the city. The next morning, Colonel Jennings received orders from a member of General Couch's staff, Major Granville O. Haller, to march out toward Cashtown Gap along Chambersburg Pike and to delay the advance of any hostile troops. Jennings objected, stating that his men had insufficient training to stop any rebel force and would only be sacrificed to the combat veterans of Lee's army.[25]

Jennings marched his regiment out across Marsh Creek and ordered the men to make camp. As the 26th rested in camp, Jennings rode forward toward Cashtown, and about two miles from camp, he spied Confederate cavalry coming down the road past the McKnights' property. Returning hastily to camp, he ordered his men to pack up, led them across a dirt road to Mummasburg, and turned his column toward Hunterstown.[26] Henry Melchoir Muhlenberg Richards of Company A, 26th Pennsylvania, gave this account: "We, a few hundred men at the most, were in the toils, what should be done? . . . Our colonel, left to his own resources, wisely decided to make an effort to return to Harrisburg." According to Richards, they quickly broke camp and were harassed by Confederate cavalry. Finally, a rearguard action took place near Witmer's house about four and a half miles from Gettysburg on the Carlisle Pike. The 26th lost nearly 200 men in the retreat.[27]

Also responding to the crisis was the 27th Regiment of the Pennsylvania Volunteer Militia. These men came from a variety of Pennsylvania counties: Companies A, B, C, E, G, and I from Schuylkill County; Companies D and K from Northampton and Berks Counties; and Company F from Huntingdon County.[28] The recruits gathered at Camp Curtin, were organized into companies of eighty men, and became the 27th Volunteer Militia Regiment. Like the 26th Militia, they were issued equipment, were mustered into Federal service, and elected their officers in two days. The 27th Pennsylvania Militia elected Jacob Frick as colonel—a very good choice, as his leadership would be instrumental in their later success.

Frick, a Pennsylvania Dutchman from Pottsville, was thirty-six years old when he took command. He was a veteran soldier and had seen considerable service with the 96th Pennsylvania Volunteer Infantry until August 1862. After returning to Pottsville, he was given command of the nine-month regiment of the 128th Pennsylvania Volunteer Infantry, which saw extensive action at Fredericksburg and Chancellorsville and was mustered out of service on May 18, 1863. Frick returned to Pottsville again, and within a month he was given command of this new emergency unit. A substantial number of the men in his command were of Pennsylvania Dutch ethnicity, with some companies being 90 percent Dutch. These soldiers did not have to wait long for their orders; they were immediately sent to guard the all-important Wrightsville-Columbia Bridge area.

The Wrightsville-Columbia Bridge spanned the Susquehanna River. It was said to be the longest covered bridge in the world, with a span of

5,620 feet from shore to shore. It had been built in 1834 as a toll bridge, and in 1846, railroad tracks were laid across it. On the downstream side was a covered towpath that serviced the canal running from Harrisburg along the northeast bank to Columbia and then to Baltimore. The bridge and the towpath made the area an important military target.[29] Capturing the bridge would allow Southern forces easy access to Harrisburg and the important Pennsylvania Railroad bridges there. It would also provide direct railroad access between Harrisburg and the Army of the Potomac. Aware of the bridge's strategic significance, Robert E. Lee had directed Richard Ewell, in command of the Confederate Second Corps, to capture it.[30]

Several hundred ex-slaves and free blacks had begun working on the defenses at Wrightsville as early as June 18. Gun emplacements of heavy earth and timbers were erected on the Columbia side of the river, and on the Wrightsville side, entrenchments were dug across the York Pike.

Colonel Frick, in his after-action report, chronicled the actions of the 27th Pennsylvania Militia at Wrightsville. He had been ordered to leave Harrisburg on June 24 for Columbia and Wrightsville. Arriving later the same day, he immediately detached four companies to cross the Susquehanna River and take up defensive positions on the Wrightsville approaches to the bridge. In the meantime, work continued on the defensive fortifications guarding the bridge. On June 27, Frick learned that the Confederates were in York, which caused him to send all the troops to the Wrightsville side of the river. He was fearful that the enemy might suddenly appear and capture the bridge. During the night, four militia companies from Columbia came over to assist the 27th; one of those companies consisted of African-Americans. The next day, convalescent soldiers from the hospital in York, the Patapsco Guard, and elements of the 20th Pennsylvania Volunteer Militia also arrived. (The 20th also had a large number of Pennsylvania Dutch in its ranks.)[31] In all, Colonel Frick now had roughly 1,500 men to defend the bridge crossing.

During the day of June 28, the militia continued to work on their defensive fortifications until around 5:30 P.M., when a large body of the enemy came into view. Alarmed, Frick and one of General Couch's aides selected key positions to be defended. A force of 2,500 rebels quickly attacked the Pennsylvania militia. Frick's skirmishers were brushed aside, and enemy artillery began bombarding the Pennsylvanians. Frick had no artillery at hand and was forced to retreat, but he had also received orders from General Couch to destroy the bridge, if necessary.

Colonel Frick had already made arrangements for the bridge's destruction by placing black powder charges at key spots. Frick ordered that the bridge be blown up, and the men assigned to that task began to saw archways and tresses to expedite the downing of the span. After some time had passed and Frick felt certain that all his troops had reached the Columbia shore, the powder was ignited. According to Frick, "The explosion took, but our object in blowing up the bridge failed. It was then that I felt it to be my duty, in order to prevent the enemy from crossing the river and marching on Harrisburg in the rear . . . [to] order the bridge to be set on fire. The bridge was completely destroyed, though a vigorous attempt was made to save a part by the soldiers."[32] One result of the bridge's burning was that a group of Pennsylvania Dutch from Adams County—a home guard unit under Captain Robert Bell—was left on the other side. These Adams County horsemen rode into Wrightsville only to discover that it was occupied by the enemy. Bell's men immediately scattered, and all but one made their escape. That man's horse was shot out from under him, so he hid in a local house, waited until the rebels had left, and then returned to safety.[33]

The militia soldiers in Pennsylvania and the regular troops in the Shenandoah Valley had performed their duties as well as their limited training and the leadership of their officers permitted. It was not a banner effort, but these units, composed of a high percentage of Pennsylvania Dutchmen, had answered their state's call and helped blunt the initial efforts of the Southern invasion. Many more Pennsylvania Dutch citizens, however, refused to rush to the colors and remained safely in their homes, hoping the Confederate menace would pass them by. For many, it did not.

In the days preceding the battle of Gettysburg, Pennsylvania was exposed to a major Confederate effort to gather supplies. They raided from Chambersburg through Carlisle and on to Mechanicsburg. Reflective of much of the action is a diary entry of a citizen of Newville: "June 27, 1863. About 50 Rebels in town. . . . The calvary are raiding our corn cribs tonight. June 28. Johnny Reb left this morning with almost 300 cattle." The citizens of Shippensburg were concerned about the rebel incursion into their town but found enough pluck to joke with the invaders that they "were in the Union now." In Carlisle, the rebels collected ransom from the town fathers.[34]

In the early phases of the Gettysburg campaign, men of Pennsylvania Dutch stock had made their presence known. The results of their efforts were often reflective of their leadership. Nevertheless, from the Shenandoah

Valley to the Susquehanna River, the Dutch men of Pennsylvania were slowly heeding their state's call. Not all Pennsylvania Dutchmen felt inclined to fight the rebel invasion, but for the most part, the Pennsylvania Dutch soldiers acquitted themselves well.

The rebels were deep into Pennsylvania, and what would happen next was anyone's guess. The Union Army of the Potomac was closing in on the Army of Northern Virginia. Lee's army was spread out from Chambersburg to York, and he definitely did not want to bring on any action until his command was reunited. Major General Jeb Stuart's cavalry was still in the hinterland of Pennsylvania, and until Lee gained intelligence as to the whereabouts of the Union army, he wanted no contact with the enemy. This would all change on the morning of July 1, 1863, when elements of Major General A. P. Hill's Third Corps, Army of Northern Virginia, tangled with a cavalry reconnaissance force under Brigadier General John Buford on the hills and ridges north of the small, predominantly Pennsylvania Dutch town of Gettysburg, Pennsylvania.

CHAPTER 4

The Pennsylvania Dutch and "the Hard Hand of War"

Christian B. Keller

The civilians of southern Pennsylvania were unique within the Northern population. Three times during the Civil War—in September 1862, June and July 1863, and late July 1864—they were subjected to occupation by Confederate forces. Although the duration of each of these raids was short-lived, the death, property damage, and losses to foragers were not soon forgotten or easily remedied. Of the three Confederate incursions, the Gettysburg campaign was by far the longest and most memorable for the Pennsylvania Dutch, who accounted for a large percentage of the population in the southern-tier counties. Their behavior during late June and July 1863 not only sheds light on the experiences of Northern civilians during the war but also clearly demonstrates the influence of their German ethnicity and its effect on their decision making. Unlike the vast majority of Northerners, the Pennsylvania Dutch experienced the war firsthand.[1]

Spared the post-Chancellorsville criticism unleashed on their German-American compatriots, the Dutch were not free from commentary during the Gettysburg campaign. The Northern press complained about the apathy of southern Pennsylvanians, who failed to rally to the colors prior to Lee's invasion of the state. Once the two armies crossed the Mason–Dixon line, both Union and Confederate soldiers remarked on their experiences with the Pennsylvania Dutch, and the Dutch themselves wrote accounts that portrayed their diverse reactions to invasion. Some passively resisted the Southern invaders. Others panicked and fled, but most endured the occupation. A few may have even purposefully aided the Confederates. Whatever their experiences in the Gettysburg campaign, the Pennsylvania Dutch clearly exhibited ethnic traits in their actions and reactions. The unique ethnicity of these people—a combination of American and German—remained as strong as ever under "the hard hand of war."[2]

Southern Pennsylvania was home to large numbers of Pennsylvania Dutch in 1863. According to one historian's estimates, Adams County's population was almost 50 percent German, York's more than 50 percent, and Franklin's almost 40 percent.[3] Nearly all these people were farmers, spoke the Pennsylvanisch Deitsch dialect as well as English, and retained strong allegiance to the Democratic party. Most of them had voted against Abraham Lincoln in the 1860 election and lamented the advent of the draft, emancipation, and other war-related disturbances, which threatened their traditional, agricultural way of life. Although some Dutch families had sent sons as volunteers in 1861 and 1862, many refused to be involved in a conflict that they believed had been instigated by "black Republicans" against the constitutional rights of the South. Hence, they avoided participation in the Northern war effort without evincing outright resistance. Some families bought substitutes for their drafted men when the time came, and others advocated evasion. Accused of copperheadism, most of the Pennsylvania Dutch were actually lukewarm war Democrats or neutralist in their sympathies.[4] Members of the peace denominations in the southern counties—the Mennonites, Dunkers, and Amish—avoided military service because of their anticonfrontational doctrines, but ironically, they were more supportive of the war than were their Lutheran and German Reformed neighbors. The pacifists were a minority among the larger Pennsylvania Dutch population but contained a Republican majority as a result of their general anti-slavery views.[5] No matter their denomination or political affiliation, however, the Dutch of southern Pennsylvania lived directly in the path of the invading Confederates and could no longer avoid the war. The war had come to them.

J. E. B. Stuart's September 1862 cavalry raid into southern Pennsylvania caused little damage to civilian property but strongly alarmed the Dutch of Franklin County. For the first time, they became aware that their proximity to the border exposed them to a constant threat from Confederate raids. Dunker Samuel Cormany of Chambersburg enlisted in a cavalry company out of fear for "our Homes, our firesides," and to avoid being drafted. His religious principles had delayed his decision, but the presence of the main Confederate army in nearby Maryland jolted him into action.

He and his wife, Rachel, spent "a great deal of time on our knees, before our God—and agreed that as a loyal, patriotic Man I should enlist."[6]

By June 1863, the anxiety of the previous September had subsided. Although the Confederates were approaching Pennsylvania again, the Dutch watched Lee's advancing columns with apprehension but without a sense of panic—at first. Weathered by months of false alarms about impending cavalry raids, they also remembered that Lee's last "invasion" of the North had been stopped before reaching the Keystone State. Few in the Dutch communities believed that Lee's most recent thrust northward spelled mortal danger to either themselves or the Union. The Democratic majority among them viewed the recent defeat at Chancellorsville as a shame, but they blamed the Republican administration and its bungling generals. Moreover, the frantic appeals from Governor Andrew Curtin for men to enlist in emergency militia were ineffective among the Dutch, mainly because they sensed no immediate threat. Until the Confederate infantry reached Chambersburg, life among the Pennsylvania Dutch remained basically the same.[7]

Confederate officers and enlisted men wrote numerous accounts of their encounters with the Pennsylvania Dutch. Most of their descriptions of these frugal Germans were derogatory; comments about Dutch obstinacy, female ugliness, or mercenary attitudes, as well as ethnic slurs, highlight many soldiers' anecdotes. Some also deal with the Dutch reactions to Confederate foraging, which was greeted by protest and even some resistance. A few soldiers, though, viewed the Pennsylvania Dutch in a positive light, treating them with courtesy and remarking favorably on certain cultural traits. Perhaps influenced by postwar reunionist sympathies, certain former Confederates remembered the Dutch welcoming the invaders and perhaps collaborating with them. Regardless of the varying perceptions, one of the problems in reconstructing the history of encounters between Dutch civilians and Confederates is the accuracy of anecdotal material. Many postwar reminiscences by former Confederates are suspect, and in the case of the Gettysburg campaign, some Southerners wanted to prove that their army behaved honorably compared with the Union armies, which ravaged the South. These histories, however, such as Gordon's *Reminiscences,* also contain vivid descriptions of Confederate-Dutch interactions and cannot be discarded out of hand. Thus, post-1865 remembrances should not be ruled out as source material, but they need to be carefully examined in light of the times in which they were written.[8]

Confederate staff officer G. Moxley Sorrel remarked in his recollections that the Pennsylvania Dutch were "a queer lot" whose women possessed "hard features" and who had "huge road-wagons like ships at sea" that carried the incredible amounts of food raised on their farms. He correctly surmised their ethnicity but added an insult, calling them "an ignorant off-shoot of a certain class of Germans long settled there." Sorrel was not the only Confederate to remark negatively on the ethnicity of the Dutch. Virginian Hodijah Lincoln Meade called them "simple ignorant and degraded," and General Dorsey Pender termed them "the most miserable people," adding that "they are coarse and dirty," with large numbers of "dirty-looking children." Another Confederate wrote that the girls in Pennsylvania were "nothing but Dutch and Irish and the dirty and . . . meanest looking creaturs [*sic*] that I ever saw." One observer even claimed that captured Dutch horses were "utterly unserviceable" and had "as little taste or talent for war as their fat Dutch proprietors."[9]

Reid Mitchell argues that such derogatory comments are characteristic of Americans at war—they degrade their enemies to make them seem less than human. It is also conceivable that anti-Dutch comments from Confederates were reflective of a general aversion to Germans. Confederates encountering Pennsylvania Dutch people on their home soil and hearing the unintelligible Pennsylvanisch Deitsch dialect might have easily equated them with the "German hirelings" they had encountered on the battlefield and so disliked. It would have been difficult for many Southerners to distinguish between the Dutch and German-Americans. It is clear they disdained the latter. An article in the *Knoxville Tennessee Register* from June 1863 asked, "Why are not all captured Dutchmen hanged?" Describing the Germans as a "stinking, sauerkraut-eating and beer-drinking mass," the editor called for the same treatment of captured Germans as that given to white officers of black regiments.[10]

Not all Confederates regarded the Pennsylvania Dutch with contempt. Mennonites Jacob and Elizabeth Grove of Greencastle were impressed by the "chivalrous courtesy" of the first Southerners to reach their town. Two officers approached their house, removed their plumed hats, bowed to Mrs. Grove, and asked if she and her husband were hiding Union soldiers. Mrs. Grove's answer was to summon her two teenaged sons, both of whom were wearing blue denim, which the Confederates had mistaken for blue uniforms. The officers, realizing their mistake, again removed their hats, "bowed from the waist, thanked her, [and] returned to their horses at the front yard gate." Lieutenant William Owen of the famous New Orleans Washington Artillery remembered that he and the officers of his battery were "well entertained" by a German couple, "the hospitable occupants" of a large farm where the battery encamped. After sleeping overnight in the farmhouse and enjoying a hearty breakfast, Owen handed them two silver half-dollars, to which the man said, "Py jimminy, dis war is big luck for some peebles!"[11]

A musician in the 26th North Carolina's band (many of whose members had a Moravian background) likewise reported favorably on the Pennsylvania Dutch. En route to Gettysburg, he struck up a congenial conversation in German with a woman in Greencastle and was invited to share a meal with her. Texan J. B. Polley recalled another incident in Greencastle in which a "well preserved lady of fifty" at first refused the entreaties of Confederates for provisions, but when told that they were "quite hungry," opened her door with a smile, claiming that the "Bible commands us to feed the hungry, and it is of higher authority than the orders of man." Based on her clear deference to the laws of God, it is likely this woman was a Mennonite or Dunker. Years later, Confederate General John B. Gordon wrote in his reminiscences of "the big red barns" of the Dutch, "representing in their silent dignity the independence of their owners." Gordon happily accepted the invitation of one "staid and laborious farmer of German descent" to dine with his family for breakfast. The former general remembered the natural spring that fed directly into a fountain in the dining room; the sound from this spring, coupled "with a hot breakfast," amazed him with "the sensation of rest which it produced."[12]

Most encounters between the Dutch and Confederates revolved around the Southerners' need for something the former had, whether it be space to camp, food, supplies, or information. Feeding a few Southern officers for a meal or two did not seem to bother most Pennsylvania Dutch, and quartering them on their land or in their houses was likewise seen as a tolerable price to pay. Confederate requisitions of Dutch property—grain, cured meats, livestock, horses, wagons, and even water—and the damages incurred while obtaining these commodities were something entirely different. The Pennsylvania Dutch reacted vociferously and even violently to what they perceived as outright robbery, and Confederate soldiers in turn reacted with surprise and amusement. After all, Southern civilians had been suffering the fate now inflicted on the Dutch for over two years, and all requisitions were legitimately paid for—in Confederate money.

Virginian Frederick Mason Colston remembered one Dutch farmer's reaction to the passage of Confederate troops through his farm. Some wheat near the road had been trampled, and soldiers with muddy boots had tracked dirt onto the farmer's front porch, where a water pump was located. Approaching the soldiers' officers, the farmer exclaimed, "I have heardt and I have readt, of de horros of warfare, but my utmost conceptions did not equal dis." Another old Dutchman refused to give up his horses to a raiding party, and after a heated argument with the Confederates, he grabbed a gun and shot five of them before being shot himself. Such acts were not indicative of patriotic resistance to Confederate invasion; rather, they were personal reactions to the theft or destruction of property, which was considered a high crime among the Pennsylvania Dutch and was tantamount to declaring war on one aspect of their ethnicity—the agricultural way of life. Additionally, the fact that many Pennsylvania Dutch farmers' survival was completely dependent on their horses and cattle and the timely harvest of crops may have instigated much of the resistance the Confederates recorded. The timing of the Confederate invasion could not have been worse for the farmers, whose summer wheat was ready for harvesting, making their horses indispensable.[13]

The Confederate invaders were not unilaterally shunned and viewed as pillagers by the Pennsylvania Dutch. Several soldiers wrote about the apparent warm welcome they received, and General John B. Gordon even hinted at possible collaboration. Although evidence suggesting Dutch happiness over the Confederate presence is circumstantial, enough exists to question whether they were only pretending to be friendly, with the hope of good treatment, or whether they truly rejoiced at the Confederate invasion. One soldier of Pickett's divison wrote about his passage through Middletown, Maryland (a town whose citizens were descended mainly from early Pennsylvania Dutch settlers) on June 26. He stared in disbelief at

> fully a dozen miniature Confederate flags waving from windows, while all along the streets were ladies waving handkerchiefs and scarfs from the piazzas and upper windows! Can it be that these people are sincere? Or, are these demonstrations merely a part of Dutch cunning to placate the oft-pictured, wild, cantankerous, ravenous Reb of whom so many lies are told that simple people

believe him a monster of cruelty? Possibly tho', these are Democratic families that have been persecuted and harassed by their abolition neighbors until they really welcome the advent of our army as a relief.[14]

It is difficult to tell from this excerpt whether the townspeople who apparently welcomed the Confederates were mainly Dutch, but the author refers to "Dutch cunning," presumably indicating his belief that they were. It is also impossible to discover whether these people truly welcomed the rebels or were merely presenting a facade of Confederate patriotism. Nonetheless, the Dutch in this instance were clearly not resisting the Confederate advance.

Good behavior and discipline among the Confederates impressed the Pennsylvania Dutch, to the point that some Southerners were welcomed among them. Chaplain James B. Sheeron of the 14th Louisiana wrote that the relatively "good behavior" of his troops "had made many friends" among southern Pennsylvanians. Some historians have argued that the good conduct of Southern troops—compared with what the local residents expected and feared—may have actually contributed to the sense of apathy during the Confederate occupation. Although such a theory is difficult to prove, it makes sense that some Pennsylvania Dutch, who were mainly anti-Republican to begin with, would find little reason to resist invaders who not only fought against the Republicans but also treated the Dutch better than anticipated. As long as their property remained relatively intact, there was no need to inspire the ire of the Confederates. Perhaps there was some truth to the accusations of copperheadism among the Dutch, but any collaboration between them and the Confederates was probably inspired by more practical considerations.[15]

By far the most blatant example of possible Dutch collaboration comes from the *Reminiscences* of Confederate General John B. Gordon. As his command marched through York on its way to cross the Susquehanna, he remembered a little girl running up to his horse with a bouquet of flowers. Closer examination of the flowers revealed a small note tucked inside the petals describing the number and position of Union forces defending the bridge at Wrightsville. The note "bore no signature, and contained no assurance of sympathy for the Southern cause, but it was so terse and explicit in its terms as to compel my confidence." When Gordon arrived at Wrightsville, he confirmed the note's veracity: "Not an inaccurate detail in that note could be discovered." It is impossible to determine whether the note's author was Pennsylvania Dutch, but at the time, York was the county seat of one of the most Dutch-populated counties in the state.[16]

While in Wrightsville, Gordon recalled another incident that might be described as "collaborative." Mrs. L. L. Rewalt's home had been spared from the fire that destroyed the bridge over the river and spread to the town. Some of Gordon's men helped save her house, and the next day, Mrs. Rewalt invited Gordon and his officers to breakfast. "The welcome she gave us was so gracious, she was so self-possessed, so calm and kind," that Gordon inquired which side she favored. Rewalt answered, "I am a Union woman," but added, "You and your soldiers last night saved my home from burning, and I was unwilling that you should go away without receiving some token of my appreciation." Perhaps Rewalt's motive was rooted purely in gratitude, but compared with other Dutch women, such as Rachel Cormany, her breakfast with the enemy could be viewed as collaborative.[17]

The other major eyewitnesses to Confederate-Dutch encounters were the Pennsylvania Dutch themselves. They left comparatively fewer accounts of their meetings with Southerners than the Confederates did, but a few diaries, letter groups, newspapers, and strong family oral traditions survive that provide a window on Dutch civilian reactions to invasion and occupation. The Dutch relished the status quo, which allowed them to pursue their agricultural vocations and religious beliefs quietly and without disturbance. All they really wanted was to be left alone, and after two years of intrusion and expense from the federal government in the form of the draft and substitution fees, their worst nightmares were realized. The war was no longer in faraway Virginia—it was about to be fought in their midst. This realization terrified most Pennsylvania Dutch farmers. Fearing economic ruin through Confederate pillaging, hundreds of them from the lower Cumberland Valley packed their wagons to the brim and fled northward to Harrisburg when the first Confederate cavalry crossed the Mason-Dixon line. We have little documentation of the experiences of these refugees, but it is important to note that flight was an option that many Pennsylvania Dutch chose to exercise. Those who opted to stay behind with their property reacted diversely to the invasion and utilized various methods of dealing with the Confederates. Most adopted a completely passive approach, giving the invaders what they wanted and offering neither resistance nor any sign of approval. Others viewed the Confederates as violent intruders and reacted strongly to their demands for requisitions. Many accounts mention the use of deception to make the Confederates think the Dutch had nothing to give them; a few others hint at open Dutch collaboration or resistance. Whatever their reaction, protection of their property appeared to be foremost in their minds.[18]

By far the most common reaction among the Pennsylvania Dutch who remained at home was passivity. Condemned by many in the North at the time for adopting this course of action, and lampooned even today for failing to resist in any substantial way, the Dutch reacted in a way that was not only intelligent but in some cases foreordained. Like most civilians under foreign occupation, the Pennsylvania Dutch knew that stirring up trouble while the Confederates were encamped among them was foolhardy. If the enemy's good behavior could be earned through compliance with his demands, or at least by remaining aloof, the Dutch stood a better chance of preserving their property and surviving the ordeal more or less intact. Of course, no one knew that the Confederates would soon be defeated at Gettysburg and retreat. Thus, the majority of the Dutch reacted as most civilians in an occupied population would have. Additionally, the pacifist sects among them forbade involvement in any kind of violence, so active resistance against the invaders was out of the question. The Chambersburg and Greencastle areas were heavily populated by Mennonites and Dunkers, and an anecdote from the historian of Brigadier General J. B. Kershaw's brigade clearly illustrates what must have been considered an act of resistance to them but was clearly a passive reaction to the author, who mistakenly called these people Quakers:[19]

> When the front of the column came to the line dividing Pennsylvania and Maryland, it was met by a delegation of those rigorously righteous old Quakers who, stepping in the middle of the road, commanded as in the name of God, "So far thou canst go, but no farther." After performing his seemingly command of God in accordance with their faith, a total abhorrence of war and bloodshed, they returned to their homes perfectly satisfied.[20]

Dunker Rachel Cormany lamented the passive approach taken by many of her neighbors. She complained of "copperheads" giving food to the enemy and providing more supplies than necessary to rebel requisitioners.

Local farmers were forced by the Confederate occupiers of Chambersburg "to take them breat—meat—&c to eat," but Cormany regretted the "dumb fools [who] carried them jellies and the like." No doubt Cormany's neighbors believed that supplying the Confederates with a bit extra would put them in the enemy's good graces. A passive reaction to invasion must have made sense to them.[21]

Cormany was not alone in condemning the passive stance of their neighbors. Nathan S. Wolle, a Moravian pastor in Lititz, wrote to his cousin on June 25 that "we have fallen into our wonted apathy and don't believe things are as bad as the papers represent it." There had been a patriotic rally the week before, which had stirred up enthusiasm for the defense of the state, but now all had quieted down. Wolle complained that the rally had done nothing but "disclose some of the copperhead venom amongst us" and "widened the breach between us loyalists and such traitors."[22] Wolle's comments are revealing. Although they did not consider themselves part of the Pennsylvania Dutch community, the Moravians shared many qualities with the Mennonites, Amish, and Dunkers. Like the sectarians, their church was Germanic in origin, and members worshipped in High German. They also tended to vote Republican and followed a nonconfrontational pacifist ideology.[23] Unlike the other pacifists, however, the Moravians did not shun active political participation and lamented the copperhead-like apathy among the larger Pennsylvania Dutch population during the Gettysburg campaign. Edward de Schweinitz, editor of the *Moravian* newspaper, feared on June 30 that the lack of patriotism among his neighbors might cause a Confederate victory. "In a few days, we may, in these counties, be under rebel sway." In a letter he wrote from Bethlehem, in Northampton County—a long way from southern Pennsylvania—de Schweinitz's fear was exaggerated, but an editorial he wrote clearly deplored the Pennsylvania Dutch inertia: "Whilst the state is languishing in the very throes of death, instead of rushing to her deliverance they stand back to see whether some other arm may not be extended for her rescue. It is a burning shame."[24]

Some of the Pennsylvania Dutch found that the passive approach to occupation and invasion failed. Even though they complied with Confederate requests, their encounters with the Confederates ended in violence. Mennonite Michael Hege of southern Franklin County kept a diary during the war and wrote a poem in German about his family's ordeal during the Confederate invasion. The verses described three rebels who appeared on June 27 and demanded access to his house and his purse. After taking all his money, one soldier lined Hege's family up against a wall and threatened to shoot them as the other two rifled through chests and drawers. Hege was sure that he was going to die: "I turned myself upon the bed so I would not see the fire [from the gun]; I closed my eyes and thought it was all over." Hege prayed to God to spare him and his family, and his prayers were answered when one of the soldiers interposed himself between his comrade with the gun and Hege. Their pillaging over, the three rebels left, and Hege and his family praised God for their salvation. Isaac Strite, also a Mennonite, was not as lucky. Confederates approached his farm looking for money, which he freely gave them. Then they decided to burn his barn, and Strite begged them to spare it. Their answer was a bullet. Strite died immediately.[25]

Most encounters between the Pennsylvania Dutch and Confederates ended less tragically, although the Hege and Strite incidents indicate that not all Confederates obeyed Robert E. Lee's Order Number 73 not to molest civilians.[26] Certainly, many Dutch farmers perceived the requisitioning of their horses, livestock, and foodstuffs by Southerners as blatant robbery. Although they were given receipts by the quartermasters and were often paid in Confederate money, the Dutch understood how worthless these vouchers were. Many attempted to keep what was theirs through deception. Rachel Cormany recounted that local merchants who had failed to hide their goods were "ruined" by the Confederate occupation. Catherine Horst Hunsecker remembered years later how Dutch farmers had tried to hide their horses in the mountains; her own father had locked his valuable papers in the floor of the smokehouse and hid the best "horse gears" in the bake oven. Henry Hege of Marion wrote to his brother that he kept his house locked to discourage intruders and "handed bread out the door" to passing Confederates, joking and smiling at them in the hope that this bold front would prevent the plundering of his house. His ploy worked, but he still lost all his horses, and his father suffered $2,000 worth of damages. It "was awful," he remarked, to see the Southerners go "through the fields to hunt horses."[27]

Although Reading was on the other side of the Susquehanna from the Confederates, its Pennsylvania Dutch citizens were just as frightened of the impending invasion as their compatriots in Adams and Franklin Counties. An announcement to rally to the colors in the June 30 edition of the *Reading Adler* clearly appealed to ethnic Dutch sensitivities:

A warning call to the men of Berks! Men of Berks! You must defend your homeland on the Susquehanna! Once on this side of the Susquehanna, the rebels are master of everything that is yours. Your horses, your cattle, your crops, your filled granaries will be seen by the enemy as welcome spoils of war.

The editor appealed to owners of mills and factories to defend them as well and stated that the time had come for men of all classes, backgrounds, and political persuasions to join together to repel the foe. This was a big step for Charles Kessler, the editor of the Democratic *Adler;* until this point, his newspaper had stood against everything the Republican state and national leadership had done since the war began and had remained unconcerned with the Confederate invasion. Yet the appeals he used toward the Democratic Dutch of Berks County did not mention anything patriotic. Instead, he concentrated on what mattered to them: their agriculture and their property. Like appeals from Confederate authorities for Southerners to enlist in the army to defend "hearth and home," some Pennsylvania Dutch leaders apparently believed that appeals for the protection of property might spur the citizenry into action.[28]

Whether or not the Confederates believed that some of the Dutch actively assisted them during the invasion, there is little evidence to confirm this belief. An editor in Gettysburg, probably of German descent, was arrested after the battle based on testimony that he had revealed some hiding Union soldiers to Confederate officers. Horses and livestock carefully concealed in remote glens and woods were systematically discovered by Confederate foragers, prompting some Pennsylvania Dutch to believe that turncoats among them had revealed the hiding places. Beyond these rumors, however, the Pennsylvania Dutch remembered producing no viable collaborators.[29]

Similarly, few references to active, patriotic Dutch resistance during the Gettysburg campaign exist. There were some instances of bushwhackers in the Allegheny Mountains ambushing lone Confederate foraging parties and women proudly defying Lee's passing troops with Union flags sewn onto their bosoms, but it is impossible to determine whether these people were of German ethnicity. Rachel Cormany, however, clearly did not welcome the Southern invaders, and her diary is rife with complaints against the Confederates. Watching passing troops on June 27, she heard a remark she did not like and "curled my lip as disdainful as I could & turned away." She positively hated the Confederate banner. "I did wish I dared spit at their old flag." Three days later, she and some young friends sang "all the patriotic & popular war songs" in her parlor, to the amusement of Southerners encamped nearby. She also reported that neighbors misdirected small detachments of Confederate troops who asked for directions to Gettysburg while the battle raged.[30]

When news of the Confederate defeat spread, however, some Pennsylvania Dutch on the southern retreat route suddenly grew more daring. David Shook of Greencastle recalled raiding the Southern baggage train himself, capturing "a fine bay horse" and witnessing many cattle mysteriously "turned into alleys." Certain horses "tied behind wagons had their halters cut, and were led away unobserved." According to General John Imboden of the Confederate cavalry, Greencastle residents also "attacked the train with axes, cutting the spokes out of ten or a dozen wheels and dropping the wagons in the streets." Returning swiftly from the front of the retreating column with his men, Imboden was prevented from retaliating by the appearance of Union cavalry. Again, it is almost impossible to determine whether the civilian saboteurs were ethnically German, but based on sheer probability, it seems likely. Greencastle was home to numerous Lutherans and German Reformed church members who would not have shunned violent activities, as the Mennonites and Dunkers did. It is also difficult to know whether the people who attacked the Confederate train and led away the animals did so out of loyalty to the Union or for their own self-interests. Perhaps it was a combination of both.[31]

German-Americans in Pennsylvania also reacted to the Confederate invasion, even though they were not in the direct path of the enemy. Newspaper editorials from Pittsburgh and Philadelphia portrayed a sense of high anxiety among the cities' German populations. Indications of dissatisfaction with the reactions of the Dutch in southern Pennsylvania also riddled some of the immigrant German newspapers. Georg Ripper of the *Pittsburgher Demokrat* found the unenthusiastic response of southern Pennsylvanians lamentable but excused the Dutch on account of political bungling in Harrisburg. Under the title "Pennsylvania's Defenselessness," Ripper placed all the blame on state Republican leaders. They had lost the citizens' trust, poorly deployed the volunteer troops who did answer their country's call, and now wondered why the pool of citizen-soldiers had dried up. "The fault lies in Harrisburg," Ripper declared. Yet Allegheny County Germans were earnestly doing their share. "Wild enthusiasm reigns" in Pittsburgh, he said. German-Americans there, like the Pennsylvania Dutch in Reading, had to surmount the crisis through unity. Although the problems attending Lee's invasion were worsened by Republican shortsightedness, Ripper believed that the time had come to set aside differences temporarily—at least economic ones. On June 29, he exhorted the rich and poor to come together in defense of the state: "If the rich become plundered, if our ironworks and factories are destroyed and burned down, where then do the poor earn their bread?"[32]

In Philadelphia, the Republican *Freie Presse* joined its Democratic counterpart in Pittsburgh in sounding the general alarm. Orchards would be picked clean, fences torn down and burned for firewood, grain and horses stolen, and "grave devastation" would reign supreme if the rebels reached Philadelphia. "Yet that is not all. Even worse fates stand before us." Using the example of Confederate General Jubal Early's demands on the city of York just days before, the editor claimed that the levy on a captured Philadelphia would be far worse. "Our city with its 700,000 inhabitants would have to come up with at least 15 million dollars." In a gibe at German Democrats both in southern Pennsylvania and in Philadelphia, he exclaimed that "German copperheads" would not be exempted from this levy. "Whoever believed up until now that the rebels would respect private property . . . must now to his shame admit to a better conviction."[33]

Many Union soldiers were also appalled at the general inertia among southern Pennsylvanians. They commented in disbelief at the lack of guerrilla warfare, which certainly would have harassed Union forces in Virginia had the strategic scenario been reversed. They also remarked on the difference between civilian receptions in Maryland and Pennsylvania. In Maryland, the townspeople all but joined them on the march, waving flags, providing refreshments, and cheering as they passed by. In southern Pennsylvania, no similar celebrations occurred. Many Dutch inhabitants of the Pennsylvania towns and farms viewed the pursuing Union troops as just the second phase of their despoliation. First the Confederates had arrived and taken all they had, and now the Federal army expected a warm welcome. Dutch Democrats blamed the war on the Republicans and hence viewed the Union troops as only slightly better than the Confederates. Dutch farmers, many of them robbed of the means to preserve their agricultural way of life, saw the

men in blue as inept protectors who arrived too late, and they feared even
further requisitions at the hands of Federal authorities. Concerned about
their future, some Pennsylvania Dutch began charging Union soldiers for
the use of their wells or dinner tables to help offset their losses.[34]

Private Samuel Hurst of the 73d Ohio remembered passing through "a
very rich farming district" on the way to Gettysburg. "We expected to see
[the citizens] rising as one man, and rushing to arms to defend their homes,"
but instead "saw them rush to the fields with scythe, and reaper, and leave
the work of driving back the foe undivided to ourselves." Another soldier,
Private Frank Sawyer of the 8th Ohio, recalled that "the people were not
glad to see us." Sawyer was particularly offended by "one dumpy sort of
woman, whom we took to be a lineal descendant of some original Hessian."
She "spoke bad English, bad French, and what [was] worst of all, good
Dutch; she refused to admit us to her kitchen . . . and wanted a dollar a gal-
lon for milk, and half dollar for a cruet of vinegar." An unknown soldier of
the 38th Pennsylvania also complained about local parsimony in his home-
town newspaper, reporting that the citizens of Greencastle were asking
ridiculous prices for food. "Allow me to say, all the bread this regiment got,
we paid a big price for. . . . Half a loaf of bread, 25 cents; pies, 25 cents; and
nothing free of charge. At Greencastle everything was double."[35]

Colonel Robert McFarland of the 151st Pennsylvania—a regiment with
many Pennsylvania Dutchmen among its ranks—was similarly disgusted at
the mercenary interests of the Dutch. Arriving late at night at a hotel near
the state line, McFarland and his officers awakened the proprietor and asked
for some food. "No sooner did he see our uniforms than he exclaimed, 'I bin
a Union man, I give Union soldiers every ting I have.'" The innkeeper then
produced "a little cold sausage and some hard bread." When the officers had
finished, they asked if there was a charge. "Fifty cents," replied the Dutchman. McFarland paid, "feeling however that the old man's unionism was
more likely in his pockets than elsewhere."[36]

Complaints about the Pennsylvania Dutch by Northern soldiers found
their way into some of the prominent Anglo-American newspapers. *Harper's
Weekly,* for instance, printed a cartoon on July 11 depicting a stereotypical
Pennsylvania Dutchman, replete with broad-brimmed hat, standing by a
table with a bucket of water and a sign in the background that read, "Susquehanna Water 6 cents a glass." A thirsty soldier confronted the would-be
entrepreneur, shaking his head in disbelief. The caption read: "Six cents a

glass rather dear, you think? Pshaw! What's the good of having you fellows from New York if we can't make something out of you to cover what we lost to the rebel raiders?" The *New York Times* ran an editorial two days earlier that contained an even more direct accusation of Dutch stinginess: The men, who had run away before the battle, returned not "to lend a helping hand to our wounded" or to "open their houses to our famished officers and soldiers" but only "to present their bills to the military authorities for payment of losses inflicted by both armies." All they cared about was receiving compensation for damages, the editor complained, and "almost entirely they are uncourteous—but this is plainly from lack of intelligence." Their charges for food were outrageous, and they manifested "a sordid meanness and unpatriotic spirit" toward the "noble army [that] had driven a hated enemy" away. Clearly, the Pennsylvania Dutch had made a bad impression on the Northern troops.[37]

The end of the battle brought an end to Confederate occupation, but it also exposed the extent of the losses suffered by the Pennsylvania Dutch. Their property losses reached the millions of dollars, and some farmers never received compensation for their damages. Grain rotted in the fields of the many farmers who had lost their horses. Orchards and larders had been picked clean, fields near roads had been trampled so badly that plowing had little effect, and fences everywhere had been vandalized beyond repair. Even worse, many local roads were almost impassable, thanks to the deep ruts caused by the continual military traffic. Broken-down wagons, animal waste, and a grimy layer of dust that covered every flat surface had to be cleared away. Those living around Gettysburg and Chambersburg suffered the worst, and some of their descendants were still petitioning state and federal authorities in the early twentieth century.[38]

The Confederate invasion also wreaked havoc among two of the dominant Pennsylvania Dutch religious denominations. The Lutheran Theological Seminary at Gettysburg was badly damaged; the last academic session of the year was suspended, and the institution's buildings were hastily converted into field hospitals. Divinity professor Samuel Schmucker, who had spoken against slavery before the war, lost most of his personal papers to Confederate pillagers. He was one of several faculty members who suffered losses. The directors of the seminary reported that $5,000 to $7,000 in donations from Lutheran congregations across the state would be required just to repair the physical damage. The German Reformed Seminary at Mercersburg was likewise afflicted; it too became a makeshift hospital, although the physical destruction was milder. Even the Moravians felt the effects of Gettysburg: The congregation in York was forced to suspend its services immediately after the battle, since its pastor had gone to Gettysburg to care for Moravian wounded from North Carolina.[39]

The wounded of both sides suffered in field hospitals and private homes all across southern Pennsylvania. Despite their property losses, some of the Pennsylvania Dutch did their best to help the wounded and needy. Fannie Buehler, a Gettysburg resident who had risked reprisals from the Confederates for nursing wounded Union soldiers, remembered another German, a "Mr. Frey, the German [who] came from Berks county." He had been wounded in the first day's fight and found safety in Mrs. Buehler's house. He soon proved indispensable to her. "I could not have done all I did without their help, and I believe it was by God's appointment they came to my relief," she said of Frey and a few other slightly wounded soldiers who assisted her with the more serious cases. Frey risked his life finding baker's yeast for Mrs. Buehler, who then baked bread for the wounded men in her care. Another Dutch farmer just north of Emmitsburg offered "thirty ton of hay, several thousand bushels of corn, [and] plenty of flour, wheat and buckwheat" to General John Buford's weary cavalry division as it followed the retreating rebels on July 4. Isaac Dunkleberger of the 1st Cavalry remembered how welcome these supplies were: "I wonder if any mortal man ever made six thousand men more happy and grateful than that Dutchman did. I regret that I never met him afterwards to personally thank him." The unnamed Dutchman did not want to take a voucher for these supplies, but the division quartermaster insisted.[40]

The Gettysburg campaign strongly affected the Pennsylvania Dutch. They, along with Confederate and Union observers, recorded their reactions to invasion, occupation, and war, but these reactions varied significantly, depending on whose account it was and how closely affected the chronicler was by the events. Confederates viewed the Dutch both negatively and positively, whereas Union soldiers were generally displeased with the reception they received from the Dutch. The Pennsylvania Dutch themselves adopted numerous courses of action: flight, passivity, deception, and possibly collaboration, although the fragmentary evidence supporting this last contention emanated mainly from Southern sources.

Importantly, regardless of who left the account, most Pennsylvania Dutch behavior was influenced at least partially by their ethnic identity. Passive responses, for example, were often prompted by the religious principles of certain Dutch denominations. Similarly, those who resisted Confederate foragers did so not as a result of patriotic urges but probably because of ethnic considerations. The theft of private property, especially agricultural supplies, was tantamount to a direct attack on the Pennsylvania Dutch way of life and directly threatened the survival of the families in question. Additionally, the evidence supporting collaboration points more toward the Dutch desire to preserve the cherished status quo—which allowed them to pursue their vocations independently and without interference—than to outright copperheadism.

As the theater of operations once again transferred to Virginia after Lee's retreat, the Pennsylvania Dutch calculated their losses, surveyed their trampled fields, and thanked God for sparing their lives. They had experienced something that few other Northerners would endure: occupation by the enemy. After the Union victory at Gettysburg, they believed that they would never have to face that nightmare again. Unfortunately, the burning of Chambersburg the next summer would prove them wrong.

CHAPTER 5

The Campaign and Battle of Gettysburg

Scott Hartwig

Following his stunning victory at Chancellorsville in early May 1863, Robert E. Lee, commander of the Confederate Army of Northern Virginia, and the leadership of Jefferson Davis's Confederate government pondered how to exploit the initiative that Lee's success had wrested from the enemy. The knotty question was what strategic option the Confederacy should pursue in the summer of 1863.

Despite Lee's victory at Chancellorsville, the odds were accumulating against the Confederacy. By the third week in May, a Union army under Ulysses S. Grant had bottled up the Confederate army of John Pemberton in Vicksburg, Mississippi. Unless Pemberton could be relieved, Vicksburg would be lost, giving the Union virtually complete control of the Mississippi River. Despite the passage of a conscription act in the spring of 1862, requiring men between the ages of eighteen and thirty-five to serve in the army, battle and nonbattle losses from disease, desertion, and other causes were greater than the South's ability to replace them. The South was running short of manpower. Its rail system, which had started the war greatly inferior to the North's, was sagging under the strain of the demands placed on it, and all Confederate armies suffered from shortages of food and other supplies. Additionally, Abraham Lincoln's Emancipation Proclamation had dashed any realistic hope of intervention by England or France.

Lee argued that the Confederacy's best hope for independence lay in carrying the war to Northern soil. He had attempted this once before, in September 1862, when his army crossed the Potomac River into Maryland, intending to push into Pennsylvania. But circumstances forced Lee to give battle in Maryland. The battle of Antietam, as it came to be called, cost both armies a total of 25,000 killed and wounded—the bloodiest single day of the war. The battle ended in a draw, but Lee's army was spent, and he withdrew to Virginia. Now, the victory at Chancellorsville offered a fresh opportunity to carry the war to the North. Such an operation entailed many risks, but Lee believed that these were outweighed by the gains that might be reaped. Invading Pennsylvania would enable Lee to keep the initiative and disrupt the Union army's plans for a summer campaign. Pennsylvania offered a rich landscape untouched by war, where Lee could supply his army and accumulate additional supplies for the fall. This would relieve Virginia from the burden of feeding his army and allow that state a respite from the occupying armies. Lee might temporarily capture Harrisburg, Pennsylvania's capital, and threaten Washington, Baltimore, and Philadelphia. Even the temporary occupation of Harrisburg would be an embarrassing blow to the Lincoln administration and would help fuel the fires of a growing Northern peace movement. If Lee could fight the Army of the Potomac on Northern soil under favorable circumstances and defeat it, this might create an even greater crisis for Lincoln. Although Lee did not march north seeking such a major battle, he would not avoid one if conditions were favorable.

In mid-May, Lee met with Confederate President Jefferson Davis and Secretary of War James A. Seddon in Richmond to discuss his proposed plan for an invasion of Pennsylvania. Initially, both men were inclined to support Lee's plan, but when news arrived that Grant had bottled up Pemberton's army in Richmond, Davis suggested that perhaps they should draw troops from Lee's army to help relieve Vicksburg. Lee did not agree; he believed that keeping his army strong would do more to positively influence the war than would detaching troops in reaction to the enemy's advances. Davis relented and gave approval to go forward.

THE ARMY OF NORTHERN VIRGINIA

In preparation for the summer campaign, Lee reorganized his army. Previously, the army had consisted of two infantry corps and a cavalry division. Each corps numbered nearly 30,000 men—too many, Lee believed, for one man to command and control effectively. Following the death of Second Corps commander "Stonewall" Jackson from wounds suffered at Chancellorsville, Lee reorganized the army into three corps of approximately 20,000 men each. Lieutenant General James Longstreet, Lee's most trusted and experienced subordinate, remained in command of the First Corps. Lee filled Jackson's position with Lieutenant General Richard S. Ewell. A new Third Corps was organized by taking a division each from the First and Second Corps and creating a third division from other troops. Command of this corps went to Ambrose Powell Hill. Major General James E. B. ("Jeb") Stuart remained in command of the cavalry division. A flamboyant and somewhat egotistical man, Stuart was an outstanding cavalry officer, serving ably as Lee's "eyes and ears" when the army was on campaign.

The army prepared for the summer campaign with great confidence. After the victories of 1862 and the recent triumph at Chancellorsville, many enlisted men and officers alike believed that the next battle might decide the war in favor of Confederate independence. With high spirits and a complete trust in the ability of their commanding general, the soldiers of the Army of Northern Virginia were eager to meet the enemy again and defeat him.

Some modest reinforcements were received to strengthen the army, so Lee began the summer campaign with a force totaling approximately 77,000 officers and men. This powerful force included nearly 10,000 cavalry—the strongest cavalry force yet assembled in the eastern theater of the war by the Confederates and nearly 280 pieces of artillery. It was a splendid army, and victory seemed to be its destiny that summer.

THE ARMY OF THE POTOMAC

On May 14, 1863, Captain Francis Donaldson of the 118th Pennsylvania Infantry wrote to his brother, "the army is in a very unsettled condition. The men are morose, sullen, dissatisfied, disappointed, and mortified." From the perspective of the fighting men of the Army of the Potomac, Hooker had lost the battle of Chancellorsville, not them. "I don't see how we can hope to succeed if we are not better handled," observed Donaldson. Many in the army shared the captain's opinion. Since July 1862, the army had served under four different commanders. First, had been the beloved George B. McClellan, the original army commander; then John Pope; followed by McClellan again, who led the army to its near victory at Antietam. Ambrose Burnside replaced McClellan in November and led the army to its most depressing defeat at Fredericksburg. Hooker took Burnside's place, reorganized the army, and restored its flagging morale. Chancellorsville did not undo the positive changes Hooker had made to the army's organization, but it did strike a blow to its morale and to its confidence in Hooker's ability to deliver victory. General Darius Couch, the senior corps commander with the army, was so disgusted with Hooker's generalship that he refused to serve under him any longer and requested a transfer. Not only the army had lost confidence in Hooker. President Lincoln also doubted Hooker's ability to defeat Lee, but he hesitated to remove him from command.[1]

Despite the many changes in army commanders and the string of dismal defeats it had suffered at the hands of Lee and the Army of Northern Virginia, the Northern army remained remarkably resilient. "Why, do you know that not withstanding our discouragements we are now fast recovering and could make a big fight today if we had someone to inspire us with confidence," wrote Captain Donaldson. Thousands of others in the army echoed the captain's sentiments. Given competent leadership, they believed that they could defeat Lee and his vaunted army.[2]

Besides a small number of regular U.S. Army soldiers, the Army of the Potomac was composed exclusively of volunteers. Like their Southern counterparts, they represented some of the best and enthusiastic of their section's manpower. But unlike the Confederate army, the Union army contained many men of foreign birth, including many Irish, German, Scandinavian, and Scottish immigrants, and a scattering of Canadians, Italians, Swiss, and other nationalities. The army was organized into seven infantry corps of about 10,000 to 15,000 men each: the First, Second, Third, Fifth, Sixth, Eleventh, and Twelfth Corps. The Eleventh Corps contained the largest number of soldiers of German origin, but there were substantial numbers of Germans in every corps in the army. For instance, the three Wisconsin regiments in the famous Iron Brigade of the First Corps, the 2d, 6th, and 7th Wisconsin Infantry, had German-born men sprinkled throughout their companies. The 88th and 151st Pennsylvania, also of the First Corps, had many Pennsylvania Dutch in their ranks.

All the army corps except for the Third Corps were commanded by experienced West Point–trained professionals. A powerful cavalry corps of nearly 15,000 superbly equipped and mounted horsemen and an artillery reserve consisting of five artillery brigades rounded out the army, which could carry about 95,000 men into action. Despite their unhappy past, the army looked forward to the summer with confidence. "There was never a better army," wrote General Alpheus Williams, "because from long service and few recruits we are hardened down to the very sublimation of muscle, health, and endurance."[3]

THE CAMPAIGN TO PENNSYLVANIA

The Gettysburg campaign commenced on June 3 when Lee ordered Ewell's and Longstreet's corps to leave their camps around Fredericksburg, Virginia, and move west to Culpepper Court House. Most of Stuart's cavalry had already assembled at that point in preparation for the Northern campaign. Hill's corps remained in the entrenchments at Fredericksburg, where they could keep an eye on the Army of the Potomac and conceal the movements of the rest of the army. Hooker did not divine Lee's intentions, but he did learn of the large concentration of Confederate cavalry near Culpepper. He ordered his entire cavalry corps under Major General Alfred Pleasonton to cross the Rappahannock River and "disperse and destroy" the rebel force. This resulted in the battle of Brandy Station, the largest cavalry battle of the war. Although Pleasonton surprised Stuart, the Confederate horsemen rallied and checked the Federals, but it took their hardest fighting. In the end, Brandy Station provided Hooker with little information about Lee's plans and proved to be no more than an interruption to Lee. On June 10, he ordered Ewell's corps to march west toward the Shenandoah Valley. In two days, Ewell's corps marched more than forty-five miles, crossing the Blue Ridge Mountains and arriving in front of Winchester, which was occupied by a Union garrison of 5,100 men under Major General Robert H. Milroy. Over the next two days, Ewell attacked and routed Milroy's forces, capturing 3,358 prisoners and twenty-three guns at a cost of only 269 Confederate casualties.

Up to this point, Hooker had not stirred from his position on the north bank of the Rappahannock, but Ewell's sudden appearance in front of Winchester was a wake-up call. The enemy was around his flank and poised to cut him off from Washington, D.C. On June 14, he started marching his army north.

Between June 15 and 16, the head of Ewell's corps crossed the Potomac River at Williamsport and Shepherdstown and pushed north toward Pennsylvania. Fear and excitement swept the Keystone State as the Confederates neared its borders. Governor Andrew Curtin called out the state militia, and New York State dispatched several thousand militiamen to bolster the state's thin defenses. These forces might buy some time, but only the Army of the Potomac could provide Pennsylvania the protection it needed, and that army remained south of the Potomac, its commander undecided as to which course of action he should pursue.

Between June 22 and 27, the main body of the Army of Northern Virginia moved into Pennsylvania. The bulk of the army concentrated in the vicinity of Chambersburg, in the Cumberland Valley, but Lee dispatched Ewell's corps east of South Mountain.

By June 28, Lee's campaign had enjoyed remarkable success. "Everything thus far has worked admirably," wrote one of Lee's generals.[4] But nothing had been heard from Stuart, who had taken his three best brigades and cut loose from the main body of the army in northern Virginia, bent on riding around the Union army. Stuart's absence left Lee without reliable information about the Army of the Potomac. Was it still south of the Potomac, or was it marching toward Pennsylvania? On the night of June 28, a spy in the employ of Longstreet arrived with important information. He reported that the Army of the Potomac had reached Frederick, Maryland, only thirty miles south of Gettysburg, and that Major General George G. Meade had replaced Hooker. This news substantially changed the strategic situation. With the enemy so close, Lee had to concentrate his army and maneuver to gain the advantage of position. Lee recalled Ewell from his efforts to capture Harrisburg and directed that the entire army concentrate around Cashtown, at the eastern base of South Mountain and about eight miles west of Gettysburg. By concentrating his army east of the mountains, Lee posed a threat to both Harrisburg and Baltimore. He knew that Meade would be under great pressure from his superiors to protect both these cities and Washington, as well as to drive the Confederates from Pennsylvania. If Lee could gain the advantage of position, Meade would be compelled to attack him, and when Robert E. Lee selected the field of battle, the odds were that he would win the day.

The last days of June saw both armies on the move. Lee believed that he had a respite of several days before he would make contact with the Federal army, so his army moved easily to complete its concentration. By June 30, only Henry Heth's and Dorsey Pender's divisions of Hill's corps had crossed South Mountain. Robert Rodes's and Jubal Early's divisions of Ewell's corps camped that night near Heidlersburg, about ten miles northeast of Gettysburg. The rest of the army were still west of South Mountain. Stuart's whereabouts remained unknown to Lee.

On June 30, General Heth sent Pettigrew's brigade to Gettysburg to search the town for supplies. Pettigrew was warned that he might encounter some Pennsylvania militia in the vicinity, but he was positively ordered not to engage them, for General Lee did not want the army to be drawn into a battle yet. When Pettigrew arrived at the edge of Gettysburg, he discovered a Union cavalry force entering it from the south. Obedient to his orders, he turned around and started back for Cashtown. The movements of the cavalry convinced him that they were veteran troops of the Army of the Potomac, not militia. Pettigrew reported his observations to Generals Heth and Hill. Both doubted the accuracy of the report, but Hill nevertheless decided to move on Gettysburg on July 1 with Heth's and Pender's divisions to disperse the cavalry in his front and to occupy Gettysburg. Lee offered no objection to this movement, probably because he did not believe that any substantial elements of the Army of the Potomac were nearby. The information on which Lee based this opinion was dead wrong, as he would soon discover.

Hooker reacted swiftly to Lee's move north of the Potomac, and in several days of severe marching during a brutal heat wave, he moved the Army of the Potomac from northern Virginia to Frederick, Maryland. What Hooker intended to do next is unknown, because on June 27 he submitted his resignation over a disagreement with the War Department about the use of the garrison at Harpers Ferry, Virginia. Lincoln gladly accepted Hooker's resignation and replaced him with Fifth Corps commander Major General George G. Meade, an experienced regular officer who was highly respected by his peers. The pressure on Meade was enormous. The fate of his nation might be determined by the outcome of the approaching battle.

Meade moved the army north from Frederick along a broad front extending thirty miles, from the base of South Mountain to Manchester, Maryland. By June 30, he had shifted the main strength of the army in the direction of the crossroads town of Gettysburg. That day, he grouped three army corps near South Mountain—First, Third, and Eleventh—into a wing under the command of Major General John F. Reynolds, an excellent soldier whom Meade trusted implicitly. Reynolds's orders for June 30 were to move his wing closer to Gettysburg, where a cavalry division under Brigadier General John Buford had been ordered.

Buford's command reached Gettysburg about 11 A.M. on the thirtieth and found the town "in a terrible state of excitement" over the approach of Pettigrew's brigade. Buford posted his division to cover the Chambersburg Turnpike and dispatched patrols to hunt for information. By late that night, he had assembled an impressive amount of accurate intelligence on Lee's army that he forwarded to Reynolds. While Lee labored in the dark about the precise movements and position of the Union army, Buford gave Reynolds and Meade a blueprint to the Confederate army's dispositions.[5]

Reynolds's orders for July 1 were to move the First and Eleventh Corps to the vicinity of Gettysburg to support Buford. The stage was set for the bloodiest battle in North American history, yet few men in either army suspected it. Buford was among those who sensed the coming clash. He told his subordinates that the rebels "will attack in the morning and they will come booming—skirmishers three deep. You will have to fight like the devil to hold your own until supports arrive."[6]

JULY 1

Heth's division of nearly 7,000 men, accompanied by a battalion of artillery, left its bivouac around Cashtown at 4 A.M. and started toward Gettysburg. The day promised to be humid, with a threat of showers. Around 5:30 A.M., five miles west of Gettysburg, they traded shots with one of Buford's picket posts. The troopers fell back to sound the alarm. The battle of Gettysburg had begun.

Heth advanced cautiously along the Chambersburg Pike. By about 9:30 A.M., he came within sight of Herr Ridge, where Buford had advanced several squadrons of troopers (a squadron is two companies of cavalry, or about sixty to eighty cavalrymen). The troopers dismounted to fight on foot with their carbines, with every fourth trooper holding the horses of his comrades. Heth ordered up artillery and shelled the Yankees, then he ordered the brigades of Archer and Davis to deploy from column to line of battle. A Civil War line of battle consisted of a two-rank line of men, formed shoulder to shoulder. The purpose of this formation was to mass their firepower and facilitate easier command and control of the fighting men by the officers. The infantrymen on both sides carried muzzle-loaded rifled muskets, which were accurate to about 200 to 300 yards but possessed killing power to a range of 1,000 yards or more. A trained soldier could get off about three shots a minute.

While Heth confronted Buford's dismounted line on Herr Ridge, General Reynolds arrived on the field. He reacted decisively to the rapidly developing situation. The best defensive terrain around Gettysburg was south of the town, but Reynolds knew that on July 1, due to their closer concentration of forces, the Confederates would be able to bring more men to the battlefield. Therefore, his plan was to fight the Confederates west of Gettysburg and try to keep them from reaching the high ground south of town before the rest of the Union army could reinforce him. In the grim arithmetic of war, Reynolds planned to trade the blood and lives of his men for time. He asked Buford to hold on, then dashed off to direct the leading elements of the First Corps to the point of danger.

Meanwhile, Archer's and Davis's brigades quickly swept Buford's advance line off Herr Ridge and pushed on toward McPherson's Ridge, about three-quarters of a mile to the east. Here, Buford had placed his main line, but it was no match for Heth's nearly 3,000 infantrymen. Fortunately, Reynolds arrived around 10:30 A.M. with the leading elements of the First Corps, Wadsworth's division of 3,500 men. Reynolds hastily sent the division into action along McPherson's Ridge. A hard-fought clash ensued in which both of Heth's brigades were defeated and driven back to Herr Ridge. In approximately one hour of fighting, nearly 2,000 of the 6,000 men engaged were killed, wounded, or captured. Among the fallen was Reynolds. "He would never order a body of troops where he had not been himself, or where he did not dare to go," wrote a member of his staff. In the initial exchange of fire between the Iron Brigade and Archer, a bullet struck Reynolds in the head and killed him instantly. Command of the field devolved upon the Eleventh Corps commander, thirty-two-year-old Major General Oliver O. Howard, and Major General Abner Doubleday assumed command of the First Corps.[7]

Reynolds's aggressive tactics paid off for the Army of the Potomac. Heth's defeat bought time for the rest of the Union First Corps to reach the field and take up defensive positions. Heth, meanwhile, reformed his division. What had begun as a reconnaissance with minimal risk had assumed a more dangerous character. The Army of the Potomac was present—but how much of it?

Between 11 A.M. and noon, the rest of the First Corps arrived on the field. Doubleday used his reinforcements to bolster the line on McPherson's Ridge. The Iron Brigade still held Herbst Woods, which Doubleday considered the key to this part of the battlefield because of the cover and concealment it offered the defender. He placed Biddle's brigade on the Iron Brigade's left to cover the open ground from the woods to the Fairfield Road. Colonel Roy Stone's brigade of Pennsylvanians took position on the Iron Brigade's right, filling the space between the woods and the Chambersburg Pike. North of the pike, Cutler's brigade moved up to eastern McPherson's Ridge. Doubleday held Robinson's division in reserve around the Lutheran Theological Seminary but put them to work throwing up a breastwork in the woodlot directly west of the seminary building.

Around noon, the leading division of the Eleventh Corps reached Gettysburg after a tiring march, much of it at the double-quick. Major General Carl Schurz, from Liblar, Prussia, commanded the Eleventh Corps; Howard commanded the entire field. Schurz had fled Prussia after the 1848–49 revolution and eventually settled in Wisconsin. His strong anti-slavery feelings led him to the Republican party, in which he played a prominent role in his adopted state. His political clout with Lincoln helped him get a brigadier general's commission in 1862 and a major generalship in 1863. He proved to be a brave man and a competent soldier. Howard ordered Schurz to move Brigadier General Alexander Schimmelfennig's division through town and take position on Doubleday's right, along an extension of Seminary Ridge called Oak Ridge. Brigadier General Francis Barlow's division arrived soon after Schimmelfennig's, and Barlow was ordered to follow and form on Schimmelfennig's right and rear. Howard retained Brigadier General Adolphus von Steinwehr's division as a general reserve on Cemetery Hill. Steinwehr hailed from Blankenberg, Brunswick (Germany). He had received a military education at the Brunswick Military Academy and served for a time in the Brunswick state army. He first moved to the United States in 1847 but went back to Brunswick and stayed until 1854, when he returned and settled first in Connecticut and then in New York. When the war began, he raised the all-German 29th New York Infantry and was appointed its colonel. Within several months, he was promoted to brigadier general. Steinwehr was not a flashy soldier, but he was a good one.[8]

The Confederates were also receiving reinforcements. A. P. Hill arrived at the front toward the close of Heth's action and ordered Pender's division to move forward in close support. Artillery was unlimbered along Herr Ridge, and a steady bombardment of the Union position commenced. Hill had alerted Ewell earlier that Heth would advance on Gettysburg, and as a precautionary measure, Ewell redirected his two divisions toward Gettysburg: Rodes on the Carlisle Road, and Early on the Heidlersburg or Old Harrisburg Road.

General Lee crossed South Mountain to Cashtown early on July 1. The rumble of artillery from the direction of Gettysburg troubled him. He did not want to be drawn into a battle until his entire army was east of South Mountain. Lee felt Stuart's absence keenly now. Without Stuart scouting and screening the front of the army, Lee was in utter ignorance of the disposition of the enemy force in front of him.

General Meade was at his headquarters at Taneytown, Maryland, when the battle began. At an early hour on July 1, he had issued a circular to his corps commanders, instructing them to fall back to a preselected defensive position behind Pipe Creek, near Taneytown, if the enemy were encountered in Pennsylvania. Reynolds never received the Pipe Creek Circular, as it came to be called, and initiated the battle at Gettysburg. The first Meade knew of the fighting in Pennsylvania was when one of Reynolds's staff officers galloped up to army headquarters and reported that the First Corps was engaging the enemy west of Gettysburg and that if it was driven back, Reynolds intended to barricade the streets of the town. "Good," replied Meade, "that is just like Reynolds."[9] Shortly after noon, Meade received the sad news that his friend Reynolds was dead, leaving Howard in command. Meade lacked confidence in Howard, so he ordered the Second Corps commander, Major General Winfield S. Hancock, to ride to Gettysburg and assume command of the Union forces there. Hancock suggested that this might pose a problem, as he was junior in rank to Howard, but Meade pointed out that he had received authority from the secretary of war to make whatever changes he felt necessary among his commanders. Hancock soon departed for Gettysburg, thirteen miles distant.

ORGANIZATION OF THE FIRST AND ELEVENTH ARMY CORPS, ARMY OF THE POTOMAC

FIRST CORPS
Maj. Gen. John F. Reynolds (killed)
Maj. Gen. Abner Doubleday
Maj. Gen. John Newton (took command night of July 1)

First Division
Brig. Gen. James S. Wadsworth

First Brigade (Iron Brigade)
Brig. Gen. Solomon Meredith (w)
19th Indiana
24th Michigan
2d Wisconsin
6th Wisconsin
7th Wisconsin

Second Brigade
Brig. Gen. Lysander Cutler
7th Indiana
76th New York
14th Brooklyn (84th New York)
95th New York
147th New York
56th Pennsylvania

*(w) denotes men wounded

ORGANIZATION OF THE FIRST AND ELEVENTH ARMY CORPS, ARMY OF THE POTOMAC, Continued

Second Division
Brig. Gen. John C. Robinson

First Brigade
Brig. Gen. Gabriel R. Paul (w)
Col. Samuel H. Leonard (w)
Col. Adrian R. Root (w)
Col. Richard Coulter
16th Maine
13th Massachusetts
94th New York
104th New York
107th Pennsylvania

Second Brigade
Brig. Gen. Henry Baxter
12th Massachusetts
83d New York
97th New York
11th Pennsylvania
88th Pennsylvania
90th Pennsylvania

Third Division
Brig. Gen. Thomas A. Rowley
Maj. Gen. Abner Doubleday

First Brigade
Col. Chapman Biddle
20th New York State Militia
    (80th New York)
121st Pennsylvania
142nd Pennsylvania
151st Pennsylvania

Second Brigade
Col. Roy Stone (w)
Col. Langhorne Wister (w)
Col. Edmund L. Dana
143d Pennsylvania
149th Pennsylvania
150th Pennsylvania

Third Brigade
(12th and 15th Vermont not present on the field)
Brig. Gen. George J. Stannard
13th Vermont
14th Vermont
16th Vermont

ORGANIZATION OF THE FIRST AND ELEVENTH ARMY CORPS, ARMY OF THE POTOMAC, Continued

Artillery Brigade

Col. Charles S. Wainwright

Battery B, 2d Maine Light Artillery

Battery E, 5th Maine Light Artillery

Battery L, 1st New York Light Artillery

Battery B, 1st Pennsylvania Light Artillery

Battery B, 4th U.S. Artillery

ELEVENTH CORPS

Maj. Gen. Oliver O. Howard

Maj. Gen. Carl Schurz (July 1)

First Division

Brig. Gen. Francis C. Barlow (w)

Brig. Gen. Adelbert Ames

First Brigade	*Second Brigade*
Col. Leopold von Gilsa	Brig. Gen. Adelbert Ames
Col. Andrew L. Harris	17th Connecticut
41st New York	25th Ohio
54th New York	75th Ohio
68th New York	107th Ohio
153d Pennsylvania	

Second Division

Brig. Gen. Adolphus von Steinwehr

First Brigade	*Second Brigade*
Col. Charles R. Coster	Col. Orland Smith
134th New York	33rd Massachusetts
154th New York	136th New York
27th Pennsylvania	55th Ohio
73d Pennsylvania	73d Ohio

ORGANIZATION OF THE FIRST AND ELEVENTH ARMY CORPS, ARMY OF THE POTOMAC, Continued

Third Division
Maj. Gen. Carl Schurz
Brig. Gen. Alexander Schimmelfennig

First Brigade
Brig. Gen. Alexander
   Schimmelfennig
Col. George von Amsberg
82d Illinois
45th New York
157th New York
61st Ohio
74th Pennsylvania

Second Brigade
Col. Wladimir Krzyzanowski
58th New York
119th New York
82d Ohio
75th Pennsylvania
26th Wisconsin

Artillery Brigade
Maj. Thomas W. Osborne
Battery I, 1st New York Light Artillery
13th Independent Battery, New York Light Artillery
Battery I, 1st Ohio Light Artillery
Battery K, 1st Ohio Light Artillery
Battery G, 4th U.S. Artillery

On the battlefield, Confederate Major General Robert Rodes's division of more than 8,000 men, accompanied by Ewell, arrived on Hill's left around noon and immediately occupied Oak Hill at the northern end of the battlefield. Rodes sent one of his five brigades, Doles's, into the valley to the east to protect his flank and confront the advance of the Eleventh Corps from Gettysburg. The presence of this division on Oak Hill placed a large force on the flank of the First Corps forces facing Hill and prevented the Eleventh Corps from moving up to their immediate support. Doubleday responded to this threat to his flank by pulling Cutler's brigade back into the woods on Seminary Ridge and sending Baxter's brigade, of Robinson's division, north along Oak Ridge (the northern extension of Seminary Ridge). General Schurz formed Schimmelfennig's division between

the Mummasburg and Carlisle Roads and ordered Barlow to place his
division to Schimmelfennig's right and rear. Buford's scouts also reported
the approach of Early's division along the Harrisburg Road, which deeply
concerned Schurz. His two divisions numbered less than 6,000 men, and
Oak Hill completely commanded his position. The level terrain north of
Gettysburg offered his troops no strong position on which to form a
defense, and Early's approach on the Harrisburg Road threatened his right
flank. Schurz appealed to Howard for one of Steinwehr's brigades to protect his right flank, but Howard refused. He did not wish to release his
reserves yet.

From noon to 1:30 P.M. Hill's corps and Rodes's divisional artillery
shelled the First and Eleventh Corps positions. Then, at about 1:30 P.M.,
without attempting to coordinate his attack with Hill, Rodes sent forward
O'Neal's and Iverson's brigades, supported by Daniel's brigade, to strike the
right flank of the First Corps line. The attack ended in disaster. Robinson's
division easily repulsed O'Neal and mauled Iverson's brigade, inflicting 902
casualties on the 1,500 in the brigade.

While Iverson's and O'Neal's brigades suffered their reverse along Oak
Ridge, elements of Daniel's brigade became heavily engaged with Stone's
brigade at the McPherson farm. The Pennsylvanians fought off Daniel's
initial attack, but the North Carolinians were only checked, not defeated,
and they reformed for a renewed effort.

A skillful, aggressive Union defense had blunted Rodes's attack, and
he paused to reorganize his division. Meanwhile, on Herr Ridge, General
Lee had arrived to observe the battle. General Heth approached him and
requested permission to advance his division, but Lee refused; he did not
wish to be drawn into a general engagement. But by 2:30 P.M., it appeared
that the Federals were shifting troops from Heth's front to fight Rodes.
Somewhat reluctantly, Lee gave Heth permission to attack. Heth advanced
with three brigades, Archer's, Pettigrew's (which alone numbered nearly
2,400 men), and Brockenbrough's. Davis's brigade had been so badly battered during the morning fight that it was left out of the action. Confronting this powerful force was Meredith's Iron Brigade in Herbst Woods,
the 150th Pennsylvania at the McPherson farm, and Biddle's brigade on
eastern McPherson's Ridge, about 200 yards in the rear of Meredith's line.
Watching the advancing Confederate line from near Biddle's position,
a Union officer observed that "there was not a shadow of a chance of
our holding this ridge."[10] Nearly all the regimental officers in Meredith's

On the first day at Gettysburg, Pennsylvania Dutch soldiers fought in several regiments of the First Corps defending McPherson's and Seminary Ridges. Note the Lutheran Seminary's cupola in the background in this sketch. BATTLES & LEADERS, VOLUME III

brigade had earlier requested permission to withdraw from what they felt was an exposed and difficult position to defend. Each request received the same answer: Hold your position at all hazards.

Moving with "rapid strides and yelling like demons," the men of Pettigrew's 11th and 26th North Carolina, with nearly 1,500 men in their ranks, rushed down to the banks of Willoughby Run.[11] Meredith's men opened fire, which the North Carolinians immediately returned. The fighting in Herbst Woods became a hellish nightmare for its combatants. "The fight was for some time carried on at forty to twenty yards interval," wrote one of Pettigrew's men.[12] At such short range, the carnage was appalling, and the bodies of the dead and wounded strewed the woodlot. Those still standing were assailed by choking clouds of black powder smoke and the deafening noise of hundreds of muskets being discharged. In the 26th North Carolina, nearly 500 men were killed or wounded. The 11th North Carolina lost 250. The 24th Michigan lost the most men of any Union regiment in the battle—363, including 99 killed or mortally wounded. Slowly, the Iron

Brigade gave ground, falling back fighting through Herbst Woods, pressed by men of equal courage from North Carolina.

On Meredith's left and rear, Pettigrew's right regiments, the 47th and 52d North Carolina, attacked Biddle's brigade. The Carolinians far out-flanked Biddle's line and, in a bloody, close-range musket battle, shot up the Union line and forced it to retreat back toward the Lutheran Seminary.

In a desperate attempt to stabilize his crumbling line, Doubleday committed his only reserve, the 151st Pennsylvania (whose ranks included many Pennsylvania Germans), to the support of the Iron Brigade. As they approached Herbst Woods, Colonel George F. McFarland cautioned his men not to fire unless they had a clear shot at the enemy. McFarland reported that his orders were "strictly observed, and during the next hour's terrific fight-ing many of the enemy were brought low."[13] So were many Pennsylvanians. The 151st lost more than 72 percent of its numbers before being compelled to fall back. Meredith's Iron Brigade had preceded them, withdrawing in good order back toward Seminary Ridge.

At McPherson's farm, Stone's brigade endured the pressure of both Brockenbrough's and Daniel's brigades. Every regiment in the brigade lost well over half their men, but they inflicted severe punishment on their attackers, too. When Meredith's brigade withdrew from Herbst Woods, Stone had no choice but to retreat as well, leaving McPherson's barn, house, and outbuildings crowded with wounded, and the farmyard and pasture littered with dead.

Along Oak Ridge, to the north, Rodes had renewed his efforts to dis-lodge Robinson's division. Baxter's brigade exhausted its ammunition and withdrew to the rear of Seminary Ridge, leaving only Paul's brigade to hold the line.

While the battle raged along the ridges west of Gettysburg, things were going badly for the Eleventh Corps on the level ground north of town. Instead of forming on the right of Schimmelfennig when he arrived, Barlow led his division forward to occupy a knoll overlooking Rock Creek, today called Barlow's Knoll. Barlow was an aggressive, fearless officer, and he had been assigned to command the First Division after Chancellorsville because it was thought that he could restore its sagging morale and put some fire into it. But there was mutual dislike between Barlow and the German troops under his command. The position he selected was well forward and to the right of the one occupied by Schimmelfennig's division. Barlow's advanced position stretched Schurz's line perilously thin. Again he called on Howard for reinforcements, and again Howard hesitated to draw from his reserves. To support Barlow's exposed position, Schurz ordered Colonel Wladimir Krzyzanowski's brigade forward.

On Barlow's front, powerful Confederate forces were assembling. General Jubal Early's division arrived around 2 P.M. along the Harrisburg Road. An irritable and temperamental man, Early was nonetheless one of Lee's best division commanders. He swiftly arranged his division for action and brought his artillery to open up on Barlow's line. Around 3 P.M., he sent Gordon's brigade of Georgians forward to attack the front of Barlow's line. As Gordon's men went forward, they were joined on their right by Doles's Georgia brigade of Rodes's division. The combined force of nearly 3,000 men swept forward with irresistible force. Initially, Barlow's men fought with a stubborn courage. One of his regiments, the 153d Pennsylvania, a Pennsylvania Dutch unit that had less than one month left to serve, lost 211 of its 497 men. Gordon managed to outflank Colonel Leopold von Gilsa's brigade, and the Union line began to crumble. Von Gilsa, a former major in the Prussian army, was a thorough soldier, and he did his best to check the retreat, but to no avail. Barlow too rode into the midst of retreating soldiers, recklessly exposing himself to restore his line. He was hit twice and badly wounded. Around him, his line collapsed, and the entire division streamed to the rear in a disorganized retreat.

Krzyzanowski's brigade came up as Barlow's line gave way and was greeted by Doles's onrushing brigade. Colonel Wladimir Krzyzanowski had fled Prussia after the Polish revolution and settled in New York City in 1846. When the war began, he was elected colonel of the 58th New York. In November 1862, he received an appointment as brigadier general, but the appointment was recalled and then tabled, so Krzyzanowski remained a colonel in command of a brigade.[14] The Georgians that his regiments faced advanced until the two lines were no more than seventy-five yards apart, "and the names on the Confederate flags might have been read had there been time to read them."[15] In this point-blank firefight, Doles's men prevailed, and Krzyzanowski's line melted away. The German 26th Wisconsin lost 154 killed and wounded in the clash. Another of Krzyzanowski's German regiments, the 75th Pennsylvania, also suffered terribly, with 111 casualties. In a desperate effort to relieve the pressure on Krzyzanowski, General Schimmelfennig turned to Colonel George von Amsberg's First Brigade for help. Amsberg was a Hannoverian immigrant who had fought in the Hungarian revolution of 1848.[16] He had only the 157th New York available,

*Major General Carl
Schurz. Schurz assumed
command of the Eleventh
Corps on the first day.*
MASSACHUSETTS
COMMANDERY MILITARY
ORDER OF THE LOYAL LEGION
AND THE U.S. ARMY MILITARY
HISTORY INSTITUTE

which Schimmelfenning ordered to attack Doles's right flank. The New Yorkers did so, but Doles deftly charged front with his brigade and shot up his assailants. The 157th lost 75 percent of its strength.

By this point, the Eleventh Corps line had completely collapsed and was streaming back toward Gettysburg in a disorganized retreat. Howard at last released one of his two reserve brigades, that of Colonel Charles R. Coster. Schurz met it near the town square and personally led the men to a point on the northeastern edge of the village. There was no time to select the best position, and Schurz hastily deployed the brigade, hoping that it might be able to cover the retreat of the rest of the Eleventh Corps. Coster's men had scarcely taken position when Hays's and Avery's brigades of Early's division, which the general had sent forward after Gordon had cleared Barlow's Knoll, came surging up on his front and right flank. Coster's men fought bravely, but they never stood a chance; the Confederate attack overwhelmed them. The 154th New York lost all but 18 men as prisoners, killed, or wounded, and the 134th New York lost 252 of its 400 effectives. The German 27th Pennsylvania was also engulfed in the disaster but was not as severely mauled, losing 111 of 283 men. Early's men swept into town, pursuing the fleeing Federals.

"It seemed so awful to march back through those same streets whipped and beaten," wrote Major Charles Winkler of the 26th Wisconsin; "it was the most humiliating step I ever took."[17] In less than one hour, the Eleventh Corps had lost nearly 3,000 men, including 1,400 missing or captured. The northern flank of the Union line defending Gettysburg had collapsed.

While the Eleventh Corps suffered defeat at Early's hands, Pender's division relieved Heth's battered command and launched a furious assault on Seminary Ridge, where most of the First Corps had fallen back to make a last stand. Although the First Corps infantry had suffered dreadful losses in defending McPherson's Ridge, the artillery remained a formidable force. Spread across 200-yard front near the Lutheran Seminary were eighteen pieces in position, waiting for the Confederate onslaught. Shortly after 3:30 P.M., the brigades of Scales and Perrin, of Pender's division, burst over eastern McPherson's Ridge. The Union artillery poured a murderous fire into them, ripping their lines with shrapnel and canister. The First Corps infantry added its musketry, and Pender's men went down like grain before a scythe. Scales's brigade absorbed the brunt of the First Corps artillery fire, took massive casualties, and was stopped cold. But Perrin's brigade, despite heavy losses from First Corps musketry and the carbines of some of Buford's dismounted troopers, pressed ahead. A First Corps officer looked on in admiration: "Never have I seen such a charge. Not a man seemed to falter. Lee may well be proud of his infantry."[18] One of Perrin's regiments found a gap in the First Corps defensive front, and this unhinged the Union line at Seminary Ridge. The Federals began to fall back. It was 4 P.M.

At all points, the Federal line was in retreat, with the Confederates in hot pursuit. Lieutenant Colonel Rufus Dawes, of the 6th Wisconsin, recalled the retreat: "The weather was sultry. The sweat streamed from the faces of the men. There was not a drop of water in the canteens, and there had been none for hours. The streets were jammed with crowds of retreating soldiers, and with ambulances, artillery, and wagons. The cellars were crowded with men, sound in body, but craven in spirit, who had gone there to surrender." Despite the confusion, there was no rout. Gradually, the weary soldiers straggled up to Cemetery Hill, and the "men threw themselves in a state of almost perfect exhaustion on the green grass and the graves of the cemetery."[19] Moving among them was Major General Winfield S. Hancock. Besides being ordered by Meade to assume command, Hancock was tasked with assessing Gettysburg and reporting on whether it was a favorable position from which to engage Lee in battle. Hancock was a charismatic and gifted leader, and he and Howard quickly organized a defense to meet the expected Confederate attack.

The attack never came. When General Ewell entered Gettysburg with his victorious troops, he received an order from General Lee directing him to capture Cemetery Hill, "if practicable." Ewell intended to do just that, but around the time he received Lee's order, he also received a report of a large Union force east of Gettysburg. He sent two of Early's brigades to investigate, leaving him with only Early's other two brigades and Rodes's division, which had suffered nearly 2,000 casualties in the afternoon's fighting. Ewell faced the steepest and most easily defended part of Cemetery Hill. He sent a message to General Hill and asked if the Third Corps could support an attack. Hill replied that his men were in no condition to help due to heavy losses and exhaustion. Ewell concluded that an attack was impracticable, and the first day of battle at Gettysburg came to a close.

For the combatants—about 20,000 Union and 28,000 Confederate— it had been a terrible conflict. There were more than 9,000 Federal casualties, including nearly 3,500 captured; approximately 6,800 Confederates had been killed, wounded, or captured. Tactically, the Confederates had won the day, but the sacrifices of the First and Eleventh Corps and of Buford's cavalry had given the strategic advantage to the Army of the Potomac. That army held the high ground south of Gettysburg, and with it the advantage of position. The Confederates were thrust into the role of attacker on unfamiliar ground.

JULY 2

General Meade arrived at Gettysburg shortly before midnight on July 1, stopping to meet with some of his generals at the gatehouse to the Evergreen Cemetery. He had earlier ordered the entire army to march at once to Gettysburg. When Meade asked for opinions about the army's position from those gathered, someone responded that the position was a good one. That was good news, Meade observed dryly, for "it was too late to leave it." Here, on the hills and ridges south of the town, he would offer Lee battle.

A fatiguing night march brought the Union Second, Third, and Fifth Corps to the battlefield by the morning of July 2. Before they arrived, Meade examined the ground where his army would do battle and determined where to place his troops as they arrived. He shaped his army's position to take advantage of the strong defensive terrain south of Gettysburg.

The right of the line occupied the wooded eminence of Culp's Hill, 140 feet in elevation. From there, it extended to Cemetery Hill, then curved south and ran along Cemetery Ridge, a low rise running south off Cemetery Hill, for nearly one mile. The left of the line rested on Little Round Top, with an elevation of 170 feet. Big Round Top, immediately south of Little Round Top, rose to 305 feet, but its slopes were wooded, steep, and rugged, rendering it of limited military value. The western slope of Little Round Top had been cleared in 1862, which made it an excellent observation platform. But the true key to the Union position was Cemetery Hill. Its broad, smooth summit was ideal for artillery, and its location completely commanded much of Gettysburg's road network. From above, Meade's front resembled a fishhook, with Culp's Hill as the barb, Cemetery Ridge as the shaft, and Little Round Top the eye. The front was about three miles long.

Meade's position offered him important advantages. Not only did he hold the high ground, but his position also offered interior lines and superior communication. Yet Lee held one important advantage: initiative. He could pick the time and place to attack, and Meade would have to react. The question Lee contemplated in the early hours of July 2 was where he should attack. By the early morning of July 2, eight of his army's nine infantry divisions would be on hand. Only Law's brigade and Pickett's division of Longstreet's corps were not there yet. The nature of the terrain confronting Lee suggested that an attack on the Union left flank offered the greatest prospect for success. Around daybreak, he ordered a reconnaissance to locate the Union left.

The reconnaissance party returned about 9 A.M. and reported that the Round Tops were unoccupied and that the left of the Army of the Potomac rested on Cemetery Ridge. Based on this report, Lee planned his army's attack. Longstreet's corps would march by a concealed route west of Seminary Ridge until it reached the Emmitsburg Road, near the large peach orchard of farmer Joseph Sherfy. There, Longstreet's two divisions would deploy with their left flank on the road and attack north to strike the supposed Union flank and roll it up toward Cemetery Hill. Anderson's division, of Hill's corps, would form on Longstreet's left, and when the First Corps commenced its attack, Anderson would step off and join the assault. Thus, Lee envisioned a three-division attack involving nearly 21,000 infantry that would crush the Union flank. To keep Meade off balance and prevent him from reinforcing his left, Lee ordered Ewell to demonstrate against the Union right flank when he heard Longstreet's artillery open. However, if

Ewell sensed an opportunity, he had the authority to turn his demonstration into a full-scale attack. Pender's division, of Hill's corps, was given similar orders to occupy Meade's center. Lee's plan had merit, but it proved difficult to coordinate and execute.

Longstreet's First Corps finally stepped off around noon. Their march did not add any luster to the reputation of the Army of Northern Virginia. At one point, the column reached a ridge of high ground exposed to Little Round Top, where a Union signal station had been established. Both divisions were forced to countermarch, nearly back to their starting point, and use a different route. By the time the head of Lafayette McLaws's division approached Seminary Ridge, Longstreet's infantry had marched nearly six miles to cover a distance of three miles. It was about 3 P.M.

McLaws anticipated that there would be a small enemy force holding the peach orchard, but when his leading brigade arrived on Seminary Ridge in view of the orchard, they found it teeming with Union infantry and artillery. The situation on the Union lines had shifted dramatically since Captain Johnston had conducted his morning reconnaissance.

In deploying his army on the morning of July 2, Meade entrusted his left flank to Major General Daniel E. Sickles and his Third Corps of some 10,000 men. Sickles's orders were to place his left on Little Round Top and extend his right to connect with the Second Corps, which occupied Cemetery Ridge. Of the seven corps commanders in the Army of the Potomac, only Sickles lacked professional training. He had been an attorney and congressman before the war and had a reputation as a brave man, but he also was known to be impulsive and reckless. Meade personally disliked him and had doubts about his military abilities.

During the early morning hours of July 2, the Third Corps was massed on the lower end of Cemetery Ridge north of Little Round Top. From this position, Sickles observed that west of his position there was higher ground on a ridge running from the Peach Orchard north along the Emmitsburg Road. In his opinion, this was a superior position to the one Meade had assigned him.

Around 10 A.M., Sickles ordered the 2d U.S. Sharpshooters and 3d Maine to conduct a reconnaissance to Seminary Ridge. Buford's division had been screening Sickles's front, but Pleasonton withdrew the cavalry that morning and sent it to Westminster. Sickles was left without cavalry to scout and screen his front, so he used his infantry to discover what the Confederates were up to. When the two regiments probed north of the Millerstown Road, in the woods along the ridge, they bumped into Wilcox's brigade of Anderson's division, deploying into line. A sharp fight ensued, and the sharpshooters and New Englanders fell back to report that the enemy was deploying powerful forces along Seminary Ridge. This convinced Sickles that unless he acted promptly, the enemy would advance from Seminary Ridge and seize the high ground along the Emmitsburg Road, mass their artillery there, and dominate the Third Corps' position. Around 2 P.M., without waiting for authorization from Meade, Sickles ordered his corps to advance and occupy the Peach Orchard and the Emmitsburg Road ridge.

Sickles posted most of his brigades facing west, either along the Emmitsburg Road or in support. Only two brigades deployed to guard the corps' left flank. No troops were left to defend Little Round Top. Although there were some advantages to the Third Corps' new position, such as excellent fields of fire for artillery, Sickles's infantry could not adequately defend the over one-mile front the corps occupied, and the position could be easily enfiladed by Confederate artillery. Parts of his front were also dangerously thin or held by nothing but artillery, with no infantry support. And, the position of the corps was nearly one-half mile in advance of the general Union line of battle.

Meade rode down to see what Sickles had done soon after learning of the Third Corps' unauthorized advance. Before departing, he ordered General Sykes's Fifth Corps to move immediately to the left of the army. He also had learned that the leading elements of the 13,000-strong Sixth Corps were approaching Gettysburg. Their arrival would complete the concentration of his army. He met Sickles near the Peach Orchard and expressed his disapproval of the new position of the Third Corps. When Sickles offered to withdraw to his prior position, Meade remarked that he wished he could, but the enemy would not let him pull back without a fight.[20] Meade had little choice but to try to defend the line Sickles had taken. He told Sickles that the Fifth Corps and a division of the Second Corps would reinforce him and that he could draw on the artillery reserve for additional support.

Longstreet reacted to Sickles's occupation of the Peach Orchard and Emmitsburg Road ridge by widening the front of his attack. He brought up John Bell Hood's division and moved it into line on McLaws's right, extending the line of the corps south of the Emmitsburg Road. While the infantry arranged themselves, the First Corps artillery took position at advantageous points along the corps line.

At 3:30 P.M., Longstreet's artillery opened fire, signaling the beginning of the attack. Lieutenant Colonel E. P. Alexander, who directed Longstreet's

guns that day, wrote that the response of the Union batteries "really surprised me, both with the number of guns they developed, & the way they
stuck to them. I don't think there was ever in our war a hotter, harder,
sharper artillery afternoon than this."[21] For nearly thirty minutes, the guns
of both sides blazed, sending billows of smoke upward and shaking the
landscape with their angry noise.

Around 4 P.M., Hood's leading brigades—Law's and Robertson's—
leaped the stone wall they had used for shelter and dashed forward. Law's
brigade disregarded the order to guide its attack along the Emmitsburg
Road and advanced directly toward Round Top. To maintain contact with
Law, Robertson's men were forced to do likewise. Thus, the entire division
advanced in an easterly direction rather than north, as ordered. The men
advanced at the double-quick under heavy fire from artillery and sharpshooters. Early in the advance, a shell burst near Hood, and he was severely
wounded.

When Meade rode out to meet Sickles, he sent his chief engineer,
General Gouveneur K. Warren, to examine the left end of the Third Corps
line. Warren rode to Little Round Top and was shocked to find no troops
there except for a small party from the signal corps. The signal officer in
charge told Warren that the enemy occupied Warfield Ridge and Seminary
Ridge in great strength. It was immediately apparent to the general that
Longstreet's line would outflank the Third Corps. If the enemy gained possession of Little Round Top, Sickles's position would be untenable, and the
security of the army's entire position would be in jeopardy. Warren acted
immediately, dispatching a staff officer to General Meade and another to
Sickles, requesting troops to occupy Little Round Top. Sickles responded
that he had no men to spare. While returning to Little Round Top, Warren's
aide came upon Fifth Corps commander Major General George Sykes, to
whom he explained the need for troops to defend Little Round Top. Sykes
decided to send one of General James Barnes's three brigades to the hill at
once, but when Sykes's aide arrived at the head of Barnes's division to relay
the order, the general was absent, reconnoitering a position for his men.
Colonel Strong Vincent, commanding one of Barnes's brigades, questioned
the aide and learned of Sykes's orders. Without waiting for Barnes to
approve, Vincent took the responsibility and moved his brigade to Little
Round Top immediately. It proved to be a critical decision.

Vincent's four regiments of about 1,300 men reached the southern slope
of Little Round Top shortly before 5 P.M., only minutes before regiments

from Law's and Robertson's brigades emerged from the woods covering Big Round Top and attacked his line. Vincent's men met the assault with a murderous fire that drove the Confederates back to cover. But the Southerners reformed and came again, pressing Vincent hard. Vincent fell mortally wounded, and it appeared that the attacking Southerners would carry the hill. But before the Confederates could gain an advantage, Colonel Patrick O'Rorke arrived at the head of the 140th New York of Weed's brigade—sent by Warren to reinforce the hill. The 140th swarmed down the hill, checking the Confederate advance, but O'Rorke was killed. On Vincent's left flank, Colonel Joshua Chamberlain's 20th Maine led his men in a daring bayonet charge that took the Alabamians on his front by surprise and drove them back to Big Round Top.

At nearly the same time that Vincent came under attack, regiments of Robertson's and Law's brigades attacked Ward's brigade, defending Devil's Den and Houck's Ridge. A bitter conflict ensued. Sickles sent several regiments to reinforce Ward, but Benning's entire brigade joined the Confederate attack, swinging the balance in favor of the Southerners. The Federals were forced to retreat. By the time this position fell, the Federals had managed to haul a battery to the summit of Little Round Top, and the fire of these guns prevented the Confederates from advancing beyond the position they had seized. The balance of Weed's brigade had also arrived on Little Round Top, solidifying the Union army's hold on the hill.

In their initial attack on the Union position at Devil's Den, Robertson's brigade came under a flanking fire from men of DeTrobriand's brigade, who were posted at the southern edge of the Wheatfield. Anderson's brigade moved from its position in Hood's supporting line to deal with this threat, thus expanding the front of Hood's attack. Anderson's first attack was repulsed after a hard fight, and he fell back to reform for another try. During this time, two brigades of Barnes's division, of the Fifth Corps, arrived and took position on a rocky knoll southwest of the Wheatfield, called Stony Hill. Anderson renewed his attack but initially could make no headway against the strong Union force in his front. It was now nearly 5:30 P.M., and Longstreet committed half of McLaws's division to the battle. Kershaw's South Carolina brigade, with Raphael Semmes's Georgia brigade in support—both posted south of the Millerstown Road—were ordered to attack.

Kershaw led the center and right of his brigade toward Stony Hill and ordered his three left regiments to change front to the left and attack the

Peach Orchard and the line of Union batteries on the Wheatfield Road from the south. The advance of Kershaw's center regiments, with Semmes's brigade advancing in their rear, posed a threat to the right flank of Barnes's division. Barnes had been nervous about his position from the moment he occupied it, and with hundreds of rebels bearing down on his exposed flank, he decided to clear out. Both his brigades withdrew several hundred yards north to the shelter of Trostle Woods, leaving DeTrobriand's brigade in the Wheatfield alone and unsupported. Under pressure from three different Confederate brigades, DeTrobriand's men fell back through the bloody wheat toward the Wheatfield Road.

With the positions at Devil's Den and the Wheatfield lost, Sickles's left flank was imperiled. Sickles had already drawn heavily from his reserves on the Emmitsburg Road front to bolster the line from the Peach Orchard to Devil's Den. Casualties were heavy, and many regiments were dangerously low on ammunition. An urgent request for reinforcements went to army headquarters. Meade ordered Hancock to have Caldwell's division of about 3,200 men report to General Sykes.

Caldwell led his men south quickly, toward the snarling roar of battle. His division was directed to the Wheatfield. Caldwell promptly pushed three of his four brigades into the fight, and they struck Anderson's, Kershaw's, and Semmes's men with great force. "The tumult became deafening," wrote one of Caldwell's men.[22] Another reported that they received "a withering fire from the concealed enemy."[23] Both sides suffered dreadful losses. Caldwell lost two brigade commanders who were mortally wounded early in the action. On the Confederate side, Semmes fell mortally wounded, and G. T. Anderson was wounded as well. Caldwell sent his reserve brigade into action, and the Confederate front began to give way. Stony Hill was retaken, and one of Caldwell's brigades pushed deep into Rose's Woods, south of the Wheatfield. Caldwell's counterattack had swung the tide of battle back to the Federals on this part of the line.

While Caldwell recaptured the Wheatfield and Stony Hill, events at the Peach Orchard took an ominous turn for the Federals. The initial attack on the Peach Orchard, by Kershaw's left regiments, had been repulsed, but the Union defenders at the orchard received no reprieve, coming under constant fire from Confederate artillery and small arms. Their strength gradually ebbed, and Sickles lacked the manpower to reinforce them. Around 6 P.M., a long line of Confederates emerged from Seminary Ridge, north of the Millerstown Road, followed by another. It was Barksdale's and

Wofford's brigades of McLaws's division—more than 3,500 men. Raising the "rebel yell," Barksdale's regiments moved steadily toward the orchard and Sherfy farm buildings. Union regiments and batteries blazed away in a vain attempt to stop what one observer described as "the most magnificent charge of the war."[24] The Mississippians returned the fire, and the Union line began to melt away. As resistance crumbled and Sickles's men began to retreat, Barksdale pushed his brigade across the Emmitsburg Road and changed front to the left in order to roll up the Third Corps line fronting the road.

In the wake of Barksdale's charge, Wofford's brigade swept through the Peach Orchard and advanced east, along the Wheatfield Road. As they advanced, they picked up elements of Kershaw's brigade, which moved with them. The Confederate force struck the vulnerable flank of Caldwell's division in Rose's Woods. Unable to check this new onslaught, Caldwell's regiments, as well as Sweitzer's brigade, were forced to withdraw under fire, suffering heavy losses.

Ayres's two brigades of U.S. regulars, just recently ordered into position, attempted to slow the Confederate advance. They did, conducting a disciplined, fighting retreat, but it cost them 800 casualties, nearly half their men. The Confederate line spilled over Houck's Ridge and into the valley beneath Little Round Top—later dubbed the Valley of Death. But losses and the disorder inherent to sustained combat sapped the momentum from their advance. A formidable line confronted them on Little Round Top. Part of the Sixth Corps, which had completed a grueling thirty-six-mile march in twenty-four hours, was in position there, along with a brigade of Pennsylvania Reserves from the Fifth Corps. The Federals, including the Philadelphia Germans of the 98th Pennsylvania, swept down from the heights, and the Confederate brigades fell back beyond the Wheatfield, to the cover of Rose's Woods.

To the north, the battle continued to rage. The advance of Barksdale's brigade was the signal for Anderson's division to commence its attack. The brigades of Wilcox, Lang, and Wright stepped off, one after the other, like a series of waves rolling toward the Union line. Confronted by Anderson's brigades on its front and Barksdale on its flank, Humphreys's division withdrew toward Cemetery Ridge, losing more than 1,500 men during the retreat.

Behind Humphreys's retreating division was a yawning gap in the Union line, which Caldwell's Second Corps division had earlier occupied.

The Federals were working furiously to assemble a line of artillery at this point to confront the advancing rebels, while Meade dispatched reinforcements from nearly every part of his line to shore up his crumbling left flank. To purchase time, units were thrown forward—sacrificed. The 9th Massachusetts Battery made a desperate stand at the Trostle farm against part of Barksdale's brigade; it left the battery a wreck but bought a few precious minutes. At another point, the 1st Minnesota charged Wilcox's entire brigade. Of the 262 men who made the advance, only 47 returned unscathed, but they held Wilcox off long enough for reinforcements to arrive.

On Cemetery Ridge, the Confederate attack reached its crest. Wright's brigade fought its way up to Cemetery Ridge, but the brigades that were supposed to advance on his left had failed to move forward, and Wright found himself isolated and unable to hold on to his gains in the face of increasing resistance. He ordered a retreat. It was the same story on other parts of the line. Confronted by reinforcements from the First, Second, and Twelfth Corps, Barksdale, Wilcox, and Lang also fell back. Legend has it that a Confederate soldier, confronted by one line of Yankees after another, called out in exasperation, "Great God! Have we the Universe to whip?"[25] For the first time in the war, Lee's veterans had encountered a Union general who threw everything he had into the battle. Nevertheless, the outcome of the battle had trembled in the balance that dark afternoon. When someone remarked to Meade that it had been a very close affair that day, he responded, "Yes, but it is all right now, it is all right now."[26]

When Longstreet's artillery opened fire to begin his offensive, Ewell's guns near the seminary and on Benner's Hill, east of town, opened a bombardment of Cemetery Hill and Culp's Hill. The Union batteries replied and eventually silenced Ewell's guns. Perhaps an hour after the gun duel subsided, Ewell ordered his infantry forward—much later than planned. The plan called for Johnson's division to open the attack by moving on Culp's Hill; then Early would storm the east side of Cemetery Hill with two brigades while Rodes assaulted the west side.

Johnson's division moved out around 6:30 P.M. He had to leave one brigade to guard his rear along the Hanover Road, which reduced his fighting force to three brigades, numbering about 5,000 men. Advancing over hilly terrain and crossing Rock Creek consumed a lot of time, so it was nearly dark by the time the division reached the base of Culp's Hill. Earlier in the day, the Twelfth Corps had built a formidable line of entrenchments extending from the First Corps' entrenchments on the hill's summit to its southeastern base. But by the time Johnson advanced, all of the Twelfth Corps, except for Greene's New York brigade, had left the hill to reinforce the threatened Union left.

Although Johnson's men enjoyed superior numbers, they could not overcome Greene's formidable position on the main hill. Despite several valiant efforts, neither Jones's nor Nichols's brigade reached Greene's earthworks. On their left, Steuart's brigade was able to capture the lower summit of Culp's Hill, but in the face of increasing resistance, pitch darkness, and the confusion caused by both, he chose to consolidate his position until daylight. The battle on Culp's Hill was not over—darkness had merely brought a pause to the fighting.

Soon after Johnson's men became engaged on Culp's Hill, Early's brigades emerged from a ravine where they had been under cover and dashed toward Cemetery Hill. The Union batteries immediately opened fire on them, but in the gathering darkness, their accuracy was poor, and the Confederates escaped what one soldier believed would have been a slaughter in the daylight. Within minutes, the two brigades were overrunning two depleted Eleventh Corps brigades posted at the foot of Cemetery Hill. The battered 153d Pennsylvania once again found itself attacked by overwhelming numbers. A bloody fight ensued in which one Pennsylvania Dutchman of the 153d recalled that "the bayonet, club-musket, and anything in fact that could be made available was used."[27]

Early's men ultimately overran the position and pressed up the steep slopes of the hill on the heels of the retreating Yankees, rushing the position of two of the defending Union batteries. Union gunners and Eleventh Corps infantrymen from the two retreated brigades rallied around the cannons and fought Early's men hand to hand. Just as the defenders began to give way, Second Corps brigade and several Eleventh Corps regiments, including the German 27th and 73d Pennsylvania, rushed to the threatened sector and counterattacked. With their ranks depleted and disorganized, and facing fresh enemy troops, Early's men were forced to retreat and give up their hard-won gains.

The aid that Early's men had anticipated from Rodes's attack on the western face of Cemetery Hill never materialized. Confronted by formidable Union defenses on the western slope of Cemetery Hill, Rodes chose to cancel his attack, and the fighting of July 2 came to an end.

"At last the battle was hushed and all was still," wrote a captain in the 118th Pennsylvania. "The woods and fields were strewn with the wounded

and dying, and with the ghastly forms of the dead. It is indeed remarkable
that men can lie down and sleep so tranquilly when they know the danger
that awaits them on the morrow."[28] Total casualties amounted to 18,000 or
more, of which over 10,000 were Union soldiers. July 2, 1863, ranks as one
of the bloodiest days in North American history. Both armies' leadership
had suffered severely. Sickles—the highest-ranking officer to go down that
day—lost a leg to a Confederate solid shot. Five other Union brigade commanders were killed or mortally wounded, and three were wounded. Lee
lost two division commanders, Hood and Pender, and five brigade commanders were killed or wounded.

Despite the terrible cost of the day's fighting, the battle remained undecided. Meade called a late-night meeting of his senior generals at headquarters to assess the day's fighting. The nearly unanimous opinion of the
assembled officers was to hold their position on July 3 "and fight it out."[29]

Lee held no council that night. He remained confident that victory
could be achieved. The day's fighting had secured a lodgment on Culp's Hill,
and the capture of the Peach Orchard and Emmitsburg Road provided
him with useful artillery positions. The Army of the Potomac still held the
advantage of position, but Lee knew that it had suffered heavy casualties in
the fighting on July 1 and 2. He had captured nearly 5,000 Federal soldiers,
a sign that the fighting resolve of the Union army might be weakening,
and on both days, his army had gained ground. Lee also had history on his
side. His army had never been truly defeated, and it might never again have
the opportunity that now presented itself: a chance to defeat the principal Union army in the East on Northern soil. George Pickett's division
had arrived in the afternoon of July 2, and Jeb Stuart had also reported with
his cavalry. Lee had good reason to be optimistic that his army could still
win the battle, and he issued orders that night for Longstreet, reinforced by
Pickett, to renew his attack against the Union left, while Ewell, reinforced
by four brigades, simultaneously resumed his attack against Culp's Hill.
Stuart was ordered to take his cavalry east of Gettysburg, where it could
both protect the left flank of the army and threaten the Union rear. The
attack was scheduled to commence at daylight.

Lee's plan began to unravel before daylight, however. The main body
of the Twelfth Corps returned to its position on Culp's Hill following the
conclusion of the fighting on the Union left, and it made preparations to
drive Johnson's men off the lower summit of the hill.

JULY 3

At 4:30 A.M., as the first streaks of light spread across the sky, twenty-six Twelfth Corps guns opened fire on Johnson's position on Culp's Hill. In moments, the infantries, which in places were only some 100 yards apart, commenced to blaze away at each other. Under this shelling, Johnson prepared his brigades for a head-on assault on the main hill. A look at the Union position convinced one of his brigade commanders that it "could not have been carried by any force."[30] The first advance failed. Once the attack was well under way, Ewell received a message from Lee that Longstreet would not be able to attack until after 9 A.M. The coordinated attack that Lee had planned for July 3 would not occur.

Around 8 A.M., the Confederates made a second attempt to carry the Union works. This too failed. At 10 A.M., still under the belief that Longstreet's attack on the enemy's left flank was imminent, Johnson ordered a third assault, despite the protests of some of his subordinates. This attack encountered murderous fire on front and flank. "Flesh and blood could not live in such a fire," wrote one of the attackers.[31] The assault failed, with dreadful losses.

By 11 A.M., Johnson, convinced that further attacks were futile, began to withdraw his forces across Rock Creek. The Union right flank was secure.

Lee's attack orders for July 3 had apparently been delivered verbally rather than in writing. This proved unfortunate, for Longstreet either misunderstood or misinterpreted his orders. For reasons never satisfactorily explained, he made no preparations to attack where Lee expected him to. Longstreet disliked the idea of another frontal attack against the Union left and explored the possibility of marching his corps around Big Round Top to turn Meade's left flank. What Longstreet expected to accomplish is difficult to determine, but the question is moot. When Lee rode up to Longstreet's headquarters, he discovered not only that Longstreet was not ready to attack but also that he thought Lee's plan offered little hope of success. The coordinated attack that Lee envisioned had fallen apart before it had fairly begun. Now he was forced to contemplate a new course of action. Breaking off the battle and withdrawing was not a consideration. Lee sensed that victory remained firmly within his reach, and he intended to seize it.

Lee concluded that if the Union army had strengthened its flanks, it might have weakened the center to do so. The open ground on Cemetery

Ridge, the very center of the Union position, appealed to Lee as a good place to attack. The ridge was not particularly high, and it offered little cover for its defenders, apart from some low stone walls. If the Union line could be broken here, it might force a general retreat of the Army of the Potomac. The liability associated with this point of attack was the mile of open ground that the assault troops would have to cross to reach their objective. Lee thought that he could solve this problem by subjecting the Union position, and its supporting artillery, to an extraordinarily heavy artillery bombardment before sending his infantry forward. Lee had used these tactics on a smaller scale at Chancellorsville, with great success. An assault force of eleven brigades, more than 13,000 men, was selected for the attack. The core attack force consisted of Pickett's fresh division; Heth's division, now commanded by General James Pettigrew; and half of Pender's division, commanded by General Isaac Trimble. Two more brigades from Anderson's division were also supposed to support the assault. Lee directed Longstreet to arrange the assault column so that its center would strike a vulnerable point in the Union line—a ninety-degree angle in a stone wall that generally followed the course of Cemetery Ridge and that the Union defenders were using for shelter. Nearby stood a small clump of trees and bushes—a landmark that would help guide the attacking troops.

Longstreet commanded the assault, even though eight of the brigades were from Hill's corps, a decision that reflected Lee's confidence in the Georgian. It took most of the morning to arrange all the details for the massive attack. Meanwhile, Johnson's division bled itself out on the grim slopes of Culp's Hill. Elsewhere, the troops of the two armies waited and broiled under a blazing sun.

At approximately 1 P.M., all was ready, and Longstreet gave orders for the bombardment to commence. Two signal guns fired, and then the Confederate line erupted like a volcano. "Such an artillery fire has never been witnessed in this war," wrote one Union soldier.[32] Perhaps as many as 170 Confederate cannon subjected the Union positions to a storm of shrapnel, shell, and solid shot. Gradually, the Union batteries began to reply, until eighty to a hundred Union guns were firing back. "It was one grand raging clashing of sound," wrote another soldier.[33] The firing of so many cannon generated great clouds of smoke, obscuring the aim of both armies' gunners and interfering with their accuracy. Many Confederate shells missed Cemetery Ridge completely and landed in the Union rear. But not everyone fired high, for the Union Second Corps batteries, in particular, were severely battered.

The Confederates had hoped to make the bombardment short and decisive, but the stubborn Union response caused them to continue firing in the hope that they could silence the Federals. Eventually, Meade and the Union chief of artillery, General Henry Hunt, issued orders to cease firing, intending to save ammunition for the infantry attack they believed was coming. The diminution of the Union artillery fire, combined with the apparent withdrawal of some of the artillery, offered the Confederates hope that their artillery fire had inflicted sufficient damage to pave the way for the infantry. But the length of the bombardment had nearly emptied the Confederate ammunition chests. "For God's sake, come quick, or we cannot support you," Colonel E. P. Alexander wrote in a note to Pickett.[34] It was nearly 3 P.M.

Pickett carried the urgent note from Alexander to Longstreet and asked if he should advance. "My feelings had so overcome me that I could not speak, for fear of betraying my want of confidence to him," wrote Longstreet. He merely bowed his head, despairing of the chances for success.[35]

Pickett rode to his men. Some heard him call out, "Up, men, and to your posts! Don't forget today that you are from old Virginia."[36] The long lines of Confederate infantry clambered to their feet, and the advance began.

Across the field, the Union defenders made ready to meet the advancing waves of grey-clad infantry. "I never saw troops march out with more military precision," wrote a New Yorker. The Confederate line stretched for nearly one mile, a military spectacle both imposing and frightening. The Union artillery reopened fire, and shell and shrapnel tore at the advancing line. Despite this fire, the Confederate line "came on as steady and regular as if on dress parade." The Union infantry hugged its cover and waited for the enemy to come within range.[37]

As the Confederate line neared the Emmitsburg Road, the pace increased. When Pettigrew's men reached the fences lining the road, the Union infantry of General Alexander Hays opened fire. Pettigrew's men "dropped from the fence as if swept by a gigantic sickle swung by some powerful force of nature." Men fell by the hundreds, but the majority of the survivors pushed on toward Cemetery Ridge.[38]

On the right, Pickett's men crossed the Emmitsburg Road fences under heavy fire and swept forward. As they did so, the right of the division became exposed, and Union General George Stannard ordered two of his big Vermont regiments to advance to Pickett's flank and blast his men with concentrated volleys. On Pickett's front, men of General John Gibbon's Second Corps division waited until the Virginians came within very short range, then poured in a smashing fire. A Massachusetts captain wrote, "We bowled them over like nine pins, picking out the colors first." At many points, Union firepower stopped Pickett's regiments cold, just as it did Pettigrew's.[39]

The one point where the Confederates found success was "the angle," that same angle in the stone wall that Lee had directed Longstreet to strike with the center of his column. Faced with a surge of Confederate infantrymen who threatened their front and flank, part of the 71st Pennsylvania that defended the angle fell back. Several hundred men from Pickett's and Pettigrew's divisions quickly converged on this point, which offered them some cover. It was only about twenty-five minutes into the attack, and already its success seemed doubtful, but the Confederates had won a lodgment in the Union line.

The men clustered at the angle were joined by Brigadier General Lewis Armistead of Pickett's division, the last of Pickett's brigade commanders still standing. Garnett was dead, and Kemper was badly wounded; so too were many regimental and line officers. Confusion gripped the attackers. Armistead sensed that unless the men at the angle advanced, they were doomed, for at all other points, the attack had been checked or repulsed. Shouting for the men to follow him, Armistead scrambled over the wall, followed by a hundred or more men—no one is sure exactly how many went over. But as they advanced, Armistead and many of his followers went down in a hail of fire from the 69th, 71st, and 72d Pennsylvania. The courageous general died two days later of his wounds.

Some of the men who followed Armistead attempted to outflank the Union defenders south of the angle. They ran into the largely Irish 69th Pennsylvania, which fought them hand to hand at some points. Some Virginians managed to reach the clump of trees in rear of the 69th. They were met by a vigorous Union counterattack that drove them back behind the stone wall, where they fought on with stubborn courage. The two sides blazed away at each other at a range "a little short of fifteen paces."[40] Both sides lost heavily, but the Confederates were subjected to fire on both flank and front, and it quickly became too much. Those who had not already retreated or been shot threw down their muskets and surrendered. Less than one hour after it had begun, "Pickett's Charge," as it would later be inaccurately named, had failed. In this brief span of time, nearly 5,500 Confederate soldiers became casualties, including over 1,000 killed. The disaster that James Longstreet feared had come to pass. Union losses were approximately 1,500, including Hancock, who was severely wounded.

General Lee rode out to meet the survivors of the attack. One can only imagine his feelings, seeing his proud divisions returning depleted, dazed, and bloodied. To one of his distraught officers, Lee said, "Never mind, General, all this has been my fault—it is I that have lost this fight, and you must help me out of it in the best way you can."[41]

While Lee's infantry bled on the slopes of Cemetery Ridge, three miles east of Gettysburg, Stuart's force of four cavalry brigades marched east for about two and a half miles before turning south on a crossroad that led to the Hanover Road. Despite Stuart's attempts to conceal his movement, he had been spotted, and Union Brigadier General David M. Gregg, with the brigades of Colonel John B. McIntosh and General George A. Custer, barred his way to the intersection of the Hanover and Low Dutch Roads. Around 3 P.M., the two sides engaged each other. The fighting swayed back and forth over the farm of George Rummel. It ended in a draw, but Stuart's threat to the Union rear was checked.

July 3 dashed Lee's high hopes for victory. In the three days of fighting, his army had lost more than 22,000 men and expended a large amount of ammunition. Lee had no other choice but to retreat from Pennsylvania. In preparation, he pulled Ewell's corps back to Seminary Ridge and entrenched his entire line.

On July 4, the two armies remained largely inactive, spent and exhausted by the three days of hard fighting. "No word can depict the ghastly picture," wrote a New Yorker. "I found my head reeling, the tears flowing and my stomach sick at the sight."[42] Meade has been criticized for not attacking on this day, but his army had lost 23,000 killed, wounded, and captured, plus three of seven corps commanders, including Reynolds and Hanock, who were Meade's most trusted and aggressive subordinates. Lee also occupied a very strong position. Meade chose to wait until Lee retreated before acting. The Confederates began to retreat in midafternoon, with a light rain falling. The wounded went first, in a wagon train stretching for seventeen miles. So numerous were Lee's wounded that he was compelled to leave 6,802 behind—those too seriously injured to be moved. When night fell, Lee started the main body of his army marching along the

---

THE COST OF GETTYSBURG

The Army of the Potomac gave its official losses as 3,155 killed, 14,529 wounded, and 5,365 missing or captured. But in the weeks after the battle, 2,136 men died of their wounds or were found to be dead instead of missing, raising the Union death toll to 5,291. The Union army reported 32,043 casualties for the entire Gettysburg campaign.

The Army of Northern Virginia's officially reported casualty figures for the battle are imperfect. One source gives its losses at 4,649 killed, 12,420 wounded, and 5,846 missing or captured but acknowledges that these statistics are not complete.★ The army's losses may have been as much as 28,000.

★Robert K. Krick, *The Gettysburg Death Roster* (Dayton, OH:Morningside Press, 1993).

Hagerstown (also known as Fairfield) Road. The gentle rain turned into a downpour and continued through the night.

Meade dispatched his cavalry to threaten Lee's line of retreat and harass his trains on July 4, but he did not start the main body of his army until July 7. They marched south in the direction of Frederick, where desperately needed supplies and ammunition waited, then pushed west in the hope that they might catch Lee before he could get across the Potomac River and back to Virginia. Despite the pressure of an aggressive Union cavalry, the vanguard of Lee's army reached Hagerstown on July 7. They discovered that the heavy rains had swollen the Potomac and rendered it impassable. Lee entrenched his army in a strong defensive position near Williamsport and waited for the rains to cease and the river to subside. On July 11 and 12, the Army of the Potomac came up in front of Lee's forces and deployed. It continued to rain, making movements slow and difficult. Meade made preparations for a limited attack on July 13 but canceled the order when a majority of his generals voiced their opposition to the attack until more information could be gathered about the Confederate position. Lee did not grant them any more time. The Potomac had fallen enough to be fordable, and Lee's engineers had completed a pontoon bridge over the river. Under the cover of night, the Army of Northern Virginia returned to Virginia.

The last of Lee's troops crossed on the morning of July 14. Union cavalry, sent in pursuit by Meade, pitched into them, capturing a number of prisoners and mortally wounding General Pettigrew. But the Southern infantry drove off the horsemen and completed their withdrawal. The Gettysburg campaign had ended.

THE AFTERMATH

Gettysburg was the bloodiest battle ever fought on the North American continent. In three days, nearly 51,000 men were killed, wounded, or captured; more than 6,000 men were killed outright. Remarkably, only one civilian, Jennie Wade, was killed. A Union captain described the carnage: "As far as the eye could see the dead lay in all manner of shapes, some upon their faces, others upon their backs, and as incredible as it may seem, others still kneeling behind the rocks where they had taken shelter."[43]

By July 6, the majority of the dead were buried. There were still more than 20,000 wounded—6,800 Confederate and 14,000 Union—to be cared for. The well-organized and well-equipped Union medical corps was swamped by the sheer numbers. There were not enough supplies or surgeons to provide adequate treatment to those who needed it. A volunteer nurse wrote, "There are no words in the English language to express the sufferings I have witnessed today."[44] The people of Gettysburg gave what help they could, but it would be nearly a week before adequate supplies arrived. Various relief organizations provided much help, as did hundreds of women who volunteered as nurses. Despite the Herculean work performed by many surgeons and those who assisted, hundreds of wounded died, generally from infection, swelling the battle's death toll to 10,000 or more.

Nearly 17,000 men became prisoners of war as a result of the battle—13,621 Confederates, including their wounded left behind, and about 5,000 Union. Hundreds, perhaps thousands, of these prisoners died of disease in Northern and Southern prison camps, and those who survived to be exchanged or paroled often had their health permanently impaired by diseases such as scurvy or dysentery.

The defeat at Gettysburg did not shatter the Army of Northern Virginia. Its morale and confidence remained high. But the army would never again take the offensive as it had in the summer of 1863. The fighting men noted it. "We gained nothing but glory and lost our bravest men," wrote an officer in Pickett's division.[45] The statement could have applied to the entire army. Who would replace the likes of Armistead, Garnett, Barksdale, and the thousands of other veteran troops and officers who were dead or maimed? Besides the loss of many irreplaceable men, Gettysburg may have cost the Confederacy one of its best hopes to win a peace on favorable terms.

For the Army of the Potomac, the victory at Gettysburg validated the belief of its soldiers that, if properly led, they could defeat Lee and his army. Ultimate victory, which had seemed so distant after Chancellorsville, now seemed possible. The soldiers also learned the uplifting news that on July 4 Vicksburg had surrendered to Grant. One of Meade's soldiers wrote home, "the cloud that hung over our country so long is getting lighter and I think I can see peace in the distance."[46] It was more distant than this soldier might have realized, and down a long and bloody path. But it eventually led to a quiet place in Virginia called Appomattox, where the war would end and peace would be restored to the land.

CHAPTER 6

"Fight with What Is Left"

David L. Valuska

The Southern army, under the command of General Robert E. Lee, had begun an invasion of the North that caused great concern among the people of the Northern states, particularly in Pennsylvania. The Union army was in pursuit of the invading rebels, and a major battle seemed imminent. The Pennsylvania Dutch soldiers in the ranks of the Army of the Potomac were enthusiastic as they marched across the Mason-Dixon line and into their native state of Pennsylvania. The Dutch soldiers were proud of their German heritage, but they also considered themselves American. This duality in identity was reflected in the composition of many Pennsylvania regiments; some regiments had only a smattering of Pennsylvania Dutchmen, while others were nearly 100 percent ethnic German. The Pennsylvania Dutch dialect was commonly heard among the men. This language was a sign of their separation from the newly arriving German immigrants of the nineteenth century, as well as from their "English" neighbors.[1]

These Pennsylvania soldiers delighted in their ethnicity but never questioned that they were Americans. This was a superb example of ethnic diversity in the nineteenth century and the process of ethnic Americanization that was taking place. The soldiers did not need Teutonic officers, nor did they wish to be in all-ethnic companies or regiments. When they happened to end up in a company that had a high percentage of Dutchmen, however, they often reveled in their ethnic identity.[2] These soldiers were not thinking of ethnicity in the last days of June as they marched into Pennsylvania, though. What was foremost in their minds was stopping

"Bobby" Lee and the Army of Northern Virginia. Let us now look at the role the Pennsylvania Dutch soldiers played in the first days of the battle of Gettysburg.

By the end of June 1863, Confederate commander Robert E. Lee and his vaunted Army of Northern Virginia were well into their invasion of Pennsylvania. Lee had several concerns, one of which was the whereabouts of his cavalry and its commander, Jeb Stuart. He was also worried that his army was too strung out. Lee was not quite sure where the Union enemy, the Army of the Potomac, was located, and his thin lace of cavalry support forced Lee to maneuver blindly. It was not until the night of June 28 that he learned from a Confederate spy, Henry T. Harrison, that a large Union force was near Frederick, Maryland. Harrison also informed Lee that the Army of the Potomac had changed commanders and that George Meade had replaced Joseph Hooker. This information triggered an immediate response from Lee. He sent out messengers directing his three corps to unite, without delay, in the Gettysburg-Cashtown area.[3]

A Union cavalry division, under the command of Brigadier General John Buford, had been in the field for some time attempting to pinpoint the exact location of the Confederate army. Buford had three brigades in his division commanded by Colonels William Gamble and Thomas Devin. His reserve brigade was commanded for a short time by Major Samual H. Starr, until his replacement by recently promoted Brigadier General Wesley Merritt. In Devin's brigade was the 17th Pennsylvania Cavalry, a unit that consisted of quite a few Pennsylvania Dutch troopers.

On July 2, 1862, Pennsylvania had been levied to raise three cavalry regiments, and the 17th Pennsylvania Cavalry was one of them. The recruitment for the 17th was as follows: Company A in Beaver County, Company B in Susquehanna County, Company C in Lancaster County, Company D in Bradford County, Company E in Lebanon County, Company G in Franklin County, Company H in Schuylkill County, Company I in Perry County and the city of Philadelphia, Company K in Luzerne County, Company L in Montgomery and Chester Counties, and Company M in Mercer County. A breakdown of the approximate percentages of Pennsylvania Dutch in each of the cavalry companies is as follows: Company A, 25 percent; Company B, 30 percent; Company C, 85 percent; Company D, 40 percent; Company E, 90 percent; Company G, 84 percent; Company H, 86 percent; Company I, 72 percent; Company K, 27 percent; Company L,

61 percent; Company M, 12 percent. These figures correspond with those counties identified as Pennsylvania Dutch population centers. They also underscore the intermixing of Dutch and non-Dutch volunteers.[4]

In determining these figures, geography was a chief criterion. After narrowing the regiments down to counties with a high density of Pennsylvania Dutch, it was necessary to research the regimental histories and Samuel P. Bates's all-important reference on the Pennsylvania volunteers in the Civil War. A reading of journals, diaries, and histories also aided in identifying Pennsylvania Dutch units. Finally, a knowledge of genealogy was critical. It was important to look at the names and, in consultation with trained genealogists, determine whether the names were Germanic or otherwise. Unlike the German-American regiments that attempted to maintain a pure German organization and were led by German officers, the Pennsylvania Dutch did not make such distinctions. Certainly, the dialect was spoken among the soldiers, and letters home were often written in German, but for the most part, the Pennsylvania Dutch saw themselves as Americans first and Pennsylvania Dutch second. They maintained many of their German cultural traits but accepted the mores of the American society. The 17th Pennsylvania Cavalry is a study in microcosm of the Pennsylvania Dutch society and its relationship to the greater Anglo-American society.

The various companies of the 17th Pennsylvania rendezvoused at Camp Simmons near Harrisburg, and on October 8, Colonel Josiah H. Kellogg was given command of the regiment. In Kellogg's regimental staff were many men of Pennsylvania Dutch stock, including Majors Coe Durland, Reuben Reinhold, and David B. Hartranft. There were also many Dutchmen serving in the ranks. One of them was Aaron Reuben Woomer from Myerstown, who had enlisted in Company E. His background was reflective of that of many Pennsylvania Dutch soldiers. Aaron had been born in the heart of Pennsylvania Dutch country along the Berks-Lancaster County line and baptized in the Lutheran Tulpehocken Church.[5]

Buford's division, including the 17th Pennsylvania, had been on the move since the climactic cavalry battle at Brandy Station on June 9, 1863. On June 26, the division had moved from Aldie, Virginia, through Leesburg and on to Poolesville, Maryland. On June 27 and 28, the division went into camp at Middletown, Maryland. On June 29, General Merritt took the Reserve Brigade to Mechanicstown (Thurmont), Maryland, and remained there until July 2. Buford led the brigades of Gamble and Devin in a sweep across South Mountain up to Boonesboro and then back across the mountain to Monterey Gap. The division went into camp at Fountaindale, south of Fairfield, Pennsylvania.

General Buford was not particularly pleased with his reception in Fountaindale. When he inquired of the mostly Pennsylvania Dutch citizens if they had any information about rebel troop movements, the people refused to answer, fearful of Confederate reprisals against them later. In many ways, this attitude reflected a constant strain of reluctance that ran through the Pennsylvania Dutch regions. Many Pennsylvania Dutch preferred to stay neutral and not assist either side—a difficult task to achieve. The locals were willing to provide food for their relatives, however, and early on the morning of June 30, a farmer and his daughter brought a wagonload of cakes and bread into the camp of the 17th Pennsylvania, where they were greeted with enthusiastic cheers.[6] Obviously, some Pennsylvania Dutch civilians were willing to support the Union cause, perhaps only because it benefited a loved one.

Buford's troopers rode down the Emmitsburg Pike on their way to Gettysburg, and Buford stopped to talk with Major General John Reynolds. On June 30, George Meade, commander of the Army of the Potomac, had ordered Reynolds to take command of his left wing, which consisted of three infantry corps: the First, Third, and Eleventh Corps. It was important that Buford have a clear understanding of Reynolds's plans.[7] After conversing with Reynolds, Buford rode at the head of his column into Gettysburg.[8] Although the townspeople seemed to be in a state of anxiety, they were also overjoyed that the Union army had arrived. The soldiers were met with cheers, flag waving, and the singing of patriotic songs.[9] One private in the 17th Pennsylvania recalled hearing different groups singing the "Star Spangled Banner," "Rally 'Round the Flag Boys," and "We Will Hang Jeff Davis from a Sour Apple Tree."[10] Buford immediately sent his two brigades out from Gettysburg to reconnoiter the area west and north of town. Devin's brigade, which consisted of the 6th and 9th New York, the 3d West Virginia, and the 17th Pennsylvania, rode down Washington Street and camped near Mummasburg Road. Gamble's brigade, consisting of the 8th and 12th Illinois, the 3d Indiana, and the 8th New York, also trotted down Washington Street but turned left at Chambersburg Street, headed west, and camped near McPherson's Ridge.[11]

The 17th Pennsylvania had 464 men available for combat on the afternoon of June 30. Three companies of the 17th had been detached to other

Private Levi A. Hocker, Co. F, 17th Pennsylvania Cavalry. BRUCE REINHOLD COLLECTION, U.S. ARMY MILITARY HISTORY INSTITUTE

duties: Companies D and H were assigned to Fifth Corps headquarters, and Company K was assigned to the Eleventh Corps. The 17th was armed with a .44-caliber Merrill and Smith carbine. The area it was to guard was north of town, and the troops were sent to Oak Ridge to picket the Mummasburg Road and the surrounding road network. Their headquarters was at the John Forney farmhouse. Patrols were sent out from there to cover the roads leading from Carlisle, Newville, and Middletown (Biglerville) and other points north.[12]

Shortly before daybreak on July 1, a detachment of the 17th under Major J. Q. Anderson was guarding the Carlisle Road and spotted rebel skirmishers advancing on their position. Anderson sent word back to headquarters and ordered his men to fall back. They retreated for a little over two miles until they met reinforcements coming up to support them. They stopped, dismounted, and took up defensive positions behind a stone wall. The troopers of the 17th began firing at the enemy, and many historians claim that the 17th fired the opening cavalry rounds of the battle of

Gettysburg. The skirmish north of Gettysburg had begun before 6 A.M., and the surgeon of the 17th, J. Wilson DeWitt, reported treating wounded at 7 A.M.—two hours after the firing had started.[13]

In the meantime, an elderly gentleman dressed in "Quaker" garb and carrying a cane approached the commander of the 17th, Colonel Kellogg, claiming to have vital information. The old man drew a piece of paper from his cane and handed it to Kellogg. The paper contained information that General Ewell's corps was near Gettysburg and would be marching on the town that morning. Just then, a rider approached with news from Major Anderson's patrol that a large body of rebels was advancing on his front—the old man was right![14] Once it became apparent that the rebels were advancing in force, Buford made the decision to contest the Confederates. He gathered his brigades and took up a defensive position along McPherson's Ridge.

Buford had made a conscious decision to stay and fight at Gettysburg. He gambled that Reynolds would support his decision, and based on that assumption, he positioned his troops. Buford counted on Battery A of the 2d Artillery under Lieutenant John H. Calef to be a central part of his defensive plans. Battery A had six three-inch ordnance rifled guns. These weapons were lighter than the standard army brass Napoleons, and they allowed the mobility that Calef's horse artillery required.

Buford's plans called for the distribution of the six guns to cover his front. Calef put two guns each on the right and left sides of the Chambersburg Pike. His remaining two guns were positioned near the southeast corner of McPherson's Ridge. Gamble's brigade took up defensive positions along the eastern arm of McPherson's Ridge, and Devin's brigade hooked onto Gamble's right flank and extended the line to the Mummasburg Road. The 17th held the far left of the line, guarding the Mummasburg Road and Oak Hill.[15]

Heth's division included four brigades, with Brigadier General J. J. Pettigrew commanding the First Brigade, Colonel J. M. Brockenbrough commanding the Second Brigade, Brigadier General James J. Archer commanding the Third Brigade, and Brigadier General Joseph R. Davis commanding the Fourth Brigade. In a short period, Gamble and Devin were facing the onslaught of Archer's and Davis's attacks. According to Buford, the two lines soon became hotly engaged, and Gamble fought for over two hours, holding the enemy at bay until the arrival of the First Corps. Devin's troopers were pressed to the limit as they contested the rebel advance on four separate roads. Devin held his ground until relief came in the form of the "German" Corps—the Eleventh Corps.[16]

Once infantry support arrived and took over the bulk of the fighting, Devin's brigade, with the 17th Pennsylvania, moved off the line at Oak Ridge along the Mummasburg Road. The cavalry moved out to protect the army's flank and guard roads north, including Harrisburg Road; during the remainder of the day's action, it guarded the flanks and protected communication and supply lines. The 17th helped cover the retreat of the Eleventh Corps as it fell back through town to the safety of Cemetery Hill. The 17th also retreated to Cemetery Hill, passing through the Henry Culp farm. They were next sent into the area of the Sherfy farm and an orchard of peaches that would soon become famous. Early on the morning of July 2, Buford's men got into a small firefight with enemy sharpshooters, but soon the cavalry was relieved by the arrival of Major General Daniel Sickles's Third Corps. Buford's division retreated through Emmittsburg and Taneytown and then on to Westminster.[17]

The 17th Pennsylvania performed well during the Gettysburg campaign. Although the 17th had a heavy Pennsylvania Dutch influence, the men did not fight as an exclusively Dutch organization; instead, they fought bravely with their English counterparts. All Buford's brigades had to do was hold on until the infantry arrived. Meade had directed Reynolds to send support to the beleaguered Federal cavalry, and that support was coming from the First and Eleventh Army Corps rapidly marching toward the sounds of battle.

The First Corps was commanded by Major General John Reynolds and consisted of three divisions containing seven infantry brigades with thirty-two infantry regiments—eleven of those from Pennsylvania. A close look at those regiments indicates that four of them had a solid number of Pennsylvania Dutch soldiers in their ranks: the 88th, 107th, 149th, and 151st Pennsylvania Volunteer Infantries. Many of the remaining Pennsylvania regiments also had Pennsylvania Dutch soldiers on their rolls.

The 149th had a smattering of Pennsylvania Dutch soldiers in many of its companies, but Company C from Lebanon County was extensively Pennsylvania German. Most of the company came from Myerstown, twenty-five miles east of Harrisburg. Nearly half the recruits were students from the Myerstown Academy who had been influenced by the patriotic speeches and parades of 1861 and decided to form a company. Their principal, twenty-eight-year-old John Bassler, had said that if they could get enough men to fill a company in the Bucktail Brigade within a fortnight, he would serve as captain. The young men quickly went to work, and within eight days, they had recruited the 100 men needed. The other half of the recruits were young men of the Jackson Guards militia.[18] The raising of Company C underscores the recruitment and use of Pennsylvania Dutch companies. The men were recruited from their local areas and then combined with units from various parts of the state; it was often an ad hoc proposition and reflects the indiscriminate placement of Pennsylvania Dutch units. They entered Federal service as Americans, but their unique background only intensified the personal bonds among the men.

The 149th was one of two bucktail units recruited by Colonel Roy Stone; the other was the 150th Pennsylvania Volunteer Infantry. Once at Camp Curtin, the 149th and 150th were partnered and immediately shipped to Washington, D.C. While in Washington, the 149th and 150th were assigned to the Third Division, First Army Corps, Army of the Potomac. In February 1863, the 143d Pennsylvania was added to Stone's brigade but did not wear the distinctive bucktails. The 149th saw little action before the battle of Gettysburg. It took part in the Chancellorsville campaign but did not engage the enemy.[19] This fact, as well as the flavor of the Pennsylvania Dutch influence, comes through in a letter from Franklin Weidle, a soldier in Company C, to his father in Myerstown, explaining his regiment's role in the recent campaign. As Pennsylvania Dutch linguist Edward Quinter points out, Weidle's dialect reflects the assimilation of the Pennsylvania Germans into the larger English community. Weidle often uses English loan words, and his letter is a combination of the Pennsylvania Dutch dialect and occasional English.[20]

Camp Near Patomac River

May 9th, 1863

Viel Geliebter vater:

　　Ich neme die Gelegenheit zu schreiben par Zeilen und las euch wissen das ich noch frisch und gesund bin so lange das der herr will und ich hoffe das die par Zeilen euch auch so antreffen werten. Weiter las euch wissen das mier ein grose fecht gehapt hen sie hat angehalten 8 tage lange und es hat viel menschen gekost auf unsere seite aber auf der andre seite hats drey man gekost bis ein von unsren es war ein schwer geschis gewesen nahi die gansze zeit. Weiter las ich euch wissen das mir grosz glick gehabt hen das ist unser brigat mier waren ungefe[r] zwey stunde in der gefahr das sie uns geschelt hen mit bummen guglen aber es hat net viel schaten getan mier waren hinter eim grosen berg gewesen so haben si si zimlig al über uns naus geschmizen das kannunen blitzen und dunren hat man gehort 25 Meil weit da kent ihr selbst denken wie es her gegangen ist Weiter las ich euch wissen das sie noch nie mals so abgetroszen warten sind wie dies mal das bettel felt war lang 25 Meil 8 Meil unter Frederichsburg hats angefangen und ist nuf gegangen bis auf 5 Meil nahe an Felmaus. Mier haben 200.50 tausent man im felt gehabt noch ein wenich/ich hab 40 Daler gelt heim getshicht mit der expres nach Myerstaun und es wundert mich hard ob diers het oder nicht schreibt mier ob diers habt oder nicht und fergest nicht gleicht zu schreiben ich mus zum beschlusz kammen für dies Mal so viel von eurem sohn. der herr sey mit euch zu ieter Zeit.

Franklin Weidle

direcht eur brief nemlich als wi zufohr
Washington D. C. Com. C. 149 Regt. P.V.
in care of J. H. Bassler

Camp Near Potomac River

May 9th, 1863

Very dear Father:

I take this opportunity to write a few lines and let you know that I am hale and hearty, so long as the Lord wills it. And I hope these few lines will find you even so well. Further I can report that we had a big battle that lasted 8 days and cost the lives of many of our men. But the other side lost three men to each one of ours. There was heavy firing that lasted practically the whole time.

Further I let you know that we were very lucky. Our Brigade was in real danger for about 2 hours during the shelling of the cannon balls. We were positioned behind a big hill, so most of the shells were shot pretty much over our heads. The thunder and flashing of the cannons could be heard for 25 miles. You can imagine how it sounded right here. Further I can say that they [the Confederates] never yet got such a thrashing as they did this time. The battlefield was 25 miles long. It began 8 miles below Fredericksburg and extended to within 5 miles of Falmouth. We had 250,000 men in the field. Just a little yet—I sent $40 home by express to Myerstown, and I really wonder whether you got it or not. Write me whether you did get it or not and don't forget to write right away. I must now bring this to a close for this time. So much from your son. The Lord be with you at all times.

Franklin Weidle

Direct your letter the same as before, to Washington, D.C. Company C, 149th Regt. Pennsylvania Volunteers, in care of J. H. Bassler

After Chancellorsville, the 149th remained in camp, and it was not until June 12 that it and the First Corps received their marching orders. In a series of long, arduous marches, the First Corps slowly made its way north, following on the heels of the Army of Northern Virginia. By June 29, Brigadier General Thomas A. Rowley's Third Division, which included the 149th, was encamped near Emmitsburg, Maryland, and on June 30, the division advanced to Marsh Creek, right outside Gettysburg.

On the morning of July 1, the First Corps started its march down Emmitsburg Pike toward Gettysburg. The First Division, commanded by

Company D, 149th Pennsylvania, in an 1864 photo. Note the bucktails on some of the hats. Their baptism by fire on the first day proved costly. MASSACHUSETTS COMMANDERY MILITARY ORDER OF THE LOYAL LEGION AND THE U.S. ARMY MILITARY HISTORY INSTITUTE

Brigadier General James S. Wadsworth, started for Gettysburg at 8 A.M.; the Third Division, with the 149th and 151st, under the command of General Rowley, started at 9 A.M.[21]

Colonel Stone's Second Brigade of Rowley's division had bivouacked near Bullfrog Road and Emmittsburg Road, near enough to support the First Brigade, led by Colonel Chapman Biddle. On July 1, Stone's men marched up Emmittsburg Road between Wadsworth's and Robinson's divisions. Because Rowley's division had been effectively cut in two, Biddle's First Brigade took a different route to the battle.[22]

Biddle's brigade had been on the Fairfield side of the corps to cover its left flank and protect the approaches from Fairfield and Cashtown. Biddle's men marched down Bullfrog Road to Pumping Station (Millerstown) Road, where they turned right and began marching toward Gettysburg. On the evening of June 30, the 151st Pennsylvania had bivouacked on the George Spangler farm. On the morning of July 1, the regiment began its march down Pumping Station Road through unspoiled countryside, and the war seemed far away. The men made a sharp right off the road and crossed the covered Sach's Bridge. From Sach's Bridge they marched to Black Horse Tavern Road and then onto Willoughby Run. The regiment continued northward along the west bank of Willoughby Run, eventually coming to Hagerstown (Fairfield) Road and a view of the ongoing battle.[23]

The 151st Pennsylvania had a heavy Pennsylvania Dutch component. Of the ten companies in the regiment, five were clearly Dutch: Companies E, G, H, I, and K. Companies E, G, H, and K had been recruited exclusively from Berks County. The ethnic composition of Company E was approximately 81 percent Pennsylvania Dutch; Company G, 87 percent; Company H, 86 percent; and Company K, 90 percent. Company I, which had been recruited in both Berks and Schuylkill Counties, was approximately 70 percent Pennsylvania Dutch. The other companies had only small percentages, but this underscores the fact that Pennsylvania Dutch soldiers were found in most Pennsylvania regiments. For example, Companies A and C, which had been recruited in Susquehanna County, were each roughly 9 percent Pennsylvania Dutch. Company B, recruited in Pike County, also had 9 percent; Company F in Warren had 8 percent, and Company D from Juniata 33 percent. The percentage from Juniata reflects the large number of Pennsylvania Dutch in that county, and these figures hold up well when tested against the demographics of the counties.[24] The 151st would play a large role in the upcoming battle.

The last division of the First Corps to leave camp on July 1 was the Second Division under the command of Brigadier General John C. Robinson. This division included the 88th and 107th Pennsylvania Volunteer Infantries, both of which had a strong mix of Pennsylvania Dutch in their ranks.

Nicknamed the Cameron Light Guards, the 88th was composed of men from Philadelphia and Berks Counties. Companies A, B, and H had been recruited in Berks County, and, reflecting the Pennsylvania Dutch tradition, the famous Ermentrout band came with the Reading companies.[25] The 88th fought its first action in August 1862 at Second Bull Run. In the Maryland campaign, culminating in the battle of Antietam, the 88th suffered more than 225 battle casualties. In May 1863, the regiment was marginally involved in the battle of Chancellorsville. After Chancellorsville, the regiment marched north with the First Corps and was now poised for battle. The 88th would see a great deal of fighting on Oak Hill.[26]

The 107th Pennsylvania was a composite of two understrength regiments with recruits from sixteen different counties. Companies A, B, D, E, G, I, and K all came from areas with a large Pennsylvania Dutch population; therefore, the 107th had a good mix of Pennsylvania Dutch and non-Dutch soldiers. The first major action for the 107th was at Second Bull Run, where it suffered a devastating 117 officers and men killed. The 107th was next engaged at Antietam and fought with Hooker in the Cornfield, suffering 64 casualties among the 190 men present for duty. In December 1862, the 107th supported Meade on the Union left at Fredericksburg and lost 56 of 171 officers and men.[27] The badly battered 107th would also be heavily engaged on Oak Hill on July 1.

Wadsworth's division of the First Corps was hurrying along Emmittsburg Pike when a staff officer approached and told Wadsworth to take the quickest route across the open field. Near the Codori farm, the men of the 149th marched off toward Seminary Ridge and passed McMillan's and Dr. Schumacher's house as they marched to the sound of battle.[28] The cavalry had started to give way, and the infantry reinforcements were badly needed.

The battle raged throughout most of the morning, and more reinforcements were soon needed to help the First Corps hold off the attack of General Henry Heth's Confederate division. Biddle's First Brigade of Rowley's Third Division, and the men of the 151st Pennsylvania, had arrived on the Hagerstown Road (Route 116) after their march along Willoughby Run. They were sent to fill in the gap between the Hagerstown Road and the woods, with the 151st occupying the left of the line. They crossed Willoughby Run near John Herbst's farm and advanced as far as Herr Ridge, until they were forced to fall back toward McPherson's Ridge. Stone's Second Brigade had been split off from the division and was ordered to occupy the open space north of Herbst Woods on the Chambersburg Road (Route 30). The Second Brigade included the 149th Pennsylvania and the Pennsylvania Dutchmen from Lebanon County. Rowley's two brigades were separated from each other by more than 200 yards; the famed Iron Brigade had split the two units.[29]

Stone's brigade occupied an important salient in the First Corps line—an unoccupied area between Herbst Woods and the Chambersburg Pike, which included the McPherson farm. The 143d and 149th Pennsylvania formed in McPherson's Lane, and the 150th went into line just south of the farmhouse.

The 149th went into action with 450 men armed with .577 Enfield rifles. They were soon moved from their position in McPherson's Lane and ordered to face north along the Chambersburg Pike to meet an attack from that direction. The 149th was then sent forward across the Chambersburg Pike toward the railroad cut. Captain Bassler of Company C (the Pennsylvania Dutch company) stated, "The order now came for our regiment to advance to the railroad cut, but Colonel Dwight, unfortunately, took us across the cut into an unfavorable position.[30] Bassler further reported that the 149th was soon attacked by Junius Daniel's North Carolina brigade of Major General Robert Rodes's division. Realizing that they were in grave danger, the men of the 149th scrambled back across the railroad cut, but the regiment was very disorganized, with many men already shot down or taken prisoner.[31]

An interesting story at this point involves the colors of the 149th. The regiment was receiving intense fire from Confederate artillery, and to draw off some of that fire, Colonel Stone tried to deceive the enemy. He sent the colors away from the regiment to act as a target. Color Sergeant Henry G. Brehm of Company C, Myerstown (a descendant of Conrad Weiser, the famed Pennsylvania Dutch pioneer and Indian ambassador), was ordered to take the flag to the left and front of the regiment, close enough to be seen by his comrades but far enough away to draw the devastating artillery fire. Brehm was accompanied by five other men from Company C: Corporals Franklin Lehman and John Fridell and Privates John H. Hammel and Henry H. Spayd from Myerstown, and Private Frederick Hoffman of

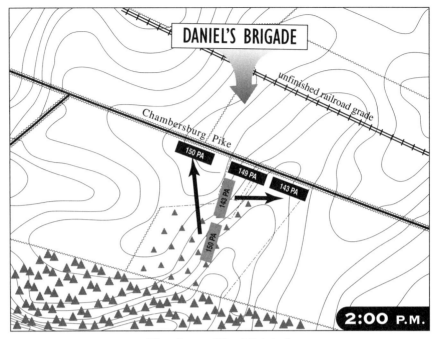

The advance of Daniel's brigade

nearby Newmanstown—all good Pennsylvania Dutchmen. The color
guard advanced and planted the colors behind a series of rails. Sergeant
Brehm carried the national flag and Corporal Lehman the state flag, and
the little group became the object of great interest from the Confederates,
holding their position during two attacks by Daniel's Confederate brigade.
Finally, Brehm and his small party attempted to retreat, only to discover
that Stone's entire brigade had retreated before them, leaving them surrounded by the enemy. Defending the colors to the last, Brehm was killed,
the flags were captured, and Lehman, Fridell, Spayd, and Hoffman were
wounded, showing great devotion to duty.[32] The 149th entered the fight
with 450 officers and men and ended it with 75 percent losses: 53 killed,
172 wounded, and 111 missing, for a total of 336 casualties—a very high
price for a regiment in its first major combat.

As Stone's brigade was engaged, the First Brigade was in line. Biddle
had placed his men on the left flank of McPherson's Ridge. The 151st Pennsylvania had been sent back to the hollow between Seminary Ridge and
McPherson's Ridge; it was the only reserve the First Corps had left. The
151st took refuge in a grove of trees and quickly made use of a series of

breastworks that had been hastily thrown up by the men of Paul's brigade. The 151st had been selected as a reserve because it was one of the largest regiments in the brigade.[33]

The Confederate attacks of Brigadier General James J. Pettigrew's North Carolinians and Colonel John M. Brockenbrough's Virginians struck Herbst Woods and drove the Iron Brigade back. Pettigrew's right regiments attacked Biddle's line, and a gap opened between the Iron Brigade and Biddle's command. It was at this juncture that the 151st Pennsylvania was ordered to fill that gap. One Confederate officer reported that "the fighting was terrible—our men advancing, the enemy stubbornly resisting, until the two lines were pouring volleys into each other at a distance no greater than 20 paces."[34]

The 151st initially held its position, but casualties quickly mounted. Second Lieutenant Charles Potts of Company I looked around and thought that the regiment could not hold on much longer. Rebel forces were attempting to take the left flank. The regiment's right flank was also being threatened; the officers of the Iron Brigade assumed that the 151st had come to relieve them and thus fell back, exposing the right flank of the 151st.[35]

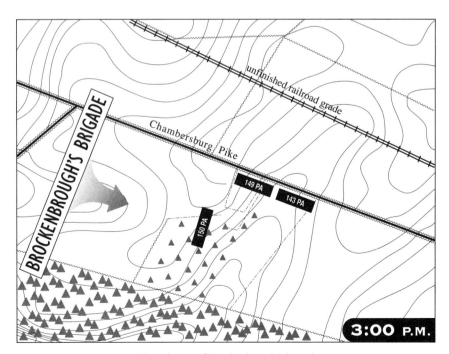

The advance of Brockenbrough's brigade

At around 3:30 P.M., the commander of the 151st, Lieutenant Colonel George McFarland, realized that his regiment was nearly isolated and about to be overrun, and he ordered a retreat. The 151st, along with Stone's brigade, was the last to retire from McPherson's Ridge. The remnants of the 151st regrouped behind entrenchments in front of the seminary, but the worst was yet to come.[36]

The remaining Federal force regrouped in the breastworks in front of Seminary Ridge. They were supported by twenty-one pieces of artillery that were lined hub to hub from the seminary toward the railroad cut. The Confederates began their renewed attack against Seminary Ridge around 4 P.M., with the South Carolina brigade of Abner Perrin attacking the front held by McFarland's 151st Pennsylvania. The Union command structure had been badly fractured, and each regimental commander conducted his own tactical maneuvers for the rest of the day. McFarland had the 19th Indiana to his right and the 142d Pennsylvania to his left. Captain William Gray of Company I approached McFarland and stated, "Colonel, my men are nearly all killed and wounded, what shall I do?" McFarland replied, "Fight with what is left," and that is exactly what the 151st did.[37] As the South Carolinians pressed their charge, they were met by a tremendous volley from the Federals. The Confederates recognized the futility of attacking the 151st head-on and soon began working toward the right, trying to flank their enemy. The 151st stood almost alone as the other Federal regiments began to retreat. Even the indomitable Iron Brigade was forced to retire. Little could be done against the irresistible rebel onslaught, and the men of the 151st were also forced back. McFarland (staying with his command) had stopped to observe the pursuing enemy (approximately twenty feet from the northwest corner of the seminary building) when he was shot in the left ankle and the lower right leg. The Confederates finally took Seminary Ridge, capturing 173 wounded officers and men of the 151st Pennsylvania.[38]

The remnants of the 151st under Captain William Beltz retreated through town, and many men were taken prisoner as they attempted to flee. Lieutenant Charles Potts of Company I wrote of his experience, "we made directly for the town, thinking that we would be [able] to make another stand, but, to our great surprise, the rebel cavalry had cut off our retreat, and we were bottled up. It had never occurred to me that I might be taken prisoner, and when I found I was in their hands, my feelings can't be described."[39] Most of the men followed the Chambersburg Pike and then possibly Washington Street to Cemetery Hill. The flag of the 151st was

Lt. Colonel George F. McFarland, 151st Pennsylvania. Wounded twice on the first day.
ROGER D. HUNT COLLECTION,
U.S. ARMY MILITARY HISTORY
INSTITUTE

raised in the rear of the cemetery, where the survivors of the regiment were able to rally. Only 113 men did so; the rest had been killed, wounded, or captured.[40] The 151st suffered 81 killed, 181 wounded, and 75 captured out of 467 men engaged, giving it the dubious distinction of ranking first among all Federal regiments at Gettysburg in the number of men wounded, fifth in total killed, and ninth in total percentage lost. Most of the casualties occurred in less than one hour of combat in McPherson's Woods. Lieutenant William Blodget wrote home to his wife after the battle and remarked that the men of the 151st had fought tenaciously, without a single exception. "Our poor boys fell around me like apples in a rain storm."[41] Among the regiment's killed was Sergeant Alexander Seiders, a Pennsylvania Dutchman from Reading. He had written home to his wife before July 1, stating how he longed to see her and their one-year-old daughter, Annie. A neighbor of Seiders, musician Michael Link, lost his eyesight while fighting at Gettysburg.[42] As with the 149th Pennsylvania, this had been the first combat experience of the 151st, and its soldiers paid a horrible price for their bravery and devotion to country.[43]

While the left flank of the First Corps was fighting for its life along the hills and dales of McPherson's Ridge, the right flank along Oak Ridge was also putting up a determined fight. As the battle along McPherson's Ridge was developing, the Second Division of the First Corps under Brigadier General John C. Robinson had arrived on the scene. General Doubleday immediately ordered Baxter's brigade to take up positions on the far right of McPherson's Ridge and on Oak Hill to cover the gap between the First Corps and the recently arrived elements of the Eleventh Corps.

Earlier, Doubleday had sent two regiments of Baxter's brigade to cover the area around Oak Hill, but his right flank was now weak. He was compelled to use up the last of his reserve and send the remainder of Baxter's brigade and all of Paul's brigade to hold the right. The 88th Pennsylvania of Baxter's brigade had three companies with a large number of Pennsylvania Dutch soldiers. Companies A, B, and H had all been recruited in Berks County, with Company H coming from the city of Reading. Approximately 60 percent of these companies consisted of Pennsylvania Dutch recruits.[44]

The men of the 88th had been held in reserve until about noon, when reports came in that a large body of Confederates was approaching Oak Hill. The regiment was called to arms, and after loading their weapons, the men marched north along McPherson's Ridge and over a cut to reach the fields near the Mummasburg Road. Skirmishers were sent to probe the enemy. The 88th, along with the 90th Pennsylvania and 83d New York, moved into a position that paralleled the Mummasburg Road and protected the rear and right flank of the division.[45] The skirmishers quickly met lead elements of Colonel Edward O'Neal's Alabamians and were pushed back. A general firefight commenced that ultimately forced O'Neal's men back. Before long, however, another Southern detachment was seen forming to attack across Forney's Field, hoping to "roll up" the Federal left flank. Baxter readjusted his line, which brought the 88th onto the ridge of Oak Hill.

Preparing to attack was a North Carolina brigade under Brigadier General Iverson. As the soldiers of Baxter's brigade watched with amazement,

Private Michael Link,
Co. E, 151st Pennsylvania.
Shot through the eyes on
the first day of Gettysburg.
Notice the First Corps
badge on his cap. DALE E.
BIEVER COLLECTION, U.S.
ARMY MILITARY HISTORY
INSTITUTE

Iverson confidently marched his lines straight, as if on parade. The North Carolinians seemed unaware that Baxter's brigade was waiting for them behind a stone wall on Oak Hill. Iverson did not have skirmishers out, and his men walked into a death trap.[46] When the Carolinians were about 100 paces distant, the men of Baxter's brigade rose up and poured a withering volley into the oncoming rebels. Hundreds of Confederates fell with the first volley and lay on the battlefield in neat rows of dead and wounded. Those who were uninjured ran to the rear, taking refuge in a small depression about 200 yards away.

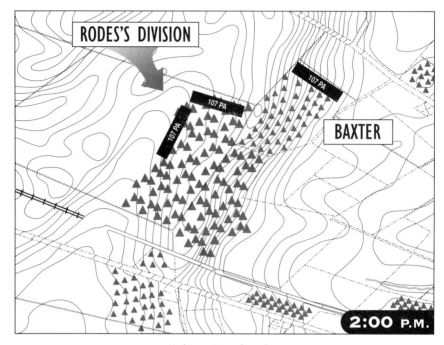

Robinson's northern line

It was at this juncture that General Baxter ordered his men to give the enemy cold steel—a charge with bayonets. The men of the 88th rushed after the demoralized Southerners and, in the process, captured many prisoners from the 5th, 20th, and 23d North Carolina. The 88th captured the regimental flag of the 23d, and a flag from another regiment. Baxter claimed that he took 1,000 prisoners, and Iverson reported 820 men captured. Iverson further reported being shocked at the sight of white handkerchiefs being waved by his troops, but when he saw his 500 dead or wounded men lined up where they fell, he exonerated the survivors.[47]

After Baxter's men had captured their prisoners, they found Paul's brigade coming to give them much needed support. Although Paul's brigade was smaller than Baxter's, numbering only about 1,500 officers and men, it included the 107th Pennsylvania's numerous Pennsylvania Dutch soldiers.

Paul's men arrived none too soon. Facing superior numbers, Paul aligned his regiments with large intervals between them, hoping to cover a greater front. Baxter's men were out of ammunition and left the line. Paul's brigade now held the right end flank of the First Corps, and the troops patiently awaited the next rebel attack. They did not have to wait long, as

General Junius Daniels was positioning his brigade of North Carolinians to assault Oak Hill again. Daniels maneuvered his right wing regiments to attack Shead's Woods and the troops of Generals Cutler and Baxter. The remnants of Iverson's brigade, along with troops from O'Neal's brigade, began forming for an attack against that portion of the line held by the 107th Pennsylvania.[48]

The 107th fired at the advancing enemy from behind a stone wall. At one point, someone yelled out that the Federals should charge the oncoming rebels, and that is what they did. The 104th New York began this impromptu attack and was soon joined by the 107th Pennsylvania. Both regiments were punished for their bold behavior. The 107th fell back to the wall and remained there for the rest of the fight on Oak Hill, blazing away at the enemy. Before long, the 107th had expended most of its ammunition,

First Lieutenant and Adjutant Benezel F. Foust, Co. A, 88th Pennsylvania. Company A was recruited in Berks County and assisted in the capture of two Confederate battle flags on the first day. DIVISION OF ARCHIVES AND MANUSCRIPTS, PENNSYLVANIA HISTORICAL AND MUSEUM COMMISSION

and the men were forced to rummage through the cartridge boxes of the dead and wounded. This may have proved difficult, since the 107th was armed with both the Austrian Lorenz rifle, which was a .54 caliber, and the .58-caliber U.S. Springfield.[49]

The 107th was one of the last units to fall back from the hill, and it suffered grievously there and on the retreat through Gettysburg. When eventually forced to fall back, the men were disorganized and exhausted, and many were easily taken prisoner by the pursuing Confederates. After a harrowing retreat through town, the survivors finally rallied at Ziegler's Grove on Cemetery Hill. The 107th had gone into action with 333 officers and men and lost 10 killed, 40 wounded, and 60 captured, for a total loss of 33 percent of the command. That regiment ranks fourth in the number of men captured at Gettysburg, a testimony to the men's steadfastness and devotion to duty.[50]

As the First Corps valiantly fought to hold the line along McPherson's and Seminary Ridges and Oak Hill, the Eleventh Corps was marching to its aid. The Eleventh Corps was called the German Corps because many of its regiments consisted of German immigrants. From Pennsylvania came the 27th, 73d, 74th, and 75th Pennsylvania, each composed largely of recent German immigrants. Also in the Eleventh Corps was the 153d Pennsylvania, which probably had the highest percentage of Pennsylvania Dutch (80 percent) of any regiment on the field. It was a nine-months regiment, and all the companies had been recruited in Northampton County.[51] The German Corps, commanded by Major General Oliver O. Howard, marched into Gettysburg about noon on July 1. The troops were ordered to protect the right flank of the First Corps but were unable to close the gap of about half a mile that separated Robinson's division and the Eleventh Corps. The First Corps held the high ground on Oak Ridge, and the left flank of the Eleventh Corps occupied the Gettysburg plain, extending the Union line from the Mummasburg Road to the Harrisburg Pike. The command structure of the Eleventh Corps was a little confusing. Howard assumed tactical command of the fighting in the Gettysburg area after Major General John Reynolds had been killed in the first day's fighting. Howard ordered Major General Carl Schurz to assume temporary command of the Eleventh Corps, and Schurz turned the command of his Third Division over to Brigadier General Alexander Schimmelfennig.

Schurz brought two divisions of the Eleventh Corps up to the Gettysburg plains; the last, under Brigadier General Adolphus von Steinwehr, was held in reserve on the heights of Cemetery Hill. The truncated Eleventh went into action with the Third Division, attempting to hook up with the right flank of the First Corps. In support of the Third Division was Brigadier General Francis Barlow's Second Division. Barlow was ordered to remain aligned with the Third, but for some unknown reason, Barlow moved his men to higher ground on Blocher's Knoll (Barlow's Knoll). This move by Barlow would prove to be costly.[52] Barlow's two brigades were led by Brigadier Generals Adelbert Ames and the German-born Leopold von Gilsa. Von Gilsa's brigade contained the 153d Pennsylvania.

The 153d Pennsylvania had been recruited in response to the 1862 militia draft. The regiment formed at Camp Curtin and was mustered into service in October 1862. After receiving uniforms and equipment, the men were sent to Washington, D.C., where the regiment was attached to the Eleventh Corps. The regiment arrived in Fredericksburg, Virginia, in mid-December 1862.[53] During the battle of Chancellorsville, the 153d had the distinction of being the first Federal unit in the Eleventh Corps to be attacked by Lieutenant General "Stonewall" Jackson's famous flank attack. It received the first shock of the Confederate assault and managed to get off only a few volleys before being swept from the field.[54]

On July 1, 1863, the 153d Pennsylvania and the rest of the Eleventh Corps approached Gettysburg on two parallel roads. The two divisions of Schurz and Steinwehr entered Gettysburg via the Taneytown Pike, while Barlow's division came down the Emmitsburg Pike.[55] Barlow's division followed Schurz's (Schimmelfennig's) through town and entered the Gettysburg plain from Washington Street. The troops proceeded east until they came to the Harrisburg Pike, where they turned left and marched to the vicinity of the Almshouse.[56]

When Barlow blundered by sending Ames's brigade farther to the right to hold Blocher's Knoll, he sealed the fate of the Union right. Von Gilsa, realizing the danger to Ames, double-quicked his men to the barn near the Almshouse; the men dropped their knapsacks and threw them into an outbuilding as the brigade began to form en masse. (The men of the 153d went into battle thinking that their enlistment had expired, but it had not. That fact proved to be inconsequential, however, because the men were willing to fight for their home state).[57] As the 153d formed its battle line, it created a "two-company" division front. In such a configuration, the color company was out in front. Elements of the 153d were then ordered out as brigade skirmishers, and the Second Division was held in reserve. It would have been

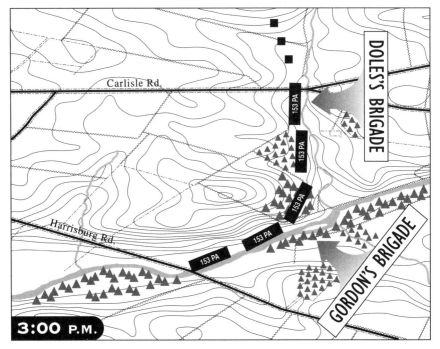

Carlisle Rd.

153 PA

153 PA

153 PA

Harrisburg Rd.

153 PA

153 PA

153 PA

DOLE'S BRIGADE

GORDON'S BRIGADE

3:00 P.M.

The attack on Barlow's flank

disastrous to send the color company out on the skirmish line, and von Gilsa (who could swear in German as well as in English) knew it. Angered, he let out a curse and asked why the color division was deploying. The problem was quickly remedied, the color party retired, and Companies A and F maneuvered to the front as skirmishers.[58]

Altogether, von Gilsa sent the 54th and 68th New York and two companies of the 153d forward as skirmishers. The other eight companies of the 153d were held in reserve immediately behind the skirmish line. The skirmishers rushed over the crest of Blocher's Knoll and pressed on toward Rock Creek. Von Gilsa rode among his men, admonishing them not to shoot unless they could see the enemy and not to mind the minié balls whizzing past their heads.[59]

Soon the Confederates of Lieutenant General Richard Ewell's corps began marching down the Carlisle Pike to show themselves en masse. The brigades of John Gordon and Robert Doles began a vigorous attack against the two divisions of the Eleventh Corps. Much of Gordon's attack was aimed against von Gilsa. The skirmish line of the 153d felt Gordon's attack first and soon found itself in jeopardy of being flanked. Private Reuben

Ruch of Company F gave a detailed account of the fight of the 153d as he stood in line in support of the skirmishers. Ruch reported that the rebels first charged far to their left, but the next charge came closer to the 153d. Ruch remarked to his mates that it would not be long before their turn came, and within ten minutes, the skirmish line started coming back. Following the skirmishers of the 153d were three rebel battle lines. Soon, the skirmishers had fallen back to the main line of the regiment.

Ruch was fighting quite hard, and he considered taking a rebel color-bearer in his sights but opted for another target. As he was firing, he heard the order to fall back. The enemy was only two or three paces away, and the brigade line was broken on the left and flanked on the right. There was nothing to do but surrender—or run. Ruch wrote that they passed the red barn by the Almshouse as they retreated toward Gettysburg. The brigade made it all the way back to York Street—about a mile and a half from the original line—and von Gilsa was still attempting to form a battle line.[60]

The remnants of the two divisions of the Eleventh Corps retreated through town, and confusion reigned in the streets of Gettysburg as men from the First Corps intermingled with men from the Eleventh. Many Unionists were wounded and sought out the many makeshift hospitals in town. The 153d's retreat was reminiscent of the retreat of many a Union soldier on that first day at Gettysburg. The First and Eleventh Corps had fought themselves to the point of exhaustion, and the Pennsylvania Dutch soldiers had performed admirably. But how did their comrades in arms, the German-Americans, fare in their struggle on the Gettysburg plains?

CHAPTER 7

Pennsylvania's German-Americans, a Popular Myth, and the Importance of Perception

Christian B. Keller

First Lieutenant Louis Fischer of the 74th Pennsylvania's Pioneer Company looked over the plain north of Gettysburg with an acute sense of helplessness and dread. Standing on a "boxed post some eight feet in height" near the edge of Pennsylvania College, Fischer had a clear view of the unequal fight that his regiment and the rest of the Eleventh Corps faced on July 1, 1863. "As far as my eye could reach I saw thousands of Ewell's men come toward the rear and flank of my corps, completely enveloping it," and "a foreboding of the coming massacre kept me riveted to the spot." Rebel infantry entered Gettysburg, almost cutting off the two divisions of the Eleventh Corps fighting north of it, "but the men of the two divisions [were] still grimly trying to hold their ground." Fischer could no nothing but watch, as he and his men were unarmed, but the panorama before him touched him deeply. Four years later, he could write as if he were still riveted to that post, observing "stretcher bearers . . . unable to get the severely wounded from the field," the "dull thud" of a bullet striking the body of "Lieut. Roth, of my company . . . his reeling body sink[ing] to the earth before me," and the deaths of comrades, "without them having any show for their lives." Still indignant about the results of the first day at Gettysburg, Fischer added, "my poor comrades had to be sacrificed, just as they were sacrificed at Chancellorsville two months previous."[1]

Were he alive today, Fischer probably would not be pleased by the dearth of scholarship on the Eleventh Corps, and specifically the German-American regiments in it. He would be even less sanguine about the popular memory of his corps and comrades that exists in the public mind. Of the hundreds of books written about the battle of Gettysburg, only a handful have specifically examined the role of the German-American regiments, and even fewer have critically assessed German-American perceptions of the battle. Moreover, a popular legend passed down through the years claims that the Germans ran once again and fought only marginally better at Gettysburg than they had at Chancellorsville. "D—d Dutchmen of the Eleventh Corps broke and ran like sheep, just as they did at Chancellorsville," one Union survivor of the first day's battle said. This general impression of the performance of the German troops has stuck like a burr in both historians' and the general public's image of the German-American soldiers. The persistence of the legend of the cowardly Dutchmen at Gettysburg, however, cries out for further examination.[2]

Several recent scholars, including David G. Martin, A. Wilson Greene, and D. Scott Hartwig, have analyzed the battle performance of the Eleventh Corps as a whole and, although not focusing exclusively on the German regiments, have provided fair and impartial assessments of the corps' contributions to the overall Union victory. Martin claims that the Eleventh Corps was overpowered by the greater number and superior generalship of the Confederates but fought as well as could be expected under the circumstances. Greene concludes that "the Eleventh Corps performed with honor on July 1, 1863, and deserves a better reputation," and Hartwig notes that "the rank and file of the 11th Corps had fought with courage and frequently with tenacity." So although the battle history of the German-American regiments, including those from Pennsylvania, is at least partially covered in the scholarly literature about the Eleventh Corps, a closer look at the 27th, 73d, 74th, 75th, and 98th Pennsylvania at Gettysburg may shed some light on the truth—or lie—behind the myth of the cowardly Dutchmen.[3]

More critical to discovering the background behind this legend, however, are the personal reactions of both German and non-German soldiers and civilians to the performance of the Eleventh Corps, and specifically the German troops in it, on July 1 and 2, 1863. Despite the reality of how well or how badly the German-American regiments actually fought, in the end, the perceptions of that reality decided how the Germans would be viewed after the battle by historians, by their fellow soldiers, and by the English- and German-language press.

The perceptions of the non-German soldiers at the battle were important. They biased earlier Gettysburg scholars against the Germans, thus perpetuating the "cowardly Dutchmen" idea, and may have preempted the reorganization and ultimate dispersal of the German regiments of the Eleventh Corps during the summer and early fall of 1863. Not surprisingly, the few sources written by German-American soldiers from Pennsylvania indicate that they fought a hard fight to the best of their ability and deserved recognition. Lieutenant Colonel Alexander von Mitzel of the 74th Pennsylvania, for example, recalled that his regiment had "held the position [north of town] to the last" on July 1. Naturally, soldiers are reluctant to criticize their own battlefield prowess, so von Mitzel's statement is not unusual. His voice, however, and the voices of Louis Fischer and countless other German-Americans were lost amidst the plethora of accusations by Anglo-American soldiers that claimed the Eleventh Corps and its Germans had run again.[4]

Just as important as the observations of the soldiers were the responses in the English- and German-language press to the July 1 fight. Newspapers published in both languages exhibited a significant reversal of attitude from their reportage of the Chancellorsville battle. After Chancellorsville, the Anglo-American press had strongly criticized the Germans, and Pennsylvania's German-American press had responded in an outraged, defensive manner. After Gettysburg, the major Anglo-American papers, caught up in the celebration of the Union victory, provided sparse coverage of the first day's battle and delegated even less space to reports of the Germans' performance. What little the papers said, however, was positive: The Eleventh Corps' Germans had actually fought well, despite being pushed back from their positions north of town.[5]

Pennsylvania's German-language press also changed its tone. The reaction to Gettysburg was far less incendiary than that which resulted from Chancellorsville because the battle ended in Union victory and the anti-German backlash was almost nonexistent. Instead of defending the record of the German troops' performance against Anglo-American critics, the editors seemed to revel in the accomplishments of the Eleventh Corps and its German-American regiments, highlighting their sacrifices and importance at the expense of non-German organizations in the army. To the readers of the German-language newspapers, the German soldiers not only appeared uncowardly but also became the bravest of them all.

A brief examination of the actions of the primary German-American regiments from Pennsylvania argues against the legend of the "flying Dutchmen." Although these regiments were outnumbered by their New York

*Colonel Adolph von Hartung,
74th Pennsylvania.* U.S. ARMY
MILITARY HISTORY INSTITUTE

counterparts (seven to five), they represented a considerable chunk of the Eleventh Corps as a whole and an even larger component of the Germans in it. Retracing their experiences on July 1 and 2 therefore provides a window, however limited, into the overall performance of the Germans in the Eleventh Corps at Gettysburg.

The 74th Pennsylvania, of Brigadier General Alexander Schimmelfennig's division, had almost half its numbers detached to various guard duties prior to the battle and thus entered the fight on July 1 with only 134 officers and men. About 1:30 P.M., despite their low numbers, the Pittsburgh Germans were ordered by brigade commander George von Amsberg to hold the line between the Carlisle and Mummasburg Roads. As soon as the men took position, Confederate batteries on Oak Hill found the range and pummeled the Germans with case and solid shot. Within a few minutes of the end of this barrage, Brigadier General George Doles's Georgia brigade

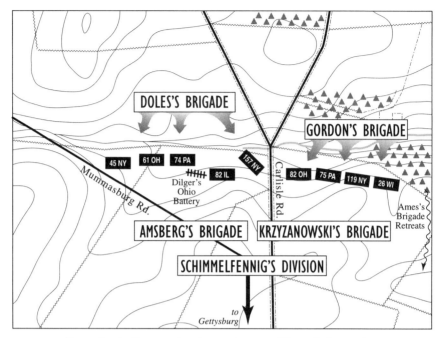

Pennsylvania German-American regiments at Howard's front, July 1

advanced against the 74th and picked off most of its officers, including
Colonel Adolf von Hartung, who took a bullet that shattered his left leg.
Command devolved upon Lieutenant Colonel Alexander von Mitzel, who
recalled that "things were getting hot, I had two horses shot under me but
I held my position with the bayonett, and though being pressed harder and
harder by the Rebels yet I held the position up to the last." Von Mitzel held
his position too long. The 74th's line broke under the extreme Confederate pressure and, outflanked on both sides, was in danger of being completely surrounded. Von Mitzel later argued that "it would have been more
prudent to retreat yet the order did not come from my superior," so finally
he decided to "fight my way through to the city." He led the few standing
soldiers of his command through thick Confederate fire back to the town
but found it "already in the enemy's hands." To his immense chagrin, von
Mitzel was captured, along with a few dozen of his men. Major Gustave
Schleiter assumed command, managed to elude capture with twenty-one
others, and rallied on Cemetery Hill with approximately 200 other men of
the regiment who had just returned from guard duty. Statistical sources on
the losses of the 74th vary; Louis Fischer's 1869 account stated that three

officers were killed, "six or seven wounded," and two taken prisoner, along with sixty-three enlisted casualties (many of whom were killed or wounded). Another source points to higher losses, approaching 85 percent of all the men engaged. Regardless of the exact figures, the high numbers of killed and wounded do not point toward cowardice.[6]

The 75th Pennsylvania in Colonel Wladimir Krzyzanowski's brigade numbered 185 officers and men when it was thrown into the battle at about 2 P.M. to support Brigadier General Francis Barlow's crumbling First Division. Taking position to the right of the Carlisle Road between the 82d Ohio and the 119th New York, the Philadelphia Germans advanced with the brigade against Doles's Georgians and succeeded in temporarily surprising them in the flank. The Confederates shifted to meet the threat, however, and for several minutes the two lines fired at each other at point-blank range. Men fell everywhere. Lieutenant Henry Hauschild, a Gettysburg native, was shot in the heart. Color Sergeant Charles Busch died from a bullet to the head. Sergeant Major Claus Kahl fell severely wounded in the leg, and Captain Conrad Schuler was shot through the abdomen. Second Lieutenant Louis Mahler, brother of Colonel Francis Mahler, also fell dead. Both sides suffered grievously. When the neighboring Union brigade (Adelbert Ames's) to the right gave way, however, Brigadier General John Gordon's Confederates overlapped Krzyzanowski's right flank and began systematically destroying first the 26th Wisconsin and then the 119th New York, which supported the 75th's flank. Carl Wickesberg of the 26th remembered that the "bullets came as thick as hail."[7]

Time was running out for the 75th Pennsylvania. After both the 26th Wisconsin and the 119th New York fell back under the Confederate onslaught, the neighboring 82d Ohio suddenly retreated, purportedly leaving the Pennsylvania Germans alone against more than 1,000 rebels.[8] Realizing the danger of being flanked on both sides, Colonel Mahler rushed to the left flank to direct his men there, but his horse collapsed beneath him, killed by a minié ball. Mahler, hurt by the fall, nonetheless reached the left flank on foot and began rousing his men with a quick speech in German, but he was mortally wounded. Lieutenant Albert Steiger carried Mahler to the rear, where he was found by Carl Schurz, who had known Mahler in Germany. "He reached out his hand to me in a last farewell," Schurz recalled. In the meantime, Major August Ledig took over command and ordered the regiment to fire to the left oblique in a gamble to check the enemy. Further resistance, however, was futile, as the understrength regiment had been

Colonel Francis Mahler,
75th Pennsylvania.
PENNSYLVANIA HISTORICAL
AND MUSEUM COMMISSION
COLLECTION, U.S. ARMY
MILITARY HISTORY INSTITUTE

reduced to the size of a company and was now in danger of being completely cut off. It was time to give up the field. Sergeant Hermann Nachtigall recounted that "the regiment retreated in good order" to the town and
retained cohesion as it reached Cemetery Hill.[9]

The cost of the 75th's half-hour ordeal was extremely high. Of the 184
men who had entered the fight, only 71 remained unscathed. A surviving
officer of the regiment, probably Adjutant Frederick Tiedemann, wrote to
the *Philadelphia Freie Presse* after the battle with a comprehensive list of
the dead and wounded. He claimed that the regiment lost 116 dead and
wounded, but later sources disputed that figure—lowering the number, but
not by much. Tiedemann, however, was clearly bitter about the losses and
added a scorching note:

This, our loss, is not to be ascribed to our generals or other commanders, but clearly to the "noble" soldiers of the 2nd Brigade, First Divsion, who were ashamed after the battle of Chancellorsville, VA to fight any longer next to or with the Dutchmen. They broke right after the first shot, and we received the entire fire of the enemy, through which our beloved Colonel Franz Mahler found his early death.

Tiedemann was clearly referring to the brigade of Adelbert Ames, containing several non-German regiments that had officially protested being in the Eleventh Corps with the Germans after Chancellorsville and whose officers had requested that their regiments be transferred. The transfers did not occur, but the bad feelings between the survivors of the 75th and Ames's men persisted throughout the war. Many soldiers of the 75th also blamed their regiment's decimation at Gettysburg on the supposed flight of the 82d Ohio. In truth, the German regiment was so reduced in numbers after the battle that it barely escaped amalgamation with another unit.[10]

Captain Frederick K. Tiedemann, Co. G, 75th Pennsylvania, in a postwar image.
MASSACHUSETTS COMMANDERY MILITARY ORDER OF THE LOYAL LEGION AND THE U.S. ARMY MILITARY HISTORY INSTITUTE

Assigned to Colonel Charles Coster's brigade of Brigadier General Adolphus von Steinwehr's reserve division, the 27th Pennsylvania, another Philadelphia German unit, was commanded by Lieutenant Colonel Lorenz Cantador during the first day's battle and numbered 283 men. Ordered into the fight late on the afternoon of July 1 to shore up Barlow's and Schimmelfennig's retreating divisions, Coster's brigade was too small and too late to stem the Confederate advance that had earlier compelled the 74th and 75th Pennsylvania to retreat. Carl Schurz himself led the 27th and its sister regiments, the 134th and 154th New York, to Stratton Street, on the northeast border of town. Isaac Avery's and Harry Hays's Confederate brigades approached the hastily formed Union line confidently, expecting little resistance. Suddenly the command to fire was given, and the men of the 27th fired in unison. Avery's North Carolinians staggered under the blast, but Hays's men continued their advance and soon enveloped the right flank of the 134th New York, forcing a gap between it and the 154th. Colonel Cantador realized the danger and called for the 27th's Second Battalion to fill the gap, but only Lieutenant Adolphus Vogelbach and about fifty men could hear the order. Vogelbach's detachment hurried to its new position, but the Confederates had completely broken through. Vogelbach's men fought on with the 154th New York after the 134th disintegrated and the rest of the 27th Pennsylvania had been ordered to retreat. Vastly outnumbered, outflanked on both sides, and soon to be surrounded, Vogelbach's troops refused Confederate appeals to surrender and tried to cut themselves out of the trap. Then Vogelbach fell badly wounded, and after several more minutes of close-quarters fighting, the Philadelphia Germans finally threw down their rifles and gave up. The rest of the 27th Pennsylvania succeeded in retreating to Cemetery Hill, but only after losing a total of 111 men.[11]

The 73d Pennsylvania, also composed mainly of Philadelphia Germans, saw little fighting on July 1, having been left as part of von Steinwehr's reserve on Cemetery Hill. The next day, however, the 73d participated in a critical counterattack that saved several Union batteries. Hays's Louisiana brigade—including the famous "Louisiana Tigers"—covered by the waning daylight and an artillery barrage, succeeded in reaching the Union cannon almost undetected and charged the surprised cannoneers. The 73d immediately counterattacked and, along with other troops, including the German 27th Pennsylvania and 107th Ohio, wrested back control of the batteries and the hill through vicious hand-to-hand combat. Captain Michael Wiedrich

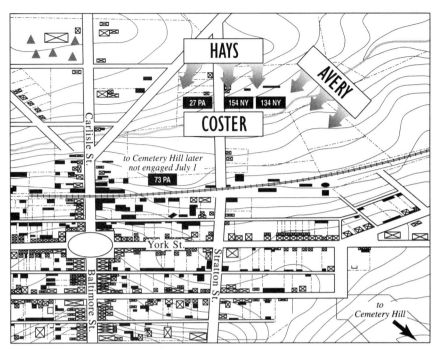

Howard's Pennsylvania German-American reserve regiments in Steinwehr's division, July 1

recalled that the 73d had been instrumental in preserving the Union line on
Cemetery Hill and recapturing his cannon: "When the Louisiana Tigers
charged my battery, and when we were in a hand-to-hand fight with them,
I saw that my position could not be held, and had ordered my battery to
limber up and fall back to the Baltimore pike, when the Seventy-third and
Twenty-seventh Regiments Pennsylvania Volunteers came to my rescue and
repulsed the rebels." Veterans of the 73d would always be proud of their performance on the evening of July 2, and when the survivors attempted to
erect a monument, the veterans of the 27th Pennsylvania protested, claiming
that they had a greater right to the location, but adding, "we unanimously
declare that they are fully and justly entitled to the position which they
claim." The 73d's action at Gettysburg cost only thirty-four casualties, most
caused by Confederate artillery.[12]

The 98th Pennsylvania, a Philadelphia German regiment assigned to
the Sixth Corps, also escaped large numbers of casualties and was not hotly
engaged at Gettysburg. The 98th and its brigade (Brigadier General Frank
Wheaton's) fought late in the afternoon of July 2 below Little Round Top,

helping to check the Confederates surging toward the critical Union position. The Confederates "retreated before us with little firing," recalled Captain Jacob Schmid, who was in the vanguard of a charge made by the 98th. The regiment advanced the entire way to the Wheatfield, then stopped and formed a battle line behind a stone wall on its edge, which it held for the rest of the battle. The 98th's performance cost only twelve casualties.[13]

Taken together, the battle record of the five Pennsylvania German-American regiments does not give an impression of frightened soldiers who failed to stand their ground, abandoned their positions quickly, or otherwise behaved in a cowardly manner. The 98th Pennsylvania was not part of the Eleventh Corps, so its record might be discounted. It could also be argued that the performance of the Pennsylvania regiments in the Eleventh Corps did not reflect that of all German-American troops in the corps and that, in the end, the 74th, 75th, and 27th Pennsylvania had been forced to retreat on July 1. Still, the historical record of Pennsylvania's German-American regiments at Gettysburg does not reveal anything that remotely substantiates the rumors of cowardice that arose later. Further, four of the five Pennsylvania regiments evaluated here *were* part of the Eleventh Corps, so their actions at Gettysburg must be taken into account when assessing the overall record of that corps' German troops. Finally, the casualty rates, particularly of the 74th and 75th Pennsylvania, testify to the fact that these men did not simply "skedaddle." Something compelled these soldiers to hold their positions as long as possible. It could be, as the German-language press argued, that they had actually fought with courage.

By late June 1863, many non-German soldiers in the Army of the Potomac identified the Eleventh Corps as the "Dutch" or German corps. Strong traces of this sentiment were evident before the battle of Chancellorsville, and afterward, they were even stronger. It did not matter that almost half the corps' regiments were non-German (twelve of twenty-seven); the performance of the Eleventh Corps at Chancellorsville and, more importantly, the postbattle excoriation of the German troops by both Anglo-American soldiers and the English-language press created the impression that the organization was all German. Certainly, better-informed Anglo-American soldiers knew that most of the Ohio regiments and several New York regiments in the corps were not German, but after the Union debacle on the first day at Gettysburg, distinctions among regiments mattered little to critics (or even in postwar histories written years later). Some non-German soldiers in the Eleventh Corps also believed that theirs was primarily a German command, and their comments about the Germans were just as negative as those from Anglo-Americans of other corps. For the most part, when Anglo-American soldiers spoke of the Eleventh Corps, they were referring to the Germans.[14]

Accounts of the battle performance of the corps were naturally dependent on the vantage point of the observer, the time of the observation, and the troops actually being observed. Some of the most telling commentary came from soldiers of Robinson's division of the First Corps, who occupied their corps' right flank. They believed that the retreat of an Eleventh Corps division on their right around 4:00 caused the outflanking of their position by advancing Confederates and, subsequently, the Union disaster on the first day.[15] A veteran of the 12th Massachusetts wrote years later, "We of Robinson's division have a very vivid remembrance of a division of the Eleventh Corps throwing away its guns and manifesting intense anxiety to regain the charming shelter of Cemetery Hill." Another survivor of the 12th, Benjamin F. Cook, wrote that the first day's fight "was made by the First Corps and Buford's cavalry: the retreat was caused by the inability of Howard's twenty-six regiments to keep eighteen Confederate regiments off the right flank of the First Corps." Cook also noted that none of the captured Confederate battle flags from July 1 were carried by men wearing "the crescent badge of the Eleventh Corps."[16]

In his assessment of the first day's battle, private Charles E. Davis of the 13th Massachusetts agreed with the other two Bay Staters that "the Eleventh Corps had done less work than the First." Major Abner R. Small of the 16th Maine was more explicit, arguing that "our [Robinson's] right flank, which had been fully exposed by the skedaddling of a part of Howard's Eleventh Corps," suffered grievously from the ensuing Confederate onslaught. The "half moon men," he continued, not only failed to hold their line but had arrived too late to be of any use: "When the Eleventh Corps reached the field, hardly a field officer had escaped [becoming a casualty], and nearly half of the First Corps lay dead and wounded." Private John Vautier of the 88th Pennsylvania was a bit more charitable, claiming that the Eleventh Corps "presented a thin and broken line, too feeble to resist the grand attack that was presently to be made on its scattered battalions." But, he observed, "it is remarkable, when compared with the First Corps, how little damage they inflicted upon their opponents."[17]

Men in the First Corps' famed Iron Brigade, which had suffered aston-
ishing casualties, likewise berated the Eleventh Corps. Sergeant James P.
Sullivan of the 6th Wisconsin recalled the evening of his first day as a Confederate prisoner, stating that his comrades "cursed the 'Flying Moon'
Corps freely and [accused] Howard for a bible thumping hypocrite." One
of Sullivan's friends, Private Hugh Talty, "wanted to go out and whip the
'damned cowards be gob'" but was reminded that he could do little as a
prisoner. Another unknown soldier, having reached the safety of Cemetery
Hill after the collapse of the Federal positions north of town, overheard a
man with a German accent ask an officer which way led to the Eleventh
Corps positions. The Anglo-American soldier burst in, "1st Corps to the
right and 11th Corps go to hell."[18]

Some of the most vitriolic commentary about the Eleventh Corps
and its German-Americans at Gettysburg came from eyewitnesses to the
defense of Cemetery Hill on the night of July 2. After the defeat of the
First and Eleventh Corps on the first day, the Unionists retreated to prepared positions on Cemetery Hill and there licked their wounds, reorganized, and strengthened their defenses. The Confederates attacked in the
evening of the second day and succeeded, for a moment, in penetrating
the Federal positions and threatening several important Union batteries.[19]
The temporary collapse of certain Eleventh Corps regiments during this
assault attracted the attention of Colonel Charles Wainwright, commander
of the First Corps' artillery:

> So soon as the rebels began to fire, the two lines of Deutschmen in
> front of the batteries began to run, and nearly the whole of them
> cleared out. . . . I pitied General Ames most heartily. His men did
> not stand at all, save one. I believe not a single regiment of the
> Eleventh Corps exposed to the attack stood fire, but ran away
> almost to a man. Stewart stretched his men along the road and
> with fence rails to try to stop the runaways but could do nothing.
> Officers and men however got a supper (they had been without
> food all day) for when they knocked a Deutschman down, they
> took his haversack from him.[20]

Wainwright's observations not only exaggerated the number of Eleventh Corps regiments that retreated (and ignored those, such as the 73d
Pennsylvania, that actually counterattacked) but also lumped all the troops

of Brigadier General Adelbert Ames's division under the rubric "Deutsch-man." In fact, Ames's command at this time included three non-German regiments (17th Connecticut and 25th and 75th Ohio), but Wainwright apparently cared little for such distinctions when assessing blame.

Second Lieutenant Oscar D. Ladley of the 75th Ohio probably best cap-tured the feeling of disgust for the German troops held by non-Germans of the Eleventh Corps. On July 16, he wrote his family a letter that described recent changes in command, his opinion of Germans, and his role in "repulsing" the rebels in the night attack of July 2:

> They have put an infernal Dutchman in command of the Div. and sent Ames to his Brig. His name is Schimmelfennig or something of that kind, he is the General who hid in a shop barrel in Gettys-burg to keep from being taken prisoner. He is a poor excuse. Gen. Ames is a young man of good judgment, a graduate of West Point and far superior to any Dutchman in the army. Western troupes [*sic*] might as well be in Halifax as here. The dutch run and leave us to fight, so we have to fight twice our numbers or run too which we don't like to do at the first fire. Well I hope we shall be out of this soon.

Ladley continued: "I had a little revenge on the night that Earleys Div. of Ewell's corps charged us, they [the Dutch] commenced running back as usual. My sword was out and if I didn't welt them with it my name ain't O. D. L. It was the only good service it has done me yet." Noting that his sword had not yet "killed a reb," Ladley expressed "satisfaction" that "it came mighty near laying out a dutchman!" Ladley's mother wrote back on July 27, stating, "I think you did good service with your sword when you welted the Dutch with it."[21]

Another member of the Eleventh Corps who specifically blamed the Germans for the corps' performance at Gettysburg was Brigadier General Francis Barlow, commander of the First Division. After the battle, Barlow wrote to a Harvard classmate, "But these Dutch won't fight. Their officers say so and they say so themselves and they ruin all with whom they come in contact." It is well known that Barlow disliked a lot of people in the Army of the Potomac, but his hatred for the Germans was legion. Because of his position of authority, Barlow's loud denunciations likely exacerbated the German regiments' already poor reputation in the army.[22]

Brigadier General Francis C. Barlow, nicknamed "Dogberry" by members of the 153rd Pennsylvania. He wrote to his mother he had "always been down on the Dutch." MASSACHUSETTS COMMANDERY MILITARY ORDER OF THE LOYAL LEGION AND THE U.S. ARMY MILITARY HISTORY INSTITUTE

Ladley's and Barlow's invective against the German-Americans of the Eleventh Corps was not echoed by every non-German in either that command or the army as a whole. Importantly, some officers and soldiers noted that certain German units had fought well or that the Anglo-American units had retreated alongside the Germans. Despite an ongoing postwar dispute between the veterans of the non-German 82d Ohio and those of the 75th Pennsylvania about who retreated first on the first day, private Arthur T. Lee of the 82d recalled that "the truth is the whole line [and] Division was 'flanked and gave way,' and the position was one which no troops in the world, of equal numbers, could have held." Witnessing the retreat of both the First and the Eleventh Corps from atop Cemetery Hill, Colonel Adin B. Underwood of the 33d Massachusetts wrote that "the two Corps fought gallantly" before both "stubbornly retreated, turning every few rods to fire a volley, facing in every direction."[23]

The actions of Captain Hubert Dilger's German Battery I, Ohio Light Artillery, received particular praise from many observers. Dilger handled his guns with great skill on the first day, holding his own against a superior number of Confederate guns on Oak Hill and conducting a fighting retreat, as he had at Chancellorsville. When his battery reached Gettysburg, Dilger ordered a portion of it to cover the infantry's retreat through town. Private Vautier of the 88th Pennsylvania conceded that "a section of Dilger's battery unlimbered near the [town] Diamond, [and] fired a canister into the faces of the pursuers." Dilger, he claimed, was not alone, as other German units in the Eleventh Corps "did their level best to breast the storm and repulse the graybacks." Vautier singled out the "plucky stand" of the 119th New York at the foot of Washington Street, which succeeded in "holding the enemy in check a little while," and admitted that the casualties of some of the German regiments, particularly the 75th Pennsylvania and 107th Ohio, confirmed that "there were undoubtedly as good regiments in this corps as in any other in the army."[24]

Unfortunately for the Germans of the Eleventh Corps, Anglo-Americans like Vautier who were willing to provide an unbiased account of the first day at Gettysburg were rare both in July 1863 and in the years to come. Most soldiers of the First Corps blamed the Eleventh Corps for putting up a poor fight in its sector of the field and retreating prematurely, thus opening up the right flank of the First Corps and precipitating the Union defeat. Their version of events was supported by certain published Confederate accounts—namely, those of Generals A. P. Hill and Robert E. Lee—although those of less prominent Southerners sometimes disagreed. The legend of the cowardly Dutchmen no doubt also survived because of the nature of the Eleventh Corps' retreat through the town of Gettysburg late on the afternoon of July 1. Variously described as a "rout," a "disorganized retreat," or simply "skedaddling," the withdrawal of the Eleventh Corps, and particularly the Germans in it, was singled out as akin to a second Chancellorsville. The image of thousands of retreating men running through the narrow streets of the town certainly conjured up remembrances of the earlier battle among observers.[25]

The famous "Schimmelfennig incident" became a favorite example of the Germans' "cowardice." Schimmelfennig, of the 74th Pennsylvania (commanding the Third Division of the Eleventh Corps at Gettysburg), was chased by Confederate skirmishers, feigned death, and hid in a woodshed

Brigadier General
Alexander Schimmelfennig.
Shown here as Colonel of
the 74th Pennsylvania.
MASSACHUSETTS
COMMANDERY MILITARY
ORDER OF THE LOYAL LEGION
AND THE U.S. ARMY MILITARY
HISTORY INSTITUTE

until the end of the battle. His stay in the "pig sty" saved him from capture but offered an irresistible opportunity for Anglo-Americans (such as Oscar Ladley) to lampoon the Germans. Early historians picked up on the story and, although more judicious in their presentation of Schimmelfennig's plight than Ladley, managed to blow the incident out of proportion to its historical significance. Today, most visitors to Gettysburg participate in a tour that mentions Schimmelfennig's ignominious adventure. Even the renowned Civil War Institute of Gettysburg College, held every summer, pokes fun at the Pennsylvania German general by singing a humorous song composed by some of the institute's founders (see appendix B for the lyrics).[26]

The derisive treatment of Schimmelfennig by modern students of Gettysburg is symptomatic of the negative perceptions of the Eleventh Corps, which historians have perpetuated to the present. Drawing mainly on the letters and memoirs of the biased soldiers of the First Corps, earlier historians succeeded in transmitting the erroneous message that the Eleventh Corps was a completely German corps and that it had performed in a cowardly fashion on July 1. Frank A. Haskell, a respected early chronicler of the battle, was typical when he wrote about the retreat of the Eleventh Corps:

> Back in disorganized masses they fled into the town, hotly pursued, and in lanes, in barns, yards and cellars, throwing away their arms, they sought to hide like rabbits, and were there captured, unresisting, by the hundreds. . . . I suppose our loss would exceed four thousand, of whom a large number were prisoners. Such usually is the kind of loss sustained by the 11th Corps.[27]

Abner Doubleday, who defended the record of the Eleventh Corps' Germans more than most, nonetheless claimed that "they were rallied with great difficulty" after the events of the first day. Bruce Catton, among other more recent writers, followed the same trend. In his famous *Never Call Retreat,* Catton argued that "taken in front, flank and rear by the expanding Confederate offensive, Howard's Dutchmen finally broke and ran off, victims of sheer bad luck and their own low morale." Even James McPherson, in his masterly *Battle Cry of Freedom,* described the Eleventh Corps at Gettysburg as "General Howard's 'Dutch' 11th Corps," which subsequently "retreated in disorder" in the late afternoon of the first day while the "tough fighters" of the First Corps "were forced back yard by yard." Apparently, the stereotype of the Dutchmen at Gettysburg still lives.[28]

More directly pertinent to the German-Americans of the Eleventh Corps in July 1863 than the opinions of future historians were the perceptions of their Anglo-American comrades. The still vivid memories of Chancellorsville, the complaints of soldiers in the ranks after the first day, and the disparagement by higher-ranking officers such as Barlow apparently contributed to a series of organizational and command changes that ultimately led to the watering down of the corps' German identity and its transfer out of the Army of the Potomac. Although this theory cannot be completely substantiated by the available evidence, a close look at the events of the summer of 1863 points in that direction.

On July 14, Brigadier General George H. Gordon and several non-German regiments, formerly of the Fourth Corps of the Department of Virginia, were transferred to the Eleventh Corps. The 127th and 142d New York were added to the First Division, and three days later, Gordon was appointed division commander, replacing Schimmelfennig, who had been elevated to that post just a few days earlier. Schimmelfennig was retained in a leadership position, but only as a brigade commander; he replaced Colonel Leopold von Gilsa of the First Brigade, First Division, who had purportedly been sent away "on detached duty for three months." Slighted at his demotion and angry at the accusations against the Germans of the Eleventh Corps, Schimmelfennig officially requested a transfer from the Army of the Potomac. All the reshuffling effectively reduced German leadership of the First Division and increased the number of non-German regiments.[29]

The reorganization in the Eleventh Corps' First Division could be written off as a postbattle adjustment for casualties, but a letter from Gordon to corps commander Oliver O. Howard on July 29, 1863, suggests that the perception of the corps by others in the army had reached a new low after Gettysburg:

> The reputation of this corps in this army is so bad that good troops are demoralized and rendered worthless while they wear its badge and form part of its organization. That its reputation is bad is patent to all. It is so from its disgraceful record at Chancellorsville, and not a clean reputation at Gettysburg; from its lack of discipline; from its unsoldierly education; from its great number of poor and worthless officers. . . .
>
> I see no remedy for the salvation of the "materiel" of this corps, but the breaking up of the organization, its name and symbol cast into oblivion, the consolidation of its regiments into other corps, and pretty general dismissal of officers now or hereafter, as they shall, under other influences, prove themselves still worthless.
>
> My own command is already affected, and I desire to remove them.[30]

Gordon's appeal for the disbandment of the Eleventh Corps may have struck a chord with Major General George Meade, commander of the Army of the Potomac, or Gordon's and Meade's writings may have occurred concurrently but separately. Either way, the evidence is compelling. Avoiding Gordon's colorful language, Meade drew up an official plan to dismember the Eleventh Corps and sent it to Army Chief of Staff Henry W. Halleck on the same day that Gordon wrote his letter. Meade's plan called for the dispersal of the three divisions of the Eleventh Corps throughout the eastern theater. Howard would take a division with him when he assumed command of the Second Corps, the Twelfth Corps would get another as reinforcements, and the third division would be broken up, its individual regiments posted as guards along the Orange and Alexandria Railroad. Fortunately for the Eleventh Corps, the War Department rejected Meade's proposal, retained the integrity of the corps, and ordered all its divisions posted along the railroad, where they remained for the rest of the summer.[31]

Considering the ill feeling toward it and the earlier attempts to dissolve it, it is not surprising that the Eleventh Corps was one of two corps from the Army of the Potomac selected to journey westward to relieve the siege of Chattanooga in late September 1863. Three of Pennsylvania's German-American regiments went to Tennessee with the corps: the 27th, 73d, and 75th Pennsylvania. The 74th Pennsylvania, perhaps because it was Schimmelfennig's old regiment, traveled with the general to the Department of South Carolina when his request for a transfer was granted and served under his command on various sea islands near Charleston for the next eleven months. The stalwart 98th Pennsylvania, spared the opprobrium attached to its sister regiments in the Eleventh Corps, remained in the Sixth Corps until the end of the war, making it the only Pennsylvania German-American regiment that was permitted to stay in the Virginia theater of operations. The rest of them were effectively banished, although they "felt just as happy to leave Virginia as the Army of the Potomac did to see them go." Anglo-American soldiers' perceptions of the Germans, building since Chancellorsville and expanded at Gettysburg, had borne fruit.[32]

Reports of the performance of the Eleventh Corps on the first day at Gettysburg appeared in the English-language newspapers before the last shots were fired on the third day of the battle. Quickly overshadowed by subsequent reports and editorials proclaiming the overall Union victory, which began to appear as early as July 4, the message in the Anglo-American press was clear: The Eleventh Corps, including its German regiments, had fought well in the opening rounds at Gettysburg. Perhaps they had been pushed back by overwhelming numbers of the enemy—as they had been at Chancellorsville—but this time, the correspondents noted the bravery with which they fought before they retreated. Certain papers, such as the *Cincinnati Daily Gazette* and the *New York Post,* emphasized the retreat through

the town and portrayed it in a negative light, but a strong majority of the
thirteen major newspapers sampled praised the actions of the Eleventh
Corps. An analysis of these papers reveals that the sacrifices of the German-
American soldiers did not go unacknowledged by the greater American
public and were not, on the whole, ridiculed by them. Thus, the English-
language press apparently did not add much to the legend of the cowardly
Dutchmen at Gettysburg.

The first newspaper to publish reports of the first day's action was the
Baltimore American. Its July 2 edition contained a dramatic, if inaccurate, por-
trayal of the engagement of the Eleventh Corps as a whole. "At first they
slightly faltered," reported the unknown correspondent, but then General
Howard cried, "Remember Chancellorsville!" and "they rushed into the
fight like infuriated demons, and the whole line of the enemy gave way
before them."[33] Although unquestionably a gross exaggeration of the performance of the Eleventh Corps, the *American's* story was reprinted in seven
of the twelve other newspapers in the sample. They published the account in
their July 3 editions and then followed up the initial inaccurate report with
more detailed and reliable coverage a few days later. Two papers, the *Washington Daily National Intelligencer* and the *Pittsburgh Post,* originally printed a
different report of the first day's fighting that allegedly came from "some
gentleman of the press" in Baltimore; whether it was written by the corre
spondent for the *Baltimore American* is unknown, but based on the text, it
seems unlikely:

> Early in the afternoon both Longstreet and Hill combined their
> forces for a grand effort to turn our right flank, when Gen. How-
> ard's Eleventh Corps, which broke and ran at Chancellorsville,
> dashed in to regain their lost laurels, and right nobly repulsed these
> two veteran corps of the rebel army. The repulse was so complete
> that no further attempt was made by the enemy during the remain-
> der of the day, and night closed in with our holding the position
> chosen by the enemy to give us battle.[34]

Again, the papers got the facts wrong, but the impression created was
that the Eleventh Corps had fought well and regained its fallen reputation.

The *Chicago Tribune* and the *Pittsburgh Gazette* of July 4 did not reprint
the *American's* account but instead published a "Special Dispatch" that they

claimed had been forwarded to them. Interestingly, the dispatch read exactly the same in both papers. It reported that the First Corps had held off the rebel onslaught until the Eleventh Corps arrived on the field, but "it soon became manifest that they were largely outnumbered." The "sheer superiority" of the Confederates' numbers "completely turned our flanks and by an enfilading fire forced the 11th corps to break. They had partially redeemed themselves from their mishap at Chancellorsville, but were now forced to retire through the town, which they did in some disorder." In contrast, the First Corps retired through town "in good order." Although depicting the retreat of the Eleventh Corps negatively in comparison with that of the First, the message that the Eleventh had not broken and run but had, in fact, "partially redeemed" itself must have struck a chord among readers. Neither the *Tribune* nor the *Gazette* mentioned anything else about the Eleventh Corps as news of the Union victory traveled west.[35]

In contrast to the report printed in the *Tribune* and *Gazette,* the *Cincinnati Daily Gazette* unilaterally condemned the Eleventh Corps' performance. Correspondent Whitelaw Reid described the retreat of the corps' regiments as a panic: "Perhaps the old panic at the battle-cry of Jackson's flying corps comes over them; at any rate they break in wild confusion, some pouring through the town . . ., and are with difficulty formed again on the hights [*sic*] to the southward. They lost over twelve hundred prisoners in twenty minutes." Official accounts of the captured and missing of the Eleventh Corps average around 1,500, so Reid's estimate was not far off the mark. However, his description of the entire corps breaking into a panic, as it had at Chancellorsville, was highly suspect. The July 6 report of the *New York Evening Post* was probably more accurate and played down the retreat through town, where many of the Eleventh Corps prisoners were taken: "The conduct of the Corps partially redeemed the reputation at Chancellorsville, though in coming through the town, in retiring, there was considerable confusion, and a great many stragglers were lost."[36]

Cincinnati readers and, to a much lesser extent, some New York readers must have believed the accounts in their newspapers that the Germans had underperformed again. The majority of Anglo-American newspapers, however, portrayed them and their corps in a positive light. From the initial reports of the *Baltimore American,* reprinted in other papers, to the versions published by the two major Pittsburgh newspapers and the influential *Chicago Tribune,* the general reaction among the major English-language newspapers of the North was positive. The *Philadelphia Inquirer* boasted that "General Howard's 11th Corps, which ran at Chancellorsville, regained their lost laurels," and the *Cleveland Plain Dealer* was openly eulogistic:

> The eleventh—German—corps behaved with conspicuous brav- ery, and amply relieved its escutcheon from any stain acquired on the unfortunate field of Chancellorsville. All honor to these brave German patriots who are offering up their lives in defence of their adopted land, its government and its free institutions!

Even L. L. Crounse, the *New York Times* correspondent who had defamed the Germans after Chancellorsville, said little about the Germans or the Eleventh Corps as a whole but did include a sentence of praise for the soldiers of both the First and the Eleventh Corps for their efforts on the first day.[37]

The most comprehensive coverage of the experiences of the Eleventh Corps was contained in a dispatch from J. H. Vosberg to the *New York Herald* on July 3. Using a map and two columns of print, Vosberg documented the first day's battle in surprisingly accurate detail. Barlow's division "fought bravely, and lost heavily," he declared, and "the Third division, General Schimmelfennig, was meanwhile striving to hold the position it was directed to hold." After describing the location of Schimmelfennig's men, Vosberg wrote that "the losses in this division show how well it fought." After detail- ing the fates of the brigade commanders and several regimental officers, he then examined the losses of the units themselves: "Every regimental commander of Krzyzanowski's brigade was killed or wounded. . . . The Twenty-sixth Wisconsin lost all but one of its officers. . . . The Seventy- fourth Pennsylvania brought off sixteen men."[38]

Turning to Colonel Charles Coster's brigade, containing the 27th and 73d Pennsylvania, Vosberg claimed, "Col. Coster and his men did all that brave men could do; but it was so late when they were called out that it was scarcely worth while for them to be slaughtered by the artillery and infantry force to which they were exposed." Waxing a bit dramatic, the correspondent overplayed the losses in the 74th Pennsylvania and painted a portrait of heroism drenched with clichés, but his closing sentence must have made an impression on readers: "The Eleventh corps did more than all the others."[39]

The story of the poor performance of the Eleventh Corps at Gettysburg clearly did not emanate from the Anglo-American press. If anything, the major English-language newspapers praised the conduct of Howard's men and refuted the negative army gossip circulating about the Germans and the corps as a whole. Perhaps Whitelaw Reid's version of the first day's battle was better circulated than that of other papers, though this seems unlikely. It is more probable that the source of the cowardly Dutchmen legend rests with the Anglo-American soldiers in the rest of the Army of the Potomac and their prejudical inclinations.

Noticeably absent after the Gettysburg campaign was one important ingredient in the post-Chancellorsville backlash: invective in the prominent English-language newspapers condemning the German soldiers as cowards. Reveling in the glory of the overall Union victory, the Anglo-American papers forgot the nativism of May and concentrated on congratulating the Army of the Potomac for its victory. A few of the minor newspapers apparently followed in the footsteps of the *Cincinnati Daily Gazette* and derided the performance of the Eleventh Corps, but these papers were exceptions. The Pennsylvania German-American press, presented with only minimal public nativism this time, thus reacted differently to Gettysburg than it had to Chancellorsville. Instead of defensive and outraged editorials responding to serious nativist attacks, the German papers reported the battle of Gettysburg by highlighting the deeds of the German soldiers and praising them for their bravery. The battle as a whole received some coverage in the German press, but the clear emphasis was on the role of the Eleventh Corps and, specifically, the German-American regiments.

Overjoyed that their soldiers had fought well, the editors focused on German contributions—and sacrifices—in the Union victory, but in the process, they lost touch with the greater significance of the battle and the efforts of non-Germans. Their myopic preoccupation with praising the German troops thus conveyed to readers the impression that Gettysburg was just as much a German-American victory as a Northern one. And from their viewpoint, it was exactly that; the honor of the Germans had been vindicated by their soldiers' battlefield performance, and the slurs of the nativists had been refuted. The German-language newspapers' concentration on German issues at the expense of wholly American ones indicates that a "flying Dutchmen" interpretation failed to surface, and it supports the inference that, in the eyes of Northern German-Americans, their soldiers were contributing the most to the defense of the Union. This, in turn, begs the question of whether the Northern German-Americans were truly being "Americanized" by the Civil War.

It did not take long for news of the victory to reach the Pennsylvania German-language newspapers. As early as July 4, the *Philadelphia Freie Presse* contained detailed accounts of the first day's battle. "General Howard sings the praises of the bravery of the 11th Army Corps, which did more than any other to stave off defeat," editor Friedrich Thomas declared. He was joined by the editor of the *Pittsburgh Freiheitsfreund,* who printed a similar editorial on July 7: "Our corps lost no less than 3,000 men, while the First Corps, although it fought bravely as well, can count only half that number." The Eleventh Corps clearly deserved national recognition for the important role it played on the first day's field, and the German soldiers in it deserved even more praise because they had decisively deflated the nativist impulse and restored the good name of the Northern German-Americans:

> Our stalwart German regiments have thus brilliantly refuted the sordid infamies which nativism flung at them. The bodies of the brave which bedeck the battlefield are numerous but clear signs of the centuries-old German courage, which hopefully no one will ever want to doubt again.[40]

Both the *Freiheitsfreund* and the *Freie Presse* then described the deeds of specific units in the Eleventh Corps in an attempt to show how bravely the Germans had fought, clearing the German-American name through their blood sacrifice. Some of the descriptions were quite vivid. Dutifully following orders to "hold the line, the German brigades under Kryzanowsky [*sic*] and Amsberg were subjected to a horrendous crossfire that shattered entire regiments." Colonel George von Amsberg, commander of the brigade that included the 74th Pennsylvania, "came within a hair's breadth of death by having two horses shot beneath him," and "all of the regimental commanders in Krzyzanowski's brigade were killed or wounded" as they "gallantly attempted to hold back the overwhelming numbers of the enemy." The 26th Wisconsin—"the German Sigel regiment—lost all of its officers but one," the editor of the *Freiheitsfreund* exclaimed, and the "74th Pennsylvania (earlier Col. Schimmelfennig's), brought only 16 men out." No doubt the editor had consulted the *New York Herald*'s report for this number, but he added, "hopefully, this is exaggerated."[41]

The *Pittsburgher Demokrat* agreed with its Republican counterpart about the valor of the German-American troops. Its July 6 issue boasted an exhaustive account of the Eleventh Corps' participation in the first day's battle. Claiming that "all correspondents are in consensus that the 11th Corps fought bravely and sustained great losses," editor Georg Ripper added that the men had reportedly been "reminded by Howard of the Chancellorsville calamity" and hence fought even harder. Von Gilsa's and Schimmelfennig's commands had particularly distinguished themselves that first day, "the casualties of the same showing their bravery." On July 7, Ripper's editorial boasted that "only the extraordinary courage and fortunately timed arrival of the 11th Army Corps prevented a terrible defeat that day." The *Allentown Unabhängige Republikaner* echoed this theme, arguing that "the heroic efforts of our troops, and namely the deathly courageous fortitude of the German regiments," had staved off overall Union defeat. Despite some hyperbolic rhetoric, these German-American editors strongly believed that their soldiers had saved the Union from disaster.[42]

Unfortunately, not all Anglo-Americans agreed. Despite the largely positive nature of the reports on the Eleventh Corps in the major English-language papers, editors of a few of the German-American newspapers alleged that nativism was not yet dead. The July 12 and 17 issues of the *Pittsburgh Freiheitsfreund,* for instance, contained editorials recounting specious comments supposedly made by non-German Union generals and the Anglo-American press after the battle of Gettysburg. Although the editor did not name the officers, he singled out the *Pittsburgh Chronicle* for blame, claiming that it and several smaller "native American" papers were beginning to print "these lies" that attacked the fighting abilities of the German soldiers. "These disguised nativists do not dare to openly challenge the bravery of the Eleventh Corps on the first of July, but instead are like hidden thieves, who plan to murder with a knife in the back." Importantly, however, such editorials were uncommon in the weeks after Gettysburg, suggesting that Pennsylvania's German-Americans generally believed that the late battle had dealt a heavy blow to nativism.[43]

That perception, however, did not indicate that the German-Americans were embracing their Anglo-American neighbors with open arms or celebrating the Union victory as Americans first and Germans second. On the contrary, the strong emphasis in the Philadelphia and Pittsburgh German press on the martial deeds of the Eleventh Corps proportionately reduced the coverage given to other aspects of the battle, including the repulse of Pickett's Charge, which received only a few paragraphs in each of the four newspapers surveyed. Moreover, the after-action reports were joined by long lists of the dead, wounded, and missing from the German regiments—with few corresponding listings for the nonethnic units—preceded by romantic phrases praising the "fallen heroes."[44]

In the weeks immediately after the battle, certain noteworthy officers or units also received special attention that highlighted their particular sacrifices or achievements. The July 9 issue of the *Freie Presse,* for example, printed a long obituary for Colonel Francis Mahler of the 75th Pennsylvania in which editor Thomas praised Mahler's tactical abilities and portrayed his death as "heroic": "Mahler is the second Colonel of the 75th Regiment who died a hero's death for his adoptive Fatherland. He leaves behind a poor widow with ungrown children and many friends, who lament his all too early death." Similarly, the *Freiheitsfreund* praised Mahler's "brave regiment" in a solemn manner, lamenting that "in the last battle . . . it was reduced to 64 men fit for duty" and was threatened with amalgamation with another unit. "This small pile of heroes," however, desired to remain independent and took pride in their new nickname, circulated throughout the German regiments: "the last tenth of the 75th."[45]

Based on the reports and editorials appearing in the Pennsylvania German-American press in the weeks after Gettysburg, it is clear that at least the editors of three of the most prominent newspapers clearly rejected the cowardly Dutchmen interpretation of the German troops' performance. Perhaps that is not surprising. More interesting, however, is the effect the editors may have had on their readers. An uninformed German citizen of Philadelphia, for instance, reading only the pages of the *Freie Presse,* might have believed that the Eleventh Corps alone had secured the Union victory. The German-language press reveled in the performance of the German soldiers, almost to the exclusion of other news about the battle, and, it could be argued, turned Gettysburg into an "anti-Chancellorsville"—an event with a historically different ending but a similar ethnic consequence: a renewed emphasis on German identity at the expense of Americanization.

CHAPTER 8

The Pennsylvania Dutch Fight for "Old Dutch Pennsylvania"

David L. Valuska

July 1, 1863, had been a brutal day for the men of the First and Eleventh Corps. Granted, they had fought the rebels to a standstill for most of the day, but eventually, superior numbers and better Confederate troop placement proved to be too much. By 4 P.M., the retreat was under way, and as the soldiers of the two corps fell back through Gettysburg, there was confusion. But even in this hasty retreat, a rough system emerged to facilitate order. The crowded streets precluded any coherent plan, but the soldiers came up with one of their own: The men of the Eleventh Corps stayed to one side of the street, and the men of the First Corps walked on the other.[1] They were all headed for Cemetery Hill and the Union reserve line, but there was little panic as the men worked their way back to safety.

The 12,000 retreating men hastily made for the Federal defensive positions on Cemetery Hill. The men had fought well, but some felt betrayed. The Eleventh Corps still carried the stigma of Chancellorsville, and at Gettysburg, they were vilified by their comrades. One First Corps officer, when questioned about where the Eleventh was regrouping, said he did not know but added, "1st Corps goes to the right & 11th Corps goes to hell." One officer even went so far as to blame the Eleventh for the first day's loss.

Finally, the two retreating corps reached Cemetery Hill, and the men began to take up defensive positions. The Eleventh Corps fortified areas around the cemetery, the region facing town, and on the east side of the Baltimore Pike. In the First Corps, the First Brigade—the Iron Brigade—took position on Culp's Hill, with Cutler's brigade in reserve. Robinson's division occupied the north end of Cemetery Hill facing the Emmitsburg Pike, and Doubleday's division was on the west slope of the ridge facing the Taney-town Road.[2]

The men of the First and Eleventh Corps and Brigadier General John Buford's cavalry brigade had been badly mauled that first day, but they remained resilient and were able to regroup. These exhausted, dust-covered soldiers had forced the enemy to pay a heavy price for his first day's success. The price was so heavy, in fact, that the Confederates hesitated to press their attack in the evening, and that hesitation gave the men in blue an opportunity to reorganize and rally. Around 5 P.M., the First and Eleventh Corps veterans began receiving reinforcements. Scattered units of both corps that had been dispatched to duties elsewhere rejoined their comrades. Elements of the Twelfth Corps also began arriving and took up positions near Little Round Top. By late that evening, more than 28,000 Federal troops were on the field.

By July 2, 1863, the Union defensive positions were beginning to take form. After some repositioning of arriving reinforcements, the Federal line began to resemble an inverted J, or a fishhook. Major General George Meade, commander of the Army of the Potomac, was placing his corps into line, and their positions were roughly as follows: The Twelfth Corps held Culp's Hill; the Second Corps was on Cemetery Ridge, facing the Emmits-burg Pike; the Eleventh and First Corps held Cemetery Hill and portions of Cemetery Ridge; and the Third Corps took up a position about half a mile in advance of the main Union battle line. The Third Corps deployment was like a half-opened jackknife, with the First Division facing the Emmits-burg Pike and the Second Division's right flank anchored at the Peach Orchard and the left flank at Devil's Den. The Fifth Corps was held in reserve, and the Sixth Corps was en route to the battle and would arrive on the afternoon of July 2.

After a victorious first day, Confederate commander Robert E. Lee had decided on a definite tactical plan for July 2. Lieutenant General James Longstreet's First Corps was to march around the face of the Union army. The purpose was to hit the Federal left flank, which was believed to be positioned somewhere around Little Round Top. What Longstreet encoun-tered first was the advance position of Major General Daniel Sickles and the Federal Third Corps.

A search of the records reveals that there was no significant contingent of Pennsylvania Dutch troops in any one regiment in the Third Corps. The

99th Pennsylvania had a few Pennsylvania Dutch, but not enough to warrant study.[3] At Gettysburg, the 99th occupied the left flank of the Third Corps battle line above Devil's Den. The regiment heroically held fast against heavy opposition and was finally forced back late in the afternoon.[4]

At 4 P.M. on July 2, Longstreet launched his two divisions under Major Generals Lafayette McLaws and John B. Hood against the lines of the Third Corps. Sickles, by taking an advance position, forced his corps to cover an extensive amount of territory, and his men severely punished the attacking rebels. The men of the Third Corps fought valiantly and in many instances held the rebels in check, but time, numbers, and position were not on their side. To hold the Union line, Sickles would need help.

Major General Winfield Scott Hancock, commander of the Second Corps, Army of the Potomac, was ordered to provide that help. Hancock turned to Brigadier General John C. Gibbons, commander of his First Division, and ordered him to assist Sickles in the Wheatfield fight. Brigadier General John C. Caldwell issued orders and immediately began to move to that area of the battle.[5] In the First Brigade of Caldwell's division were the men of the 148th Pennsylvania Volunteer Infantry.

The 148th had recruited seven companies from Centre County and one company each from Indiana, Jefferson, and Clarion Counties. The companies from Centre County had substantial numbers of Pennsylvania Dutch soldiers in their ranks, and Company A had a majority of Pennsylvania Dutch. The story of the 148th's Company A is illustrative of many Pennsylvania Dutch regiments and underscores the point that units coming from counties with large Dutch populations would always have some Pennsylvania Dutch in their ranks. Company A's history at Gettysburg also sheds light on Pennsylvania Dutch recruitment and the importance of geography.

On August 24, 1862, the recruits for Company A gathered in front of the hotel in Rebersburg, Centre County, Pennsylvania, and were administered the oath of allegiance to the United States. More than 100 individuals were sworn in that day, and the majority of them came from the Brush Valley—an area with a heavy concentration of Pennsylvania Dutch families. The regimental history states that the new recruits were "of the best families; mere boys, single with the exception of a few, used to toil, robust, temperate in their habits—good material out of which to make soldiers."[6] These were good Pennsylvania Dutch men who were willing to fight for the Union. Company A was approximately 85 percent Pennsylvania Dutch.[7]

Six men of Co. A, 148th Pennsylvania. BATTLES & LEADERS, VOLUME III

The 148th went to Camp Curtin in early September 1862, and during its stay there an amusing incident occurred that emphasized the Pennsylvania Dutch influence in the regiment. "Comrade Solomon B_____ was doing guard duty . . . and as he was slowly walking his beat . . . some fellow slipped across his trail. The sentinel, roused from his reverie, rushed after him with uplifted stick and yelled, 'Dunnerwedder holt, oder Ich farschlock dir de kup!'" The regimental historian apologized for using Pennsylvania Dutch but stated that this was appropriate, as at least half the members of the 148th could speak and understand the language.[8]

After a rudimentary period of training, the 148th was shipped off to Maryland to guard railroad lines. In December 1862, the 148th was assigned to the First Brigade, First Division, Second Corps of the Army of the Potomac. The first major engagement for the regiment was at Chancellorsville (May 1–3, 1863), where it suffered 164 casualties.[9] After that battle, the regiment went back to its permanent camp at Falmouth, Virginia, where it remained until ordered to march north at the opening of the Gettysburg campaign. On June 14, the 148th began moving and witnessed the burning of Stafford Court House. The troops' route over the next several days took them through Fairfax Court House, then on to Centerville-Gainesville and the old Manassas battlefield, and then through Thoroughfare Gap, where they halted for several days. On June 26, they moved to Poolesville, Maryland; on successive days they reached Sugar Loaf Mountain, Frederick, Maryland, and Uniontown. On July 1, the 148th bivouacked about four miles from Gettysburg.

Early on the morning of July 2, the men ate a hurried meal of hardtack and then began their march to the battle. Along the way, they met frightened civilians carrying boxes and packages of hastily gathered valuables.[10] According to an after-action report, the 148th took up a position on the left of Cemetery Hill on the farm of a Mr. Hummelbaugh.[11]

The men of the 148th marched into battle carrying a grudge against their brigade commander, Colonel Edward E. Cross.[12] On the way to Gettysburg, Colonel Cross had ordered his men to cross a stream without stopping to take off their shoes and socks. Admittedly, this was a trivial matter, but Corporal George Duffy openly complained about the colonel's lack of concern for the men's well-being, and Cross hit Duffy on the neck with the flat of his sword.[13] The officers and men of the 148th were outraged and considered Cross to be a tyrant—a feeling that was reinforced on the night of June 30, 1863.

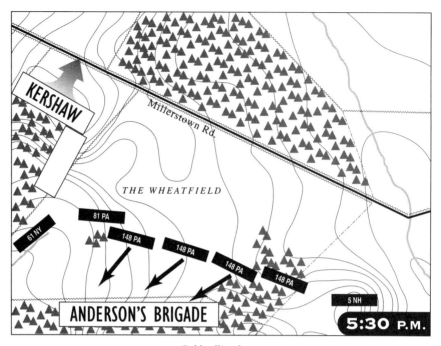

Caldwell's advance

That night, Colonel Cross summoned the officers of the 148th to meet Colonel H. Boyd McKeen, veteran commander of the 83d Pennsylvania. Since the colonel of the 148th was at home recuperating from wounds received at Chancellorsville, and Lieutenant Colonel Robert McFarlane lacked the experience to lead the regiment, Cross announced that McKeen would command the 148th in the upcoming action. Cross's decision was probably correct, but to the officers and men of the 148th, it was an insult.[14] The men of the 148th were about to enter battle with a new regimental commander and a disliked brigade commander, but they would do their duty.

When orders were received by General Caldwell to send support to the Unionists fighting in the Wheatfield, he summoned Colonel Cross, whose brigade was closest to the fighting. Cross's men began their march to the left of the Wheatfield, past the Trostle house, and then deployed in the woods and eastern edge of the Wheatfield. Cross aligned his regiments facing the field and soon received an order to shore up the Union line. The brigade moved forward with the 5th New Hampshire on the left and the 148th on the right. Next to the 148th was the 81st Pennsylvania, and on their right, the 61st New York. The position of the 148th put its left flank in the woods and its right flank in the middle of the Wheatfield.

Cross's men stood on an elevated portion of the field and were waist deep in wheat. As the brigade moved forward, Cross was mortally wounded. The 148th advanced with seven companies in the woods and three in the Wheatfield and slammed into the flank of Brigadier General George T. Anderson's Georgia brigade. The 148th drove Anderson's men from the wall bordering the woods and, in the process, captured some Confederates in its front. As the 148th was passing the prisoners to the rear, one of the rebels pulled out a pistol and shot a sergeant. Sergeant Ezra B. Walter then bashed the man in the head with his rifle butt. It was the Confederate's last act of defiance.[15]

While Cross's brigade was busily engaged, the Second Brigade, commonly referred to as the Irish Brigade, began an assault down the middle of the Wheatfield. Supporting the Second Brigade was the Third Brigade commanded by Brigadier General Samuel K. Zook, a Pennsylvania Dutchman born in Tredyffrin, Chester County, Pennsylvania. His forebears initially

Brigadier General Samuel K. Zook, killed in the Wheatfield.
MASSACHUSETTS COMMANDERY MILITARY ORDER OF THE LOYAL LEGION AND THE U.S. ARMY MILITARY HISTORY INSTITUTE

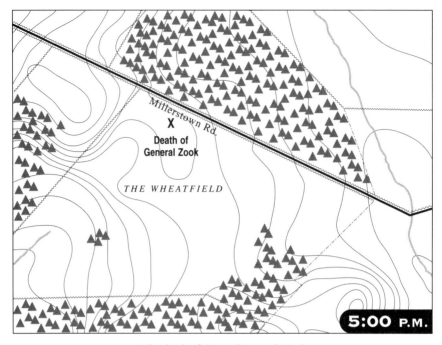

The death of General Samuel Zook

came from Switzerland via the Palatinate (Pfalz) and were practicing Mennonites. Although Zook had never been baptized a Mennonite, he grew up in a traditional Pennsylvania Dutch family and was influenced by their traditional folkways.[16]

Zook, on his own initiative, led his Third Brigade away from General Caldwell's First and Second Brigades with the intention of striking the Confederates on the far right of the Wheatfield. Zook's men crossed the Millerstown Road and moved through the northwest corner of the Wheatfield to attack the rebel brigade commanded by General Anderson. Zook's men received withering fire from the enemy and were forced to halt. The general attempted to rally his men and reform their ranks, and while mounted at the head of his brigade, he suddenly felt a severe burning in his chest. A minié ball had entered his left side and lodged in his spine. Zook fell from his horse and was carried to a field hospital, where it was determined that his wounds were too severe and nothing could be done. Later, he was taken to G. F. Hoke's Tollhouse on the Baltimore Pike, where orderlies tried to make him comfortable, and he rested there through the night. As the battle raged on July 3, Zook's aides moved the general about one mile away to an unidentified home, where he died.[17] He was the only Pennsylvania general to die at Gettysburg. While Zook lay dying, the fight around the Wheatfield intensified.

Colonel John Rutter Brooke, who commanded the Fourth Brigade in Caldwell's First Division, led an attack against the Confederates in the field. Brooke's men swept the field and forced the Confederates back into Rose's Woods. The 148th supported this attack but, in so doing, exposed its left flank to enemy fire. The fighting done by Brooke's men and the 148th was quite savage. It lasted only a short time, probably no longer than fifteen minutes, but it became evident to Brooke that he could not hold the line. Confederates were flanking and enfilading the Union force; the men of Brooke's command and elements of the 148th were forced to retreat, fighting hand to hand as they went. They fell back across the woods with the curse of a Georgian following them: "Go to the rear you d—d Yankee son of a b—h."[18] Once they reached the area of the Weikert farm, they regrouped and later took up a position on Cemetery Ridge. The 148th had gone into battle with 392 officers and men, and during the fight in the Wheatfield, nearly 32 percent of their effective strength had been killed or wounded.[19]

As the 148th fell back, there was more fighting in the Wheatfield. The U.S. regulars attempted to recapture the field and were bloodily repulsed for their efforts. Confederate troops occupied most of the terrain around the Wheatfield and were preparing to renew their attack against the Union line, which was reforming in the vicinity of Little Round Top. General Meade sent orders for the Third Division of the Fifth Corps to go to the aid of the beleaguered Third Corps. In the Third Division were two brigades of the Pennsylvania Reserves.[20] The 1st Pennsylvania Reserve, also called the 30th Pennsylvania Volunteer Infantry, was one of the units marching to the aid of the Northerners fighting in the Wheatfield.

Of the ten companies in the 30th Pennsylvania, Companies B, D, E, H, I, and K had a significant number of Pennsylvania Dutch recruits. Company B, which had been recruited from Lancaster County, had approximately 53 percent Pennsylvania Dutch in its ranks; Company D, from Lancaster and York Counties, had nearly 50 percent; Company E, also from Lancaster, had roughly 45 percent; Company H, from Cumberland County, had over 40 percent; and Company K, from Adams County and, more specifically, Gettysburg, was 55 percent Pennsylvania Dutch.[21]

As the men of Company K, 30th Pennsylvania, marched into Gettysburg on July 2, they were overwhelmed by familiar sights and faces. One aged citizen of Gettysburg recognized one of his nephews in the ranks and spoke out in a pronounced Pennsylvania Dutch accent, "Vy Chon, for vat you defil you left dem repel soljers gum up here, Hey?" John answered: "Why! Uncle Same, it was all planned out so that I could come home to see Mammy." As the men marched through Gettysburg, they would indeed see their homes and families. The 30th approached Gettysburg from the vicinity of Hanover and bivouacked the first night along the Baltimore Pike. About 4 P.M. on July 2, the 30th was ordered to sling knapsacks and to get ready for some "devilish" work.[22]

The men of the Third Division were ordered to fill a vacancy on the northwest slope of Little Round Top, and as they filed into position, the sun was setting on the battlefield. The scene before them was one of retreating Federal soldiers as the U.S. regulars fell back from the Wheatfield. A brigade of the Sixth Corps was also directed to the same general area. These troops were commanded by Brigadier General Frank Wheaton, and in that brigade were the 93d and 98th Pennsylvania Volunteers, both containing strong Germanic elements. The 98th Pennsylvania Volunteer Infantry was a German-American unit recruited in Philadelphia, and as it was marching up into line, it became separated from the rest of the brigade. The 98th ended up on the left rear of the Pennsylvania Reserves while the rest of the brigade marched to the right flank of the reserves.[23]

The Union lines had barely formed before the masses of Confederate attackers appeared. The Federal position was supported by two batteries of guns, and one of the battery commanders cried out in broken English, "Dunder und Blixen, don't let dem rebels take our guns," to which an officer in the reserves replied, "Stand by your guns, Duchy, and we will stand by you."[24]

As the Confederates attacked, a series of strange incidents occurred. The all-German 98th suddenly launched into an attack against the oncoming rebels. They rushed from the northwest slopes of Little Round Top down into Plum Run, or, as it was later called, the Valley of Death. Shortly thereafter, the Pennsylvania Reserves also attacked, and as soon as they moved forward, Wheaton's brigade of the Sixth Corps charged. The Pennsylvania Reserves swept down through Plum Run, over the valley, and up to a stone wall, where they engaged in hand-to-hand fighting. They then advanced over the wall and drove the enemy back to Stony Hill. There were quite a few Pennsylvania Dutch and German-American soldiers in this overall attack, with the men of the 98th, 30th, and 93d containing a

Company K, 30th Pennsylvania, in an 1862 photo, probably taken on the Virginia peninsula. MASSACHUSETTS COMMANDERY MILITARY ORDER OF THE LOYAL LEGION AND THE U.S. ARMY MILITARY HISTORY INSTITUTE

strong mix of Teutonic blood. They stopped the Confederate attack and established a solid defensive position.[25]

The 93d Pennsylvania had been recruited extensively in Lebanon County, although its ranks were also filled with men from Berks and Montour Counties. The regiment formed near the Weikert farmhouse and advanced when the Pennsylvania Reserves moved forward. The men of the 93d pressed on toward the Wheatfield and, in their charge, took twenty-five rebel prisoners. After the fight, the 93d returned to Weikert's farm and camped in his yard.[26]

One other unit of the Sixth Corps that came up in support but did not take part in the charge was the 96th Pennsylvania. The 96th came almost exclusively from Schuylkill County, with the exception of Company G, which had been recruited in Hamburg, Berks County. The roster of the 96th reveals a very high percentage of Pennsylvania Dutch in the ranks. The 96th was deployed as a support unit and took up defensive positions behind the Pennsylvania Reserves and saw no real fighting. The battle for the Wheatfield was over, and the Federal forces had held. The men in blue rested that night and prepared for the next day's fight.

The men of the 30th had apparently done their job well. The next morning, the German battery commander who had admonished to the 30th, "Dunder und Blixen, don't let dem rebels take our guns," visited their

Group photo of officers of the 153rd Pennsylvania in an 1863 photo. HISTORY OF THE 153RD
REGIMENT PENNSYLVANIA VOLUNTEER INFANTRY

camp and said, "The Pennsylvania Reserves saved mine pattery, by—, I gets
you fellers all drunk mit beer."[27]

An important action took place on the evening of July 2 that involved
the 153d Pennsylvania Volunteer Infantry. The 153d had been involved in
extensive fighting on the far right of the battle on July 1 and had retreated
back through Gettysburg and taken up defensive positions along Cemetery
Hill. On the evening of July 2, the Confederates launched a massive attack
against East Cemetery Hill, and the 153d was in the center of it. The rebel
attack is best described by two members of the 153d—William Simmers
and Paul Bachschmidt. Both men were involved in the struggle, and they
provide a graphic account of the action around East Cemetery Hill:

> The position occupied by us that morning was . . . at the right, or
> east, of the cemetery facing town. Immediately in our front was
> Battery I of the First New York Artillery, while in our rear was Bat-
> tery B of the First Pennsylvania and a battery of the First Regular
> Artillery. . . . When the order to advance was given and the con-
> tending armies met, the shock and the scene that followed were
> such as to defy description. It was no longer a battle. It was hand-

to-hand conflict, carried on with the valor and vindictiveness of desperation. The arms of ordinary warfare were no longer used. Clubs, knives, stones, fists—anything calculated to inflict pain or death was now resorted to. Now advancing, then retreating, this sort of conflict continued for three-quarters of an hour. At one time defeat seemed inevitable. Closely pressed by the enemy we were compelled to retire to our first line of defense, but even here the enemy followed us, while the more daring were already within our lines and were now resolutely advancing towards our piece. The foremost had already reached a piece, when throwing himself over the muzzle of the cannon, he called out to the bystanding gunners, "I take command of this gun!" "Du sollst sie haben," was the curt reply of the sturdy German, who at that moment, was in the act of firing. A second later, and the soul of the daring rebel had taken flight. . . . Here our reverses ended. Determined to conquer or die in the attempt, our men threw themselves upon the enemy with a resolution and fury that soon compelled him to retire. The batteries were saved. The day ours; Chancellorsville redeemed."[28]

Seven unidentified members of the 93d Pennsylvania in a posed wartime photo.
ROBERT DIEM COLLECTION, U.S. ARMY MILITARY HISTORY INSTITUTE

*Private Hiram J. Onlinger and
Private John D. Onlinger,
Co. I, 153d Pennsylvania.*
MRS. ESTHER BROOKS
COLLECTION, U.S. ARMY
MILITARY HISTORY INSTITUTE

The fighting quieted down along Cemetery Hill, but the action along
Culp's Hill was just about to begin. One of the units defending Culp's Hill
was the 46th Pennsylvania Volunteer Infantry, which contained several
companies of Pennsylvania Dutchmen.

The 46th Pennsylvania Volunteer Infantry had been formed from ten
different companies that rendezvoused at Camp Curtin in Harrisburg in
September 1861. Companies C, D, and E had quite a few Pennsylvania
Dutch in their ranks. Company C had been recruited in Lehigh and Northampton Counties. Company D was from Dauphin County, and Company E
from Berks County. These counties contained a high percentage of Pennsylvania Dutch, and it was inevitable that a large number of recruits would be
Germanic.[29]

After leaving Harrisburg, the regiment served with Major General
Nathaniel Banks in the Shenandoah Valley, where it was engaged in the May
25, 1862, battle of Winchester. In this fight, Confederate General Stonewall
Jackson attacked Banks's command and drove it across the Potomac. The

rout was so complete that the Confederates referred to General Banks as "Commissary" Banks, due to the vast amount of material the rebels captured from the retreating Yankees. The 46th lost more than 100 men during the battle and retreat.

The next action of the 46th was on August 9, 1862, at Cedar Mountain, Virginia, and once more the opponent was Stonewall Jackson's corps. The fighting around Cedar Mountain was intense, and the 46th paid a high price in casualties. Of the 504 officers and men who had entered the fight, 31 were killed, 102 wounded, and 111 captured; the regiment had nearly been halved. Afterward, the 46th was reassigned to the Twelfth Corps and took part in the battle of Antietam in September 1862, suffering only light casualties. It had no role in the battle of Fredericksburg but lost more than 80 men captured at Chancellorsville.

The 46th Pennsylvania was assigned to the First Brigade, First Division of the Twelfth Corps, commanded by Major General Henry W. Slocum. On July 1, Slocum had leisurely marched his corps up to Two Taverns, not far from Gettysburg, and allowed his men to break for a midday meal. Slocum stated that although he heard the sound of fighting, it did not sound like a general fight. Finally, a civilian came down the road and reported that a great battle was taking place in Gettysburg. After sending out a staff officer to verify the report, Slocum belatedly began moving his corps toward Gettysburg around 5 P.M. on July 1. Slocum moved his corps toward Hanover Road, and there his regiments took up defensive positions.

On the morning of July 2, the 46th was sent to Culp's Hill, where it constructed extensive earthworks on the slopes of the hill. Sometime later, the regiment was sent over to assist in the battle raging around the Third Corps near the Wheatfield. After the fighting had stabilized on the left, the 46th was ordered to return to its original position on Culp's Hill, but when it tried to move back, it found that the enemy had secured the trenches. The 46th took up defensive positions around the entrenched enemy and held those positions during the night. The men of the 46th were part of a holding force, and they suffered no losses during the night action, although they were exposed to intense artillery fire from Federal guns. The commander of the 46th, Colonel James L. Selfridge, searched in vain after the battle to identify the Federal guns that had caused his men so much anguish.[30]

On the morning of July 3, the 46th held its position in Pardee Field and, after the Confederate retreat from Culp's Hill, reoccupied the trenches.

Then the troops were ordered forward and placed near Meade's headquarters. From that vantage point, they were able to observe the retreating
rebels after the failed assault by the divisions of Major Generals George
Pickett and James Pettigrew.[31]

The 147th Pennsylvania Volunteer Infantry was also assigned to the
Twelfth Corps and fought along with the 46th on Culp's Hill. The 147th,
christened the "Dutch company of Snyder County" by the rest of the regiment, was representative of the indiscriminate mixing of Pennsylvania
Dutch and Anglo-American units. Most companies in the 147th were
"English," but Company G was almost exclusively Pennsylvania Dutch. In
early September 1862, Company G had been recruited from the towns of
Port Trevertown, Beavertown, Salem, and Kratzerville in Snyder County,
and its members were the only three-year men recruited completely from
that county. On September 12, the new recruits were issued the oath of
allegiance and left for Selinsgrove Junction and then on to Camp Simmons
in Harrisburg.

The chronicler of the history of Company G of the 147th, Private M. S.
Schroyer, apologized for using Pennsylvania Dutch so often in his narra-
tive. He explained that the men of Company G were all of German (Pennsylvania Dutch) descent, and they would usually speak in English. However,
if they got into an argument, they would revert to Pennsylvania Dutch,
which they felt made their arguments more emphatic. For purposes of this
study, use of the dialect and Pennsylvania Dutch folkways in the camps provides evidence of the pervasive nature of the Pennsylvania Dutch culture
among the soldiers.

One night, a recruit from adjoining Camp Curtin ran into Camp Simmons yelling that someone wanted to kill him. He ran into a tent occupied
by three men of Company G who were all sound asleep. They awoke and
pinned down the intruder. One of the three called out in Pennsylvania
Dutch, "Habe un bis ich des licht ow sthecht" (Hold him until I can turn on
this light). A light was produced, and the intruder called out, "Ich bin Johnnie Schultz. Ich cum fun Schuylkill koundy. Ich bin un gardraften mon, dot
cumma se, se welle mich dote maucha. Oh, ich bin der Johnnie Schultz.
Ich cum fun Schuylkill koundy" (I am Johnnie Schultz. I come from Schuylkill County. I am a drafted man, there they come, they want to kill me. Oh,
I am Johnnie Schultz. I come from Schuylkill County).[32] Poor Johnnie
Schultz was lucky that he ran into dialect-speaking soldiers.

Private M. S. Schroyer, Co. G, 147th Pennsylvania, in a post-war reunion photo. Private Schroyer relished his Pennsylvania Dutch identity. COLLECTION OF KEN AND SUE BOARDMAN, GETTYSBURG, PENNSYLVANIA

Private Schroyer wrote of some of the unusual characters in the 147th:

One of these peculiar characters was Michael Schaffer, superstitious and a believer in spooks, hobgoblins and powwowing. The writer was on picket duty one night at a very lonely place in the woods. It was near a low, wet place and dark as dark could be and raining all the while. The will-o-the-wisps were plentiful everywhere. When I was relieved by Schaffer, I called him aside and said: "Schaffer, Da holt di og uff." ("Schaffer, keep your eyes open.") "Fur was?" ("Why?") he asked. I said, "Du warst shunt ous finna." ("You will soon find out.") I left him and he took my place on the picket post for two hours. I knew he was worked up and that the

hours were long ones for him. When he was relieved and came
back to the reserve post, he saw me and said: "Schroyer, cum mole
har, node sancked ehr du worst recht. Dot drouse sin socha net
sauver." ("Schroyer, come here once. . . . Out there are many things
that are not clean.") "Why, did you see something?" I said. "Gawiss,
hov ich, finf de shenshda glana visa hundlin sin ols schiwicha my
ba gasprunga." ("Truly I did, five pretty little white puppies all ran
between my legs.") The poor fellow was just so worked up that
he really believed he saw five little white dogs in that dark place.
The reader must kindly pardon the Dutch. So often used in our
little stories. The boys of Company G, all of whom were of German descent, would get into an argument in English, but as the
argument would advance and they would get hot under the collar,
English was too slow; so they would finish up in Dutch, thinking
that they could make it more emphatic. The balance of the Regiment being English speaking soldiers, they christened Company G
"The Dutch Company of Snyder county." As we held up that end
of it until the close of the war, and, I am glad to say. The survivors
continue it at this late date.[33]

It was not unusual for the Pennsylvania Dutch to believe in other-
worldly powers, such as powwowing, and in the case of Private Schaffer,
those powers seemed very real. Of course, Private Schroyer helped set the
scene for Schaffer's visit from fantastic beings.[34]

Pennsylvania Dutch soldiers loved their "Dutch" food, and the men of
Company G often boasted about it. Army fare replaced the traditional cui-
sine, and the following dialogue was overheard between two Company G
brothers, Sollie and Jere App:

Someone of the mess would be selected to do the cooking for a
little while, then another. Taking turns. This gave us all a chance to
become experts in the culinary department. Sometimes we had
nothing but crackers. On one such occasion Sollie App, who was
messing with his brother Jere and was cook at this time, said to him
"Jere, wos wella mere hovva fur suppe?" Jere replied, "I, ich denk
grackers." ("Jere what are we having for supper?") ("Well, I guess
crackers.")[35]

Schroyer also distinctly remembered the march to Gettysburg:

On Tuesday, June 30th, broke camp. Passed thru Townytown and shortly came to a tree upon which was posted. "Line between Pennsylvania and Maryland." Just beyond the line in Pennsylvania, an old man stood at the gate in front of his large white house. Someone in Company G said, "Now we are in old Dutch Pennsylvania and I am going to ask the old man in German about the exact place of the line separating the two great States." When we got a little closer someone yelled out in Dutch, "Dauty, wu gade de line do dorrich?" ("Pappa, where does the line go through?") The old gentlemen turned around and pointing to the chimney on his house replied in German, "Graude dorrich de mit fun seller shonshta." ("Right through the middle of that chimney.") Then we all yelled and gave three hearty cheers for our good old German Pennsylvania. As we passed through Littlestown, the ladies came out and greeted us in true Pennsylvania style, giving us water, cakes, pies and bread. Someone noticed a sign, "James Crouse: Druggist," as we passed thru town. When someone in Company G proposed three cheers for Jimmie Crouse and three cheers were heartily given because he had his namesake living in old Selinsgrove. . . .

An old lady, who was standing with her arms folded and was looking at us marching by, said, "My grund, wu wella oll de lite schloffa de nocht? Gook wos un grosser schnopsock hut seller gla cal uff sime bookel. Orma drep wos mere se dowera. De soldauda sin oll so hallich und ferlicht sin se oll dode bis moray." ("My goodness, where are all these people going to sleep tonight? Look how big that knapsack is that the little man has on his back. I pity the poor soul. The soldiers are all so happy and perhaps they will all be dead by morning.")[36]

Schroyer reported many similar incidents.

The 147th marched on July 1 to a position north of Little Round Top. The men were used as skirmishers and advanced through the Wheatfield all the way to Sherfy's Peach Orchard on the Emmitsburg Pike. Schroyer mentioned an interesting event that took place there on July 1. Colonel Parks and John Mull got into a quarrel about some trivial matters, and Parks

Members of Co. G, 147th Pennsylvania, in a post-war reunion photo, c. 1890. COLLECTION
OF KEN AND SUE BOARDMAN, GETTYSBURG, PENNSYLVANIA

said in Dutch, "Du daitshed besser hame ga un di finger opp sheesa" (You
had better go home and shoot off your finger). Mull replied, "Well, won ich
miner opp gashosha hop sheesed du diner au opp" (Well, if I shoot mine off,
you must shoot yours off too). Sure enough, the first man wounded in the
company was Parks, with the index finger of his right hand shot off. When
Parks was wounded, Jere Moyer said, "Cal you're wounded." Parks replied,
"Tell me something I don't know," and started up the hill toward the hospital.[37] Clearly, not all Pennsylvania Dutchmen were willing to risk their
lives while in Federal service, and some resorted to self-mutilation to avoid
facing the enemy.

Despite this alleged episode of cowardice, early on the morning of July
2, the 147th moved to Culp's Hill and took up positions. Later that night,
the troops were pulled back from their trenches and camped near the Baltimore Pike. Early on the morning of July 3, the regiment marched back to
the position it had held on July 2. The regiment was soon ordered forward
to a location that commanded the right of the entrenched positions. Once
the 147th reached its new position, it began skirmishing with the enemy,

and a Confederate attempt to overwhelm the 147th failed. After the fighting ended on July 3, the regiment was moved into a reserve position and assisted in burying the dead on Culp's Hill.[38]

On July 3, the final day of the battle, most of the Pennsylvania Dutch units mentioned here had taken up defensive positions and held their places throughout the Pickett-Pettigrew attack on the center of the Union lines. One unit, the 151st Pennsylvania, had retreated from the first day's field and taken up position in a small field near the cemetery in reserve of the main Union line. Some of the 151st was located east of the Tanneytown Road and not too far from Lydia Leister's home, which General Meade had taken over for his headquarters. These men of the 151st must have observed the 1st Pennsylvania Cavalry around the house as they acted as Meade's headquarters escort.

The 1st Pennsylvania Cavalry had two companies recruited in Reading, Pennsylvania, that were formed from predominantly Pennsylvania Dutch militias: the Reading City Troop and the Reading Cavalry.[39] In the Gettysburg campaign, the 1st Pennsylvania fought at Brandy Station, Aldie, and Middleburg. During the fighting of July 3, several squads of the 1st Pennsylvania were sent to serve with the provost marshal (military police) while the rest of the regiment stayed in reserve. During Pickett's Charge, the unit dismounted and moved to the east brow of Cemetery Hill to help repulse the charge near the Copse of Trees. After the attack, the 1st assisted in rounding up and guarding prisoners.[40]

The 151st was camped about 300 yards south of the Copse of Trees and remained there during the extensive Confederate cannonading that preceded Pickett's attack. Once the assault began, the 151st advanced and fired into the flank of Brigadier General James Kemper's brigade as it was charging. The 151st was then pulled out of line and sent into action with Stone's brigade—the 143d, 149th, and 150th Pennsylvania. After the fighting on July 1, Stone's brigade had retreated to Ziegler's Grove, and during July 2, it was camped in the grove. On July 3, the brigade joined the 151st in repelling the rebel attack near the Copse of Trees.[41]

Two other Pennsylvania Dutch units that had fought on the first day and then retreated back to Cemetery Hill and Ziegler's Grove were the 88th and 107th Pennsylvania. Both these units were forced out of Ziegler's Grove as a result of the intense Confederate artillery fire on July 3, and both units played a peripheral role in helping turn back Pickett's men and, after the battle, assisted in burying the dead.[42]

One unit with a small contingent of Pennsylvania Dutch that played anything but a peripheral role in turning back Pickett's men was the 71st Pennsylvania Volunteer Infantry. The 71st took up a position to the rear of Cushing's 4th U.S. Artillery very near the angle and close to the Copse of Trees. It held this position through the great cannonading of July 3, with many men of the 71st replacing wounded gunners of Cushing's battery. The 71st played a crucial role in stemming the Confederate breakthrough at the angle. They held against terrible odds, counterattacking the rebels and stopping them in their tracks. One man, Private Joseph Copp, received a Medal of Honor for capturing the 9th Virginia's battle flag.[43]

With the repulse of Pickett's men, the battle of Gettysburg was essentially over. The 151st and 153d marched home to joyous welcomes as their nine-month term of duty ended. For the remainder of the Pennsylvania Dutch units, the ordeal of cleaning up after the battle, pursuing the retreating rebels, and rebuilding their shattered ranks would occupy the next few days. Most of these units would fight on for nearly two more years in the attempts to crush the rebellion. The Pennsylvania Dutch soldiers had done their duty, and their feats of valor would later be regaled to their families and in the many Grand Army of the Republic lodges throughout the state.

The three days of battle were over. The men were exhausted, and nerves were on edge. When they were unwinding, tempers would often flare, and it is interesting to note that the Pennsylvania Dutch soldiers often resorted to their dialect when angry or making a point. The following episode underscores the Dutchman's use of his own language with his *Landsmann* (Pennsylvania Dutch for "countryman").

On July 4th we had a great thunderstorm and very heavy rain. After the storm Samuel Jarrett made a fire to dry his clothes and shelter tent, when Henry Schreffler, of the company, came to this fire to boil a cup of coffee, and began stirring and scattering the fire. Jarrett said, "Ich will net hovva dos du my fire furdarbst. Ich will my glater un my stzelt drickala, grick un noscht mit un hocka drau and habe di coffee ivver os fire." "Ich du nix on der soch hut" der Schreffler gasaut. Well mere wella sana, un we bulfer is dis omale op gonga. De cougla sin no de bame rum gafloga un de rin opgashloga ovver des hut nix ous gamocht. Grossa worta sin au rum gaflooga. Der Sammy hut der Schreffler om holtz firicked un gasaut by gooney "des wor um Sammy si sprech wort" sell nem ich net au un hut der Schreffler wetter um daum gabacked un ene amole ains he sheesa ous sime stzelt gapaked un hut gagrisha "Go in Santy Anna." Des hut der Sammy locha mocha, un graute hen se era dru-vel gasettled un de union un de konstitution warra witter safe." ("I do not want you to put out my fire. I want to dry my clothing and my shelter. Get a tree branch and sit down and hold your cof-fee over the fire with it." "I will do nothing of the sort," Schreffler said. Well we will see, and like powder it went off. The bullets flew around the trees and the ring was knocked off but it didn't matter. Big words flew around also. Sammy grabbed Schreffler by the throat and said by golly "this was Sammy's proverb" and I will not take it and backed Schreffler against his thumb and wanted to shoot him when Kankee Garmon stuck his head out of his shelter and yelled "Go in Santa Anna." This made Sammy laugh, and they settled their problem right away and the union and the constitution were safe again.)[44]

The Pennsylvania Dutch soldiers, serving alongside their "English" counterparts, gave their all, and on those fateful days of July 1 through July 3, the Union truly was saved. As one would say in the Pennsylvania Dutch dialect, *Sie hen gut geduh* (They did very well).

Throughout the three days' fighting, the Pennsylvania Dutch soldiers demonstrated their willingness to fight and die for their country. Unlike their German comrades, they did not segregate themselves from their English counterparts, nor did they demand Dutch officers to command their ranks. They relied on their unique culture to buffer the stress and anxiety of combat, falling back on a way of life that was comfortable and reassuring. A perusal of the actions of the Pennsylvania Dutch soldiers demonstrates that use of the dialect was frequent and acted as a source of identity. In times of danger, it is always helpful to have a familiar face or, in this instance, a common cultural experience to support the soldiers in the field. Not all Pennsylvania Dutch joined exclusively ethnic regiments, but Pennsylvania's system of recruiting encouraged the ad hoc development of such regiments. A visitor might be hard-pressed to differentiate the English from the Dutch, but a closer look at the men in the ranks would confirm that the Pennsylvania Dutch ways were kept, and the men were proud of this heritage. This subtle pride of heritage stands in contrast to the more stringent demands of the German-Americans, who wanted only to be with other Germans. The two groups shared a common ethnic background, but there the similarities ended. The Pennsylvania Dutch were Americans first and then Pennsylvania Dutch. Their reasons for fighting were reflective of their own political and social beliefs, but regardless of their differing opinions, they were American soldiers from the North fighting for a common cause.

After Gettysburg

Christian B. Keller and David L. Valuska

After the battle of Gettysburg, the fates of the Pennsylvania Dutch and German-American regiments differed significantly. All the Pennsylvania Dutch regiments served out the remainder of their enlistment terms with the Army of the Potomac. Those Pennsylvania Dutch soldiers served side by side with their non-German comrades in arms, compiling an impressive record of service to the Union cause. These Dutchmen did not knowingly set themselves apart from their English compatriots, but in many ways, they shared a different wartime experience. The Dutch soldiers had the extra benefit of a common cultural background, and from that shared culture, they gained an inner identity. It is a strange irony that the Pennsylvania Dutch maintained a dual sense of identity that was only intensified by their service in the war. Through four years of bloody conflict, they maintained their Americanized German culture that had evolved over the last 180 years, and adherence to their traditions during even the most trying circumstances allowed them to maintain a unique cultural awareness while at the same time embracing a larger American identity which the war helped to strengthen. Many were cognizant that an Americanization process was taking place in their lives and pondered ways to preserve their Pennsylvania Dutch folkways. Upon their return home, they reflected on their experiences as Pennsylvania Dutch soldiers and concluded that they had fought to save the Union and must now struggle to save their culture. The Civil War experience enabled the returning veterans to articulate pride in both country and culture and led to a renaissance in the study and preservation of the Pennsylvania Dutch culture.

Not surprisingly, the men who returned home in 1865 to Reading and Lebanon, Berks and Lehigh Counties, probably believed that the battle of Gettysburg itself had not substantially changed their ethnic identity. But their experiences at Gettysburg would remain firmly embedded in their memories, evoking for some feelings of great pride and in others bitter remembrances of lost friends and comrades. As these regiments erected their monuments in the waning years of the nineteenth century, they dedicated them not as Germans but as Americans "with a difference" who had truly given their "last full measure." Celebrating their regiments' deeds in the years to come in regimental histories and newspaper articles and at reunions, the Pennsylvania Dutch veterans were quick to forget ethnic differences between themselves and the other soldiers in blue even as they preserved their Dutch heritage in literary journals and festivals in their home counties. Over time the idea of a specific Pennsylvania Dutch culture gained strength as the regiments with a strong Pennsylvania Dutch flavor faded into the general public memory of those who had fought to preserve the Union.

In 1864, however, and particularly in the political arena, the Pennsylvania Dutch were anything but unified with the majority of the Northern public. Apparently, the tradition of voting Democratic remained just as strong near the end of the war as it had been during the secession crisis. Berks, Lehigh, and most of the other Dutch counties voted decidedly for Judge George W. Woodward for governor in October 1863 and voted Democratic again in the 1864 presidential election. B. F. Ulrich from Snyder County probably spoke for many Dutch Democrats in a letter he wrote to his brother in the army: "If old Abe gets elected then he is agoing to put you in the front. . . . If I would know you wouldn't vote the Democratic ticket you wouldn't get no Respt. from me. You say Pendleton has no sympathy for soldiers[,] what sympathy has Lincoln[?] He has so much sympathy that he dont care wether you get killed or not." Ulrich was not alone in his sentiments. Terming the Union party ticket the "abolitionist ticket," Democratic newspapers reported a resounding victory for George B. McClellan over Abraham Lincoln in nearly all the Dutch counties, even though Lincoln carried the state.[1]

It is not coincidental that Lincoln fared the worst and McClellan the best in Pennsylvania Dutch country. By November 1864, despite Union victories in Georgia and Virginia, the Dutch civilians at home had probably decided that the war they had not wanted in the first place was not worth any more federal intrusion into their way of life. By voting against Lincoln, they voted against emancipation, the draft, and the continued destruction of the status quo antebellum. The Democratic *Banner von Berks* summed up the "sorrowful results" of the election: "We believe that the votes, which re-elected Lincoln, equate with an unforeseeable lengthening of the war with all its accompanying depredations, such as the draft, and the final dissolution of the Union." The continuance of the war also signaled a furtherance of "the extermination and devastation in the southern states." Before the Southern people were completely annihilated, however, the editor promised that "we will cry out to the great European powers, and hear the command, 'Halt! Enough!'" The last laugh would then be on Lincoln and the "abolitionists," he predicted.[2]

The Pennsylvania Dutch civilians in Franklin and Adams Counties were less interested in politics than in rebuilding their shattered lives in late 1864. No sooner had the hardships and bitter memories of July 1863 begun to fade when they were superseded by an event far more devastating. On July 30, 1864, the town of Chambersburg was burned by raiding Confederate cavalry under Brigadier Generals John McCausland and Bradley Johnson. Jacob Hoke, a Dunker who operated one of the larger dry-goods stores in the heart of town, "sat at [his] window on the corner of the Diamond and saw [the Confederates] enter." Hoke and his family "knelt in prayer and surrounded the breakfast-table under the conviction that it was for the last time in that dear home." Fleeing their house, which had already caught fire, they "pressed through flame and smoke, amidst burning buildings," to the outskirts of town. Looking back, Hoke watched

four hundred buildings in flames, two hundred and seventy-four of which were dwelling-houses, the affrighted occupants running wildly through the streets, carrying clothing and other articles, while screams of anguish from lost children in pursuit of their parents, the feeble efforts of the old and infirm to carry with them some endeared article from their blazing homes, the roaring and crackling flames, falling walls and blinding smoke, all united to form a picture of horror, which no pen could describe, no painter portray.[3]

John K. Shryock, a Lutheran and a bookseller by trade, lost his entire business in the flames. He wrote an explicit account of the burning for the *Philadelphia Lutheran and Missionary,* claiming that "the conduct of the rebel soldiery was barbarous in the extreme, though there were many honorable exceptions. Bundles were fired upon women's backs; ladies were forced to carry back into the houses articles of clothing they had saved from the flames; drunken wretches danced upon the furniture and articles of value and ornament." In sum, "everything was done to add to the terror of the panic-stricken women and children." Driven from their burning home, Shryock's wife rescued the sick infant of a recently deceased neighbor and presented the crying baby to a nearby Confederate officer, sarcastically yelling, "Is this revenge sweet?"[4]

Dunker Rachel Cormany was appalled at the comprehensiveness of the destruction. "The whole heart of the town is burned," she wrote. "They gave no time for people to get anything out." The fire impoverished private individuals, businesses, and families alike: 559 buildings were burned, amounting to over $783,950 in damages. The Reverend B. S. Schneck claimed that the damage to private property was incalculable. Certainly, not all these losses were incurred by Pennsylvania Dutch persons, but according to primary sources, many town dwellers were members of Lutheran, Dunker, and German Reformed congregations. The German Reformed church received an especially bitter blow when the printing offices of its weekly newspaper, located on the town square, were completely destroyed.[5]

The post-Gettyburg experiences of soldiers in the German-American regiments were not as bitter as those of the residents of Chambersburg, but they paled in comparison to the exploits of the primary Pennsylvania Dutch units. All the German regiments were detached from the Army of the Potomac and sent to different locales, where they performed duties as diverse as bushwhacker patrolling in Tennessee and garrison duty in the defense of Washington. The 75th Pennsylvania, barely able to muster enough men to avoid amalgamation with another regiment, spent the rest of the war in Tennessee, where the Eleventh Corps was transferred in October 1863. It saw very little battlefield action but was kept occupied guarding railroads and prisoners and suppressing local guerrillas. The 27th and 73d Pennsylvania, also transferred to Tennessee, were more actively engaged, distinguishing themselves first at Wauhatchie and later at Tunnel Hill during the

November 25 battle of Missionary Ridge. In the forefront of the charge on the rebel works, the two regiments "displayed a courage almost amounting to rashness," according to Major General William T. Sherman. The 73d ran out of ammunition, however, and most of the men were captured in that battle. The 27th suffered heavy casualties: 132 of the 240 men engaged. The survivors of the two regiments accompanied Sherman's army during the Atlanta campaign, fighting occasionally but serving mainly as guards for the army's trains.[6]

The 74th Pennsylvania, Alexander Schimmelfennig's old regiment, was sent with its division and former commander to Folly Island, South Carolina, in August 1863. For the next eleven months, it participated in various expeditions that probed the defenses of Charleston, "raised torpedoes" in nearby rivers, and fought minor skirmishes with the enemy. After serving as heavy artillery for two months in the forts of Washington, the regiment was reassigned in September 1864 to garrison duty on the Baltimore and Ohio Railroad in West Virginia, where it served out the rest of the war in quiet inactivity.

The 98th Pennsylvania had a more exciting career after Gettysburg. First assigned to guard duty near Harpers Ferry, it rejoined the Army of the Potomac in time for Grant's Overland campaign, where it suffered particularly heavy casualties at the Wilderness and Spotsylvania. The regiment was detached to Washington in July 1864 and received special praise for its defense of Fort Stevens during Confederate General Jubal Early's raid on the Federal capital later in the month. The 98th also participated in Sheridan's valley campaign and witnessed the disintegration of the Army of Northern Virginia at Saylor's Creek in April 1865.[7]

———————————

The battle of Gettysburg and the Civil War as a whole enhanced Pennsylvania Germans' conceptions of their ethnic identity. In some cases, particularly among the Pennsylvania Dutch soldiers, this personal understanding of their ethnicity was not strongly altered; in other cases, the change was more apparent. German-Americans, especially, emerged from the conflict more aware of their ethnicity and how they differed from the greater Anglo-American population. Nativist prejudice from non-Germans after both Chancellorsville and Gettysburg, along with a post-Gettysburg preoccupation with wholly German issues in the German-language press, reinforced German-Americans' ethnic identity. Pennsylvania Dutch civilians

Monument to the 74th Pennsylvania Infantry at the Gettysburg battlefield. This photo taken c. 1888 by W. H. Tipton. KEN AND SUSAN BOARDMAN COLLECTION, GETTYSBURG, PENNSYLVANIA

remained true to their religious scruples and the agricultural way of life in the face of perceived external threats from both within and without the Union. Despite their inherent differences, the Pennsylvania Germans of both varieties shared the experience of maintaining at least some sort of ethnic consciousness during the Gettysburg campaign and, arguably, beyond.

Although concrete evidence is scarce, several scholars have theorized that the Civil War's influence in reinforcing the ethnic identity of the

North's Germans led to a postwar renaissance. During this time, both the German-Americans and the Pennsylvania Dutch separately celebrated their unique ethnicities, stressed the contributions they could make to America, and even increased their resistance against Americanization. Don Yoder asked in a 1983 article in the *Yearbook of German-American Studies,* "Is it possible that the Civil War, with its traumatic upheaving of population and bitter sectional feelings, sent the Pennsylvania Germans back upon themselves, into a discovery of their own identity—or into the first major phase of their ethnic self-discovery?" Yoder was referring here to the Dutch—specifically, to the German Reformed among them. He believed that there had been several stages in the "development of the Pennsylvania German consciousness," but the "basic one may well have been that of the 1860s and 1870s." The changes wrought by the war allowed the flowering of a bona fide "Pennsylvania Dutch culture" long after the guns had fallen silent. Yoder cited several examples of how this ethnic identity had been created, including the founding of the Pennsylvania German Society and the postwar boom in the publication of journals, newspapers, and manuals of instruction in the Pennsilfaanisch Deitsch dialect. He did not, however, speculate about what aspects of the war had specifically created this heightening of Pennsylvania Dutch ethnic consciousness.[8]

Yoder was joined two years later by Kathleen Conzen, who questioned the role of the Civil War in the creation of a German-American ethnic identity. Conzen proposed that the Germans' experiences in the war promoted the "third phase" of their "invention of ethnicity," in which German leaders rejected the "melting pot ideal" of the prewar years—assimilation, essentially—in favor of "a perpetuation of ethnic difference" between Anglo-Americans and Germans. In that third phase, the preservation and extension of German culture and language were assisted by the growing demographic, economic, and political strength of the various "little Germanies" throughout the United States. "Deutschtum" and Americanism, Conzen noted, were not mutually exclusive or competitive. In the Gilded Age, German-Americans "remained content to stress pragmatically the advantages to the nation of citizens able to appreciate the treasures of two cultures and the insight thereby gained." In other words, by retaining their ethnic identity, German-Americans would gradually assimilate on their own terms and, in so doing, provide the greatest possible advantages to the culture of the United States as a whole. German "sociability, public morality, and an appreciation for the good, the true, and the beautiful" were gifts that the Germans would bequeath to the American nation over time, and in the end, the country would be a better place for all citizens—both German and non-German. Like Yoder, Conzen did not explain what exactly had happened during the war to spur this new growth of German-American identity, except for a vague assertion about the blood sacrifice of German soldiers.[9]

Stephen Engle also briefly engaged the postwar implications of the war for the North's German-Americans in an article in the *Yearbook*. Arguing that Franz Sigel was "a protean ethnic icon" who unified Northern Germans through the conflict, Engle wrote that demonstrations in support of Sigel (particularly in 1863) propelled the Northern German "community" in "both directions (towards assimilation and towards constructing an ethnic identity) simultaneously—creating firmer ethnic solidarity, on the one hand, and acting effectively in the public sphere, on the other hand." The Civil War, and especially Sigel's role as ethnic leader, had changed German-Americans' conceptions of their identity by 1865, because they came to regard themselves collectively as German-Americans and not as Prussians, Bavarians, Swabians, Württembergers, and so forth. According to Engle, it was Sigel who brought the Germans of the North together in the war, linking the home front and the battlefield on an almost daily basis and forging a national sense of Deutschtum. As convincing as Engle's article is about Sigel's role in the formation of a national German-American ethnic identity, it provides little information about what created the postwar ethnic resurgence among the German-Americans or how it and the postwar period were specifically linked. Certainly, Sigel alone could not have been responsible for what Conzen calls the "third phase" of immigrant German ethnic identity, which flowered from the 1870s through the 1890s.[10]

Did the Civil War, then, create—or strongly contribute to—the postwar explosion in Pennsylvania Dutch and German-American ethnic consciousness? We cannot positively prove this thesis here, and a solidly researched answer would be well beyond the scope of this book. But the hypothesis warrants further scrutiny.

German-American responses to the aftermath of both Chancellorsville and Gettysburg—two of the most critical wartime events—clearly demonstrated a staunch defense of their ethnic identity against perceived threats. The specter of nativism was unquestionably paramount in the reaction to Chancellorsville, and the lingering memory of the Know-Nothings—a political party that could have jeopardized the future of immigrant Germans everywhere—was no doubt primarily responsible for that. In the case of Gettysburg, the soldiers of Pennsylvania's German-American regiments believed that they needed to "vindicate" their marred reputation after Chancellorsville. Hence, they may have fought harder during the first day's battle than they would have otherwise, fearing the repercussions of another poor battlefield performance. Likewise, the response of the German-language press to the German troops' actions at Gettysburg was so laudatory because the editors—and, by extension, the people at home—were overjoyed that their men had retrieved their reputation and avoided the barb of nativism the second time around.

Smaller, more personal actions performed on an individual basis are harder to explain using this line of reasoning, but taken on the whole, they, too, followed a similar course. Pennsylvania Dutch farmers attempted to protect their agricultural property (key to the maintenance of their ethnic identity) during the Gettysburg campaign from Confederate requisitions and collateral damage, and they reacted through a variety of measures, including, perhaps, collaboration with the enemy. Private soldiers in the Pennsylvania Dutch units, such as the 147th Pennsylvania, spoke with one another in the Pennsilfaanisch Deitsch dialect because it made them feel comfortable in a new environment and amid a panorama of death and destruction.

Based on some of the evidence presented in the preceding chapters, we believe that the postwar flowering of ethnic consciousness among the German-Americans of the North and the concurrent growth of a collective Pennsylvania Dutch identity could have been caused by the Germans' reactions to the perceived threat to their ethnic identity during the war. Nativism, or a fear of its resurgence, played a major role by serving as the overarching threat to German-Americans, but so did intrusions by both the federal government and Confederate forces in the eyes of many Dutchmen.

Admittedly, this book is limited to the Gettysburg campaign, so positing a thesis about the entire war would be a stretch. But it appears that the Pennsylvania Germans, on the whole, may have emerged from the conflict shaken by their ordeal and questioning the benefits of further amalgamation with the greater U.S. population. After all, it could be reasoned, it was precisely that American population which was the source of the various threats to the Germans' ethnic identity. German-Americans may have realized that nativism was not dead among Anglo-Americans and thus sought to reassure themselves—and others—of their worth as American citizens by celebrating rather than reducing their ethnicity and its contributions to the United States. The Pennsylvania Dutch could have deduced that they were disdained by both the German-Americans and the Anglo-Americans alike, and that their way of life (such as religious scruples or avoidance of change) was not respected by them. A natural outgrowth of such a belief would have been the efforts among Dutch leaders in the late 1860s and 1870s to promote Pennsilfaanisch Deitsch as a bona fide written language and to unify the various Dutch denominations under a collective cultural umbrella called "Pennsylvania German."[11] Admittedly, these hypotheses are unprovable without substantial research, but they provide likely explanations for postwar German-American behavior and establish links between the Civil War and the explosion of German ethnic identity in the Gilded Age. Unquestionably, Conzen, Yoder, and Engle touched on an important concept when they theorized that events of the Civil War were key to subsequent German-American history. It is hoped that the ideas presented here will inspire future projects to specifically analyze this important connection.

Pennsylvania Dutch Music

DAS LIED VON DER UNION
(Sus und Märy singen um die Wette.)

Sus:

Hescht du am Suntag der Pit gesehne,
Wie er so schön ausgeguckt hot?
Er guckt, o mein! mer sot schier mehne,
Er guckt eksektle (exactly), wie mer gucke sot.

Märy:

Wescht ah warum der Pit so guckt?
Er is vor die Union, er is vor sei Land!
Er hot gege Jeff. Davis die Musket gezuckt
Un Schiesst die Sesseschens (secessionists?) all in der Sand.

Sus:

Ho, for die Union! die acht' ich nit g'ring—
A Mann is, wu fer die Union fecht!
But, Märy, ich hab noch a ganz anner Ding,
Wovon ich mit dir jetzt spreche möcht.

Märy:

Loss höre, Sus, ich will Dir's eksplehne,
A Ding is a Ding—verleicht wehs ichs schun;
Loss es höre, un dann will ich sehne,
Ob ich kann geben Erklärung dervun.

199

Sus:

Mei Fähwers (favors) hätt der Pit nit genosse,
Wann er so neiss (nice) nit ufgetresst (dressed up) wär;
Guck mol sei Rock, Tschecket (jacket) un Hosse—
Wu hot der Kerl die schöne Klehder dann her?

Märy:

A Kerl for die Union wehs, was er thut,
Er denkt eppes vun sich, juscht wie er sot;
Er geht noch der Stadt, un holt sich a Suht (suit),
Un dresst (to dress) sich raus wie a rechter Patriot.

Sus:

But wer in der Stadt hot die Klehder im Stohr (store),
Wo die Mannsleut so herrlicht drin gucke?
O, Märy, sag mir's geschwind in mei Ohr—
Die liebe zum Pit macht mich schier jucke!

Märy:

Ich bin vor die Union—but ich muss sage,
Der Pit in sei Klehder hot mich ah schön geropt;
Die Liebe hot mir Wunde geschlage—
O, fühl mol, Sus, wie das Herz mir klopt!

Wollenweber 1869: Seite 69–70

THE PEOPLE OF THE UNION★

(Sus and Mary sing the words.)

Sus:

Did you see Peter on Sunday,
How nice he looked?
He looks, o my! we should almost think,
He looks exactly, the way we should look.

Mary:

Do you know why Peter looks like that?
He is for the Union, he is for his land!
He looked for Jeff Davis muskets
And shot the secessionists all in the sand.

★The song is loosely translated.

Sus:

Ho, for the Union! The esteem is not slight—
For a man who fights for the Union!
But, Mary, I have yet another thing,
I want to speak with you now.

Mary:

Just listen, Sus, I want to explain it to you,
One thing is one thing—maybe I already know it;
Let me hear it, and then I will see,
If I can give an explanation of it.

Sus:

Peter did not pay attention to (or acknowledge) my favors
When he was not dressed up so nicely;
Look once at his coat, jacket, and trousers—
Where did the fellow get his nice clothing?

Mary:

A fellow for the Union knows, what he should;
He (respects) thinks something of you, just like he should;
He goes to the town, and gets a suit,
And dresses himself up like a right patriot.

Sus:

But who in the town has the clothing in store,
Where the men so cheerfully look in?
O, Mary, tell me quickly in my ear—
Your love toward Peter makes me almost jealous!

Mary:

I am for the Union—but I must say,
Peter in his clothing took me in nicely also.
I was wounded (hit) by love—
O, all the time, Sus, how my heart beats fast!

Wollenweber 1869: Seite 69–70
Translated by Mary Bittner Henry

THE UNION ARCH

by Henry Harbaugh

Sensht du sell Arch von vierundreisig ste?
Du wescht du a was sell bedeuta dut?
Es stellt die Union vor, gar grieslich shoe;
Der Keystone in der Mit steht fresht un gut.
Sell Arch loss sei!—Ke single Ste reg a;
Dort mus es steh bis Alles geht zu Nix;
Wan Epper legt sei Treason Hend dort dra.
Den schiest m'r wie en Hund mit Minnie's Bix!
Sell Arch is vesht cement mit hertzens Blut;
Es stant en harter Rebel sturm, I'll bet;
"Verreist's" kreist aus die gans Sesession Brut—
Der Lincoln watcht sie close un losst sie net!

Translation*

Do you see that arch of 34 stones?
Do you know what that means?
It stands for the Union, extremely beautiful;
The keystone in the middle stands fast and good (superior).
That arch let it be!—Don't touch one single stone;
There it must stand until everything goes to nothing;
If someone lays his treason hand on it,
Then we'll shoot him like a dog with Minnie's rifle!
That arch is like solid cement made with courageous men's
    blood;
It stood a hard rebel storm, I'll bet;
Extinguish the whole secession mob—
Lincoln watches them closely and will not let them go!

---

*Translated by Mary Bittner Henry and Dr. Michael Werner.

Ballad of the Schimmelfennig Memorial Dining Hall

Sung to the tune of "Battle Hymn of the Republic."

My mind retains the memory of the Schimmelfennig Hall.
In fact some things about it I would rather not recall.
It was not the sort of place that you would hold a festival.
Its memory lingers on.

CHORUS: I remember Schimmelfennig.
              I remember Schimmelfennig.
              I remember Schimmelfennig.
              Its memory lingers on.

The floor was paved with gravel and the walls were made of tin.
There were gaps along the bottom where some things went out
    and in.
It took embattled courage to return from where we'd been.
Its memory lingers on.

CHORUS

The young athletes who shared our space impaired our quietude.
The din they made soon caused to fade our contemplative mood.
And if we didn't get there fast, they ate up all the food.
Its memory lingers on.

CHORUS

If you don't like the food you'd simply drop it on the floor.
Cover it with gravel and it would simply be no more.
And don't forget your food pass or you'd be right out the door.
Its taste lingers on.

CHORUS

There were shortages of soda, there were shortages of milk.
And the stones that turned your ankles really drew forth great ilk.
And we don't know what the chairs were but they sure as bleep
    weren't silk.
Its grace lingers on.

CHORUS

The dirt raised off the floor would really make you blink.
The only place it wouldn't was where someone spilled their drink.
As witnesses to Gettysburg we're destined to be linked.
Its story lingers on.

CHORUS

Early broke the 'leventh and he sent them on a fly.
Schimmelfennig came here for he found his famous sty.
And unto this hour there was no worse hall you'll spy.
Its history lingers on.

CHORUS

There are some nasty rumors that he still may be alive.
As a chef or cook at some school can't be denied.
Is he in Brazil or maybe here to this hall he's ever tied.
His spirit lingers on.

CHORUS

And now our song is over and we're heading for the door.
If you want to leave a tip just drop it on the floor.
We would definitely appreciate it 'cus we're really poor.
Its legend lingers on.

CHORUS

—Miss Sterious; Ann Nonymous

(As sung by the Schimmelfennig Memorial Tuberculosis Institute
Choir, created by the Civil War Institute Alumni at Gettysburg
College in 1988. The authors wish to thank the CWI at Gettys-
burg College for supplying the text to this song.)

NOTES

INTRODUCTION

1. Ella Lonn, *Foreigners in the Union Army and Navy* (Baton Rouge: Louisiana State University Press, 1951), 663–4. Lonn claims that her statistics are drawn from the national census of 1860. According to statistician B. A. Gould of the U.S. Sanitary Commission, Germans also were the ethnic group most overrepresented in the Union armies. They surpassed the quota of men they should have supplied (according to their share of the Northern population) by almost 50 percent. Benjamin A. Gould, *Investigations in the Statistics of American Soldiers* (New York: Riverside Press, 1869).

2. Lester W. J. Seifert, "The Word Geography of Pennsylvania German: Extent and Causes," in Glenn G. Gilbert, ed., *The German Language in America: A Symposium* (Austin: University of Texas Press, 1971), 17.

3. Lonn, *Foreigners in the Union Army and Navy;* William L. Burton, *Melting Pot Soldiers: The Union's Ethnic Regiments,* 2d ed. (New York: Fordham University Press, 1998); Wilhelm Kaufmann, *The Germans in the American Civil War* (1911; reprint and translation, Carlisle, PA: John Kallman Publishers, 1999); Stephen D. Engle, *Yankee Dutchman: The Life of Franz Sigel* (Baton Rouge: Louisiana State University Press, 1993). James S. Pula, *The Sigel Regiment: A History of the Twenty-sixth Wisconsin Volunteer Infantry, 1862–1865* (Campbell, CA: Savas Publishing Company, 1998), is an excellent regimental history, and a forthcoming work by Bret Coulson will examine the 74th Pennsylvania. Both Lonn and Burton fail to treat Civil War–era German speakers as the disunified, multifaceted conglomeration of people they were; they tend to view the Germans largely as a bloc and play down the differences among them. This approach, as we will demonstrate, not only is inaccurate for the German-Americans but also completely neglects any meaningful discussion of the Pennsylvania Dutch. Beyond Lonn and Burton, there are no other comprehensive works that include a significant analysis of Germans. The dearth of scholarship on the North's largest ethnic group is puzzling, especially considering the historical profession's emphasis on social history in recent years. The language barrier has clearly been problematic, which partially explains the expanding number of Irish studies compared with the handful examining the Germans.

4. U.S. War Department, *The War of the Rebellion: A Compilation of the Official Records of the Union and Confederate Armies,* 127 vols. (Washington, DC: Government Printing Office, 1880–1901). All passages quoted from German-language newspapers were translated by the authors and appear here in English.

5. In the case of subsequent translations of these materials into English, this is made clear in the notes.

6. Kaufmann, *Germans in the American Civil War,* 105; Lonn, *Foreigners in the Union Army and Navy,* 100–1; Burton, *Melting Pot Soldiers,* 98–101.

7. Nora Helen Faires, "Ethnicity in Evolution: The German Community in Pittsburgh and Allegheny City, Pennsylvania, 1845–1885" (Ph. D. diss., University of Pittsburgh: 1981), 79; Reinhard P. Doerries, "Immigrant Culture and Religion: Church and Faith among German Americans," in Randall M. Miller, ed., *Germans in America: Retrospect and Prospect, Tricentennial Lectures Delivered at the German Society of Pennsylvania, 1983* (Philadelphia: German Society of Pennsylvania, 1984), 84–88; Stephen Longenecker, *Piety and Tolerance: Pennsylvania German Religion, 1700–1850* (Metuchen, NJ: Scarecrow Press, 1994), 170–1; Theron F. Schlabach, *Peace, Faith, Nation: Mennonites and Amish in Nineteenth-Century America,* The Mennonite Experience in America Series, vol. 2 (Scottdale, PA: Herald Press, 1988), 145–7; Yoder, "The Pennsylvania Germans: Three Centuries of Identity Crisis," in Frank Trommler and Joseph McVeigh, eds., *America and the Germans: An Assessment of a Three-Hundred Year History.* Immigration, Language, Ethnicity, vol 1 (Philadelphia: University of Pennsylvania Press, 1985); Robert P. Swierenga, "The Religious Factor in Immigration: The Dutch Experience," in Timothy Walch, ed., *Immigrant America: European Ethnicity in the United States* (New York: Garland, 1994), 121–2. Also see Steven M. Nolt's *Foreigners in Their Own Land: Pennsylvania Germans in the Early Republic,* Pennsylvania German History and Culture Series, vol. 2 (University Park: Pennsylvania State University Press, 2001). It should be noted that the German denominations tended to remain composed almost exclusively of ethnic Germans in the middle nineteenth century. Yoder and Nolt indicate that Methodism and other evangelical movements managed to plant colonies in the Pennsylvania Dutch counties and lured Germans to their congregations, but the reverse process seems to have been quite rare.

8. William L. Joyce, *Editors and Ethnicity: A History of the Irish-American Press, 1848–1883,* Irish Americans Series (New York: Arno Press, 1976), 4–5.

9. Renate Kiesewetter, "German-American Labor Press: The *Vorbote* and the *Chicago Arbeiter-Zeitung,*" in Hartmut Keil, ed., *German Workers' Culture in the United States, 1850–1920* (Washington, DC: Smithsonian Institution Press, 1988), 148–9; Ken Fones-Wolf and Elliott Shore, "The German Press and Working-Class Politics in Gilded-Age Philadelphia," in Elliott Shore, Ken Fones-Wolf, and James P. Danky, eds., *The German-American Radical Press: The Shaping of Left Political Culture, 1850–1940* (Chicago: University of Illinois Press, 1992), 73–4. Bruce Levine, in *The Spirit of 1848: German Immigrants, Labor Conflict, and Coming of the Civil War* (Chicago: University of Illinois Press, 1992) a work about the influence of 1848 on German-American labor in America, relies strongly on newspaper editorials for his analysis and says almost nothing about the possible differences between editors and readers, implicitly following the same line of reasoning presented here. An additional reason the German editors were not just printing their own opinions is summed up by James N. Primm in his introduction to Steven Rowan's book about the St. Louis German radical press. "Writers relied heavily on a body of experience shared with their readers" (i.e., the common experience of being ethnically German in their specific locality), he argues; thus the similarities between the editors and the reading public outweighed any differences that may have existed. The possibility of substantial differences between the mass of "everyday" Germans and newspaper editors (as well as between Dutch and German-American editors)—or between ordinary citizens and other Pennsylvania German leaders, for that matter—is not discounted here, but we argue that such leaders more or less represented the views of their followers. See Steven Rowan, ed. and trans., *Germans for a Free Missouri: Translations from the St. Louis Radical Press, 1857–1862* (Columbia: University of Missouri Press, 1983), introduction.

CHAPTER 1

1. Philip S. Klein, "Historical Problems with the Pennsylvania Germans," *Community Historians Annual* 8, no. 6 (December 1969): 24–33.

2. For modern examinations of the traditional melting-pot explanation, see John Higham, *Strangers in the Land: Patterns in American Nativism* (1955; reprint, New York: Atheneum, 1963), and "Interpret-

ing America: The Problem of Assimilation in the Nineteenth-Century," *Journal of American Ethnic History* (fall 1981): 7–25 (though the latter work draws on the pluralist school, especially regarding the growth of a national consciousness among Germans in America who had none in Germany); Oscar Handlin, *Boston's Immigrants: A Study in Acculturation,* rev. ed. (New York: Atheneum, 1972), and *The Uprooted* (New York: Grosset and Dunlap, 1951); and Milton M. Gordon, *Assimilation in American Life* (New York: Oxford University Press, 1964). Some of the leaders of the cultural pluralist school are Michael Novak, *The Rise of the Unmeltable Ethnics* (New York: Macmillan, 1973); Thomas Sowell, *Ethnic America: A History* (New York: Basic Books, 1981); Joseph A. Ryan, ed., *White Ethnic Life in Working Class America* (Englewood Cliffs, NJ: Prentice Hall, 1973); and Nathan Glazer and Daniel P. Moynihan, *Beyond the Melting Pot,* 2d ed. (Cambridge: MIT Press, 1970). Many of the cultural pluralist authors helped develop or contributed to the "new ethnicity" school, which grew out of pluralism and expanded on it.

3. Scholars who have provided explanations for ethnic identity include Richard D. Alba, *Ethnic Identity: The Transformation of White America* (New Haven, CT: Yale University Press, 1990); Donald L. Horowitz, "Ethnic Identity," in Nathan Glazer and Daniel P. Moynihan, eds., *Ethnicity: Theory and Experience* (Cambridge: Harvard University Press, 1975); Fredrik Barth, ed., *Ethnic Groups and Boundaries: The Social Organization of Cultural Differences* (Boston: Little, Brown, 1969); and Werner Sollors, ed., *The Invention of Ethnicity* (New York: Oxford University Press, 1989). For some novel attempts to analyze ethnic identity, see Philip Gleason, "Hansen, Herberg, and American Religion" in Philip Gleason, ed., *Speaking of Diversity: Language and Ethnicity in Twentieth-Century America* (Baltimore: Johns Hopkins University Press, 1992), on the theory of "third generation return," in which grandchildren return to the ethnic consciousness of their grandparents; Kerby A. Miller, "Class, Culture and Immigrant Group Identity in the United States: The Case of Irish-American Ethnicity," in Virginia Yans-McLaughlin, ed., *Immigration Reconsidered: History, Sociology, and Politics* (New York: Oxford University Press, 1990), on the role of political ideology in Irish-American identity; and Kathleen Neils Conzen, "German-Americans and the Invention of Ethnicity," in Frank Trommler and Joseph McVeigh, eds., *America and the Germans: An Assessment of a Three-Hundred Year History,* Immigration, Language, Ethnicity, vol. 1 (Philadelphia: University of Pennsylvania Press, 1985).

4. Don Yoder, "The Pennsylvania Germans: Three Centuries of Identity Crisis," in Trommler and McVeigh, *America and the Germans,* 42. Yoder's other works include *Pennsylvania Spirituals* (Lancaster, PA: Pennsylvania Folklife Society, 1961); *Pennsylvania German Immigrants, 1709–1786* (Baltimore: Genealogical Publication Company, 1980); *Rhineland Emigrants* (Baltimore: Genealogical Publication Company, 1982) and numerous articles.

5. Klein, "Historical Problems," 26–7; Yoder, "The Pennsylvania Germans," 42, 53; Randall M. Miller, "Introduction," in Randall M. Miller, ed., *Germans in America: Retrospect and Prospect, Tricentennial Lectures Delivered at the German Society of Pennsylvania in 1983* (Philadelphia: German Society of Pennsylvania, 1984); Kathleen Neils Conzen, "Patterns of German-American History," in ibid., 4–7, 16–8; Marianne S. Wokeck, *Trade in Strangers: The Beginnings of Mass Migrations to North America* (University Park: Pennsylvania State University Press, 1999). Wokeck identifies five great waves of German immigration to Pennsylvania (c. 1715, 1740, 1790, post-1800, and post-1848) and claims that the Americanization process naturally was more advanced among the descendants of the earlier settlers than among those who arrived later.

6. Yoder has succinctly summarized the differences between these two major Germanic groups in "The Pennsylvania Germans," 43, 51–3, and in his essay "The 'Dutchman' and the 'Deitschlenner': The New World Confronts the Old," *Yearbook of German-American Studies* (1988): 1–17. Other scholars, such as La Vern J. Rippley, *The German-Americans* (Lanham, MD: University Press of America, 1984), 52–3; Richard O'Connor, *The German-Americans: An Informal History* (Boston: Little, Brown, 1968), 113–7; and Albert B. Faust, *The German Element in the United States,* 2 vols. (New York: Steuben Society, 1927), have also recognized the inherent differences between the older population, which they lump under the title the "Greys" (a slightly inaccurate practice particularly if the Pennsylvania Dutch are included) and the newer one, termed the "Greens." It is important to note here, as Conzen and O'Connor point out, that both groups of Germans were perceived by nineteenth-century Anglo-Americans as essentially the same, particularly among those who had little daily con-

tact with ethnic minorities. Hence the label "Dutchman" was applied with equal vigor to all ethnic Germans by Anglo-Americans, especially as the nativist movement of the 1840s and 1850s grew in strength. Some readers may object to the use of the term "Pennsylvania Dutch" or "Dutch" when speaking of the older, rural-dwelling, and longer-settled group. The debate about what to call these descendants of the colonial German immigrants has raged since the nineteenth century and continues today. To distinguish between this group of ethnic Germans and the newer, urban-dwelling immigrants of the major Pennsylvania cities who arrived in the antebellum period, we call the former "Pennsylvania Dutch" (or simply "Dutch") and the latter "German-Americans." Both populations are included under the rubric "Pennsylvania Germans," since both were ethnically German or spoke a Germanic language.

7. Wokeck, *Trade in Strangers;* A. G. Roeber, *Palatines, Liberty, and Property: German Lutherans in British Colonial America,* 2d ed. (Baltimore: Johns Hopkins University Press, 1998); Klein, "Historial Problems," 28; William W. Donner, "'We Are What We Make of Ourselves': Abraham Reeser Horne and the Education of Pennsylvania Germans," *Pennsylvania Magazine of History and Biography* 124, no. 4 (October 2000): 522–46; Jürgen Eichoff, "The German Language in America," in Trommler and McVeigh, *America and the Germans,* 1: 230.

8. Don Yoder, "The Palatine Connection: The Pennsylvania German Culture and Its European Roots," in Miller, *Germans in America,* 96–7, 102–8; Walter M. Kollmorgen, "The Pennsylvania German Farmer," in Ralph Wood, ed., *The Pennsylvania Germans* (Princeton, NJ: Princeton University Press, 1942), 47–50.

9. Kollmorgen, "Pennsylvania German Farmer," 36–43; Frederic Klees, *The Pennsylvania Dutch* (New York: Macmillan, 1950), 314–7; Donner, "'We Are What We Make of Ourselves,'" 523, 532–9; Russell W. Gilbert, *A Picture of the Pennsylvania Germans,* Pennsylvania History Studies (Gettysburg: Pennsylvania Historical Association, 1971), 45–55.

10. Clyde S. Stine, "The Pennsylvania Germans and the School," in Wood, *The Pennsylvania Germans,* 105–27; Klees, *The Pennsylvania Dutch,* 293–5, 314–7; Donner, "'We Are What We Make of Ourselves,'" 532–9; William T. Parsons, *The Pennsylvania Dutch: A Persistent Minority* (Boston: G. K. Hall, 1976), 193; Yoder, "The Pennsylvania Germans," 46–8, and "The Palatine Connection," 92–3; Robert Henry Billigmeier, "The Pennsylvania Germans from the American Revolution to the First World War," in *Americans from Germany: A Study in Cultural Diversity,* Minorities in American Life Series (Belmont, CA: Wadsworth, 1974), 110–2. Roeber has also shown that Dutch Germans were even reluctant to support a publicly funded German-language academy in Philadelphia in the late 1700s. See A. G. Roeber, "The von Mosheim Society and the Preservation of German Education and Culture in the New Republic, 1789–1813" in Henry Geitz, Jürgen Heideking, and Jurgen Herbst, eds., *German Influences on Education in the United States to 1917,* Publications of the German Historical Institute, Washington, D.C. (Cambridge: Cambridge University Press, 1995), 163–5. Further evidence of the limited success of Dutch German resistance to the public school movement in the antebellum period can be found in Gustav Koerner, *Das Deutsche Element in den Vereinigten Staaten von Nordamerika, 1818–1848* (Cincinnati, 1880); he observes in his second chapter that the Pennsylvania state legislature was publishing the governor's addresses in a German translation by 1837, and German instruction in the schools was sanctioned by law. Koerner also mentions a legislative movement to establish a German teachers college and a German university. By the time of the Civil War, fewer students were learning in German in the Dutch counties than earlier in the century, but their numbers were still substantial. In Northampton County, for instance, 598 students out of 7,596 were taught in German in 1861; in Lehigh County, 1,280 out of 7,271. The report of the Berks County public school superintendent was quite revealing: "The opposition [the county's residents] have evinced in the past, did not spring—as the maligners of our general character would have us believe—from ignorance and hatred . . . or from a want of congeniality between the German spirit and the demands of the age, but from the fact that no regard was paid to the peculiar type of mind with which the Almighty endowed us. . . . There is every reason to believe that, our people once convinced that, being educated, they will not be called upon to ignore their original character, the last vestige [*sic*] of opposition to the public schools will have disappeared." *Report of the Superintendent of Common Schools of Pennsylvania, for the Year Ending June 3, 1861* (Harrisburg, PA: A. Boyd Hamilton, State Printer, 1862).

11. Gilbert provides a useful explanation for the perception among Anglo-Americans that the Pennsylvania Dutch were igonorant or dumb: "The Pennsylvania German was dumb in the correct sense of the word: because of his shyness and the haunting fear of error in the use of English, he hesitated to speak in a language foreign to his own and one in which he found it difficult to express himself. . . . Silence on his part produced the incorrect assumption of low mentality by the English." Instead of being ignorant of language, Gilbert continues, the Dutch were "actually trilingual: they could read the High German literary language which they used in the daily reading of the Bible, could speak their own dialect, and to a degree could speak and understand English." See Gilbert, *A Picture of the Pennsylvania Germans,* 17. For a fuller discussion of the "hybridization" theory, see Eric Hobsbawm and Terence Ranger, eds., *The Invention of Tradition* (New York: Cambridge University Press, 1983), 1–14, and Kathleen Conzen, David A. Gerber, et al., "The Invention of Ethnicity: A Perspective from the U.S.A.," *Journal of American Ethnic History* 12, no.1 (fall 1992): 3–32.
12. Klees, *The Pennsylvania Dutch,* 316–8; Kollmorgen, "Pennsylvania German Farmer," 48–9.
13. Kenneth W. Keller, "Rural Politics and the Collapse of Pennsylvania Federalism," *Transactions of the American Philosophical Society* 72, pt. 6 (1982): 24–34; Parsons, *The Pennsylvania Dutch,* 184–8.
14. Parsons, *The Pennsylvania Dutch,* 190–2; Arthur D. Graeff, "The Pennsylvania Germans in Partisan Politics, 1754–1965," in Homer T. Rosenberger, ed., *Intimate Glimpses of the Pennsylvania Germans,* Proceedings of the Third Rose Hill Seminar, 26 June 1965 (Gettysburg: Pennsylvania German Society, 1966), 25–8. In 1876, Samuel Tilden called Berks County "the Gibraltar of the Democracy" for its consistent Democratic voting pattern, which has been broken only a few times since. As late as 1955, a political commentator on a well-known Pennsylvanisch-dialect radio program signed off as "Der Andy Jackson," indicating the lingering appeal of Jackson's name among the modern Pennsylvania Dutch.
15. Owen S. Ireland, "Germans against Abolition: A Minority's View of Slavery in Revolutionary Pennsylvania," *Journal of Interdisciplinary History* 3, no. 4 (spring 1973): 685–706. Also see Leroy T. Hopkins, "Uneasy Neighbors: Germans and Blacks in Nineteenth-Century Lancaster County," and James M. Bergquist, "The Mid-Nineteenth-Century Slavery Crisis and the German Americans," in Randall M. Miller, ed., *States of Progress: Germans and Blacks in America over 300 Years* (Philadelphia: German Society of Pennsylvania, 1989), 27, 59, 63, 82, 86, for discussions of Dutch German apathy and antipathy toward blacks and abolition.
16. Yoder, "The Pennsylvania Germans," 43–4, and "The Palatine Connection," 98–100; Theron F. Schlabach, *Peace, Faith, Nation: Mennonites and Amish in Nineteenth-Century America,* The Mennonite Experience in America, vol. 2 (Scottdale, PA: Herald Press, 1988), particularly chaps. 5 and 6. The Moravians—who were also of German ancestry and held their church services in High German— never really considered themselves part of the Pennsylvania Dutch culture, though their political and religious influence loomed large in certain Dutch counties (such as Northampton). The scholarly debate continues about whether to include the Moravians under the Pennsylvania Dutch rubric.
17. Yoder, "The Pennsylvania Germans," 43–4; G. Paul Musselman, "The Sects, Apostles of Peace," in Wood, *The Pennsylvania Germans,* 63–79; Ralph Wood, "Lutheran and Reformed, Pennsylvania German Style," in ibid., 87–95; John A. Hostetler, "The Plain People: Historical and Modern Perspectives," in Trommler and McVeigh, *America and the Germans,* 108–15; Stephen L. Longenecker, *Piety and Tolerance: Pennsylvania German Religion, 1700–1850,* especially chap. 6. For a good analysis of the origins of the split between English- and German-language Lutheran congregations, see Steven M. Nolt's *Foreigners in Their Own Land: Pennsylvania Germans in the Early Republic,* Publications of the Pennsylvania German Society, vol. 35 (University Park: Pennsylvania State University Press, 2001), 120–7, and Wolfgang Splitter, *Pastors, People, Politics: German Lutherans in Pennsylvania, 1740–1790* (Trier, Germany: Wissenschaftlicher Verlag Trier, 1998), 309–14. The differences between the church and the sectarian Germans are best explained in Nolt's book, but they can be summarized here as follows: The Lutherans and German Reformed possessed a prescribed ritual, liturgy, dogma, and centralized governing bodies (synods, for example), whereas the sects favored a more local, decentralized authority in both church governance and worship; the sectarians were pietists and, in the case of the Mennonites and Amish, Anabaptist in origin; the church Germans were more active in their communities, protecting their cultural independence while still engaging in business and politics with their Anglo-American neighbors, whereas the sectarians shunned political participation

and avoided interaction with nonsectarians; the church Germans traditionally voted Democratic, as their fathers had, whereas the sectarians frequently espoused the ideals of "reformer parties" such as the Whigs and, later, the Republicans. The Mennonites and Amish particularly supported the Republicans because slavery was expressedly frowned on in their chuch laws.

18. Roger E. Sappington, comp. and ed., *The Brethren in the New Nation: A Source Book on the Development of the Church of the Brethren, 1785–1865* (Elgin, IL: The Brethren Press, 1976), 253, 259, 272, 276, 282–4, 288; Donald F. Durnbaugh, *Fruit of the Vine: A History of the Brethren, 1708–1995* (Elgin, IL: Brethren Press, 1997), 266–7, 280–1; Schlabach, *Peace, Faith, Nation,* 27, 95–105, 148, 199–200. Since this book covers only the era of the Civil War, the term "pacifist" may be interchanged with "sectarian," as pacifism was the official stance of all three major Pennsylvania German sectarian churches during the war.

19. Mahlon H. Hellerich, ed., *Allentown, 1762–1987: A 225-Year History,* 2 vols. (Allentown, PA: Lehigh County Historical Society, 1987), 1:91–96; Billigmeier, "The Pennsylvania Germans from the American Revolution to the First World War," 110–5; Nora H. Faires, "Ethnicity in Evolution: The German Community in Pittsburgh and Allegheny City, Pennsylvania, 1845–1885" (Ph.D. diss., University of Pittsburgh, 1981); Stanley Nadel, *Little Germany: Ethnicity, Religion, and Class in New York City, 1845–80* (Chicago: University of Illinois Press, 1990); Günter Moltmann, "German Emigration to the United States during the First Half of the Nineteenth Century as a Social Protest Movement," in Hans L. Trefousse, ed., *Germany and America: Essays on Problems of International Relations and Immigration* (New York: Brooklyn College Press, 1980), 106–7; Walter D. Kamphoefner, "Dreissiger and Forty-eighter: The Political Influence of Two Generations of German Political Exiles," in ibid., 89–99; Carl Wittke, *Refugees of Revolution: The German Forty-eighters in America* (Philadelphia: University of Pennsylvania Press, 1952); Adolf E. Zucker, *The Forty-eighters: Political Refugees of the German Revolution of 1848* (New York: Columbia University Press, 1950). The last two works are good examples of earlier scholarship focusing on the split between the "Greens" and the "Greys" and the criticality of the Forty-eighters in galvanizing the great majority of the Northern Germans behind the Republican and, later, Union cause. Subsequent scholarship, such as Kamphoefner's article, has shown that the two waves of German emigrés tended to get along much better than Wittke or Zucker would have us believe and that these leaders exercised only a limited amount of power over rank-and-file Germans (as the work of the ethnoculturalists substantiates). See James M. Bergquist, "The Forty-eighters and the Politics of the 1850s," in Trefousse, *Germany and America,* for a good explanation of this argument. However, in "'Auch unse Deutschland muss einmal frei werden': The Immigrant Civil War Experience as a Mirror on Political Conditions in Germany," in David E. Barclay and Elisabeth Glaser-Schmidt, eds., *Transatlantic Images and Perceptions: Germany and America since 1776* (Cambridge: Cambridge University Press in association with the German Historical Institute, Washington, DC, 1997), Kamphoefner makes a strong case for the idea that many common German immigrants carried with them, in various degrees of sophistication, the ideals of the 1848 revolution and viewed their participation in the Civil War as an extension of the fight for freedom that had failed in Europe: "a clear linkage can be seen between republican idealism on both sides of the Atlantic" (106).

20. Lesley Ann Kawaguchi, "Diverging Political Affiliations and Ethnic Perspectives: Philadelphia Germans and Antebellum Politics," *Journal of American Ethnic History* 13, no. 2 (winter 1994): 3–29; Nadel, *Little Germany;* Frederick C. Luebke, *Germans in the New World: Essays in the History of Immigration* (Chicago: University of Illinois Press, 1990), 8–82; Kathleen Neils Conzen, *Immigrant Milwaukee, 1836–1860: Accomodation and Community in a Frontier City* (Cambridge: Harvard University Press, 1976), particularly chaps. 1 and 4; Bruce Levine, *The Spirit of 1848: German Immigrants, Labor Conflict, and the Coming of the Civil War* (Chicago: University of Illinois Press, 1992), particularly chaps. 4, 5, 8, and 9; Michael Holt, *Forging a Majority: The Formation of the Republican Party in Pittsburgh, 1848–1860* (New Haven, CT: Yale University Press, 1969); Paul J. Kleppner, "Lincoln and the Immigrant Vote: A Case of Religious Polarization," in Frederick C. Luebke, ed., *Ethnic Voters and the Election of Lincoln* (Lincoln: University of Nebraska Press, 1971); Paul J. Kleppner, *The Cross of Culture: A Social Analysis of Midwestern Politics, 1850–1900* (New York: Free Press, 1970).

21. Nadel, *Little Germany,* 8; Kawaguchi, "Diverging Political Affiliations," 14–20; James M. Bergquist, "Germans and the City," in Miller, *Germans in America,* 40–9; Conzen, *Immigrant Milwaukee,* 6–7,

and "Patterns of German-American History," 24–5, 28–9. Conzen also makes an eloquent statement regarding the ironic situation presented by the little Germanies: They fostered "the economic, political, and cultural participation which encouraged painless adjustment and good living conditions for many but which also encouraged the postponement of assimilation" (*Immigrant Milwaukee,* 7). She and Nadel have argued that the ethnic urban neighborhoods were actually practical and necessary agents of assimilation into American society, but they created feelings of separateness and distinction from the Anglo-American majority, thus strengthening ethnic consciousness and retarding Americanization. This contention is supported by Jörg Echternkamp's work on the Baltimore Germans, which argues that the multiplicity of German clubs and societies "supported a notion of 'community' that depended upon an ethnocultural network of communication and interactions." See his essay "Emerging Ethnicity: The German Experience in Antebellum Baltimore," *Maryland Historical Magazine* 86, no. 1 (spring 1991): 1–22.

22. Conzen, *Immigrant Milwaukee,* 6–7, and "Patterns of German-American History," 28–9.

23. Ray Allen Billington, *The Protestant Crusade, 1800–1860: A Study of the Origins of American Nativism* (1938; reprint, Gloucester, MA: Peter Smith, 1963), 328–9, 388–9, 396, 430; Dale T. Knobel, *"America for the Americans": The Nativist Movement in the United States* (New York: Twayne Publishers, 1996), 94, 120–1, 123–5.

24. Tyler Anbinder, *Nativism and Slavery: The Northern Know Nothings and the Politics of the 1850s* (New York: Oxford University Press, 1992), 62–3. Interestingly, Anbinder asserts that some "Pennsylvania Germans"—most likely Pennsylvania Dutch, based on his county voting statistics and analysis—had actually voted for the Know-Nothings because of the party's virulent anti-Catholic message. Such an appeal might have been effective among Lutherans and Reformed, who, like the nativists, feared the influence of popery and other Old World hierarchies that reminded them of the Europe their ancestors had left only a few generations earlier (see 65–7).

25. Knobel, *"America for the Americans,"* 99–100; Dale T. Knobel, *Paddy and the Republic: Ethnicity and Nationality in Antebellum America* (Middletown, CT: Wesleyan University Press, 1986), 167–8; Oscar Handlin, *Boston's Immigrants, 1790–1880: A Study in Acculturation* (1941; reprint, New York: Atheneum, 1974), 203–6; Kawaguchi, "Diverging Political Affiliations," 5–11. Kawaguchi also notes that temperance issues played a role in the voting behavior of Philadelphia's Germans in the 1850s, though it took a definite backseat to concerns over nativism. Despite the nativist stigma, she notes that the Republicans were able to attract substantial (though not majoritarian) support from Germans in the city due to a complex variety of factors: lingering differences among Northern and Southern Germans in the various voluntary societies, religious conflicts between Catholics and Protestants, diverse visions for the future of Philadelphia's Deutschtum among leaders, and the skill of Anglo-American Republican leaders in disguising the nativist roots of their party. A thesis by Eric W. Bright about Richmond Germans concludes that nativism was "the key that unlocks the door to understanding German-American patriotism in Confederate Richmond." Bright's research offers an interesting comparison to the experience of Philadelphia's Germans. See his "'Nothing to Fear from the Influence of Foreigners': The Patriotism of Richmond German-Americans during the Civil War" (master's thesis, Virginia Polytechnic and State University, 1999).

26. Yoder, "The 'Dutchman' and the 'Deitschlenner,'" 1–6, and "The Pennsylvania Germans," 51–3.

27. Yoder, "The 'Dutchman' and the 'Deitschlenner,'" 1–6; Klein, "Historical Problems," 28–9.

CHAPTER 2

1. John Higham, *Strangers in the Land: Patterns of American Nativism, 1860–1925* (New York: Atheneum, 1963), 13.

2. James M. McPherson, *Battle Cry of Freedom: The Civil War Era* (New York: Oxford University Press, 1988), 339–47. Throughout the chapter, original German quotes are given in English (translated by the author) and noted as such.

3. Reid Mitchell, *Civil War Soldiers: Their Expectations and Their Experiences* (New York: Simon and Schuster, 1988), 306–13. For thorough discussions of the African-Americans' struggle to participate in the war, see Dudley Taylor Cornish, *The Sable Arm: Negro Troops in the Union Army, 1861–1865*

(1956; reprint, New York: W. W. Norton, 1966); George Washington Williams, *A History of Negro Troops in the War of the Rebellion, 1861–1865* (1888; reprint, New York: Bergman Publishers, 1968); and James M. McPherson, *The Negro's Civil War* (New York: Vintage Books, 1965). Political exiles had founded the turnverein clubs, which combined physical fitness with military preparedness for the coming fight for liberty and democracy in Europe. Horst Ueberhorst, *Turner unterm Sternenbanner: Der Kampf der deutsch-amerikanischen Turner für Einheit, Freiheit und soziale Gerechtigkeit, 1848 bis 1918* (München: Heinz Moos, 1978), 44f., 80–5; Ralf Wagner, "Zwischen Tradition und Fortschritt: Zur gesellschaftspolitischen und kulturellen Entwicklung der deutschamerikanischen Turnerbewegung am Beispiel Milwaukees und Chicagos, 1850–1920" (Ph.D. diss., Ludwig-Maximilians-Universität, Munich, 1988), 103–9; Gustav Tafel, *"Die Neuner," Eine Schilderung der Kriegsjahre des 9ten Regiments Ohio, vol. Infanterie, vom 17 April 1861 bis 7 Juni 1864* (Cincinnati: S. Rosenthal, 1897), 15. The following works are still the only comprehensive sources for research on the German-American element in the Union army: Wilhelm Kaufmann, *Die Deutschen im Amerikanischen Bürgerkriege* (1911; reprint, Carlisle, PA: John Kallman Publishers, 1999) (hereafter cited as *Germans*); Ella Lonn, *Foreigners in the Union Army and Navy* (1951; reprint, New York: Peter Smith, 1969); and William L. Burton, *Melting Pot Soldiers: The Union's Ethnic Regiments* (1988; reprint, New York: Fordham University Press, 1998).

4. Louis Blenker to Simon Cameron, July 25, 1861, in *The War of the Rebellion: A Compilation of the Official Records of the Union and Confederate Armies,* 127 vols. (Washington, DC: Government Printing Office, 1880–1901), ser. III, vol. 1, 458f. (hereafter cited as *OR*).

5. Brig.-Gen. Louis Blenker to Maj.-Gen. McClellan, Commanding Army of the Potomac, August 27, 1861, *OR,* ser. III, vol. 1, 458.

6. Translated from Wolfgang Helbich and Walter D. Kamphoefner, eds., *Deutsche im amerikanischen Bürgerkrieg: Briefe von Front und Farm 1861–1865* (Paderborn: Ferdinand Schöningh, 2002), 256; Wolfgang Helbich, Walter D. Kamphoefner, and Ulrike Sommer, eds., *Briefe aus Amerika: Deutsche Auswanderer schreiben aus der Neuen Welt* (Munich: C. H. Beck, 1988), 13–5; Bruce Levine, *The Spirit of 1848: German Immigrants, Labor Conflict, and the Coming of the Civil War* (Urbana: University of Illinois Press, 1992), 67f., 119; Bell I. Wiley, *The Life of Billy Yank: The Common Soldier of the Union* (Baton Rouge: Louisiana State University Press, 1952), 37f.; Helbich and Kamphoefner, *Deutsche,* 76–9, Burton, *Melting Pot Soldiers,* 67; LaVerne Rippley, *The German-Americans* (Boston: Twayne Publishers, 1976), 65–70. See also case studies that discuss the motivations of individual German Americans: Earl J. Hess, *A German in the Yankee Fatherland—The Civil War Letters of Henry A. Kircher* (Kent, OH: Kent State University Press, 1983); Dieter Cunz, "Civil War Letters of a German Immigrant, Ferdinand Cunz," *American-German Review* 11 (1944): 30–3; Robert C. Goodell and P. A. M. Taylor, "A German Immigrant in the Union Army: Selected Letters of Valentin Bechler," *Journal of American Studies* 4 (February 1971): 145–62; Antonius Holtmann, ed., *"Für Gans America Gehe ich nich Wieder Bei die Solldaten . . .": Briefe des Ochtruper Auswanderers Theodor Heinrich Brandes aus dem amerikanischen Bürgerkrieg* (Bremen: Edition Temmen, 1999).

7. Hartmut Keil, "German Immigrants and African-Americans in Mid-Nineteenth Century America," in Ragnhild Fiebig-von Hase and U. Lehmkuhl, eds., *Enemy Images in American History* (Providence, RI: Berghahn Books, 1997), 143. Thus, Lonn's judgment may be a little too simplistic when she asserts that "probably the motive which usually swayed the common soldier among the foreigners as a whole was the desire to extirpate slavery; this gave the struggle a moral aspect and turned the war in a sense into a holy crusade." Conforming to the myth of a general anti-slavery sentiment among immigrants, she added that "the contact of the foreign-born soldier with slavery during the war only deepened his feeling against it." Lonn, *Foreigners,* 78; Hans L. Trefousse, *Carl Schurz: A Biography* (Knoxville: University of Tennessee Press, 1982), 58–79; Kaufmann, *Germans,* 276; Fritz Anneke, *Der Zweite Freiheitskampf der Vereinigten Staaten von Amerika* (Frankfurt am Main: J. D. Sauerlander, 1861).

8. Stephen D. Engle, "A Raised Consciousness: Franz Sigel and German Ethnic Identity in the Civil War," *Yearbook of German-American Studies* 34 (1999): 1f.; Christian B. Keller, "Pennsylvania and Virginia Germans during the Civil War: A Brief History and Comparative Analysis," *Virginia Magazine of History and Biography* 109, no. 1 (2001): 37f. To a large extent, the influence of the German-language newspapers forged a general sense of ethnic togetherness among immigrants from

German-speaking Europe. The highly publicized fates of famous officers such as Franz Sigel and Ludwig Blenker further strengthened ethnic bonds within the German-American population, which was ever suspicious of nativist treatment. Robert E. Cazden, *A Social History of the German Book Trade in America to the Civil War* (Columbia: Camden House, 1984), 526; Carl Wittke, *The German-Language Press in America* (Lexington: University of Kentucky Press, 1957).

9. Figures about ethnic participation in the Civil War are necessarily rough estimations, given the incomplete regimental records and the irregular recording of soldiers' national and ethnic backgrounds. The numbers of German Union soldiers are discussed in Benjamin A. Gould, *Investigations in the Military and Anthropological Statistics of the American Soldier* (New York: Hurd and Houghton, 1869), 27f.; Joseph G. Rosengarten, *The German Soldier in the Wars of the United States* (Philadelphia: J. B. Lippincott, 1886), 90f.; Kaufmann, *Germans,* 77, 102; Lonn, *Foreigners,* 577f.; Burton, *Melting Pot Soldiers,* 110; Diary of August V. Kautz, August 16, 1861, Manuscript Division, Library of Congress.

10. I use the term "myth of 1860" to explain the transformation of the Civil War into a moral conflict by most postwar ethnic spokespersons. Claims that the Germans had elected Lincoln and afterward saved Missouri for the Union settled in the ethnic consciousness during and after the war and decidedly shaped the way German-Americans viewed their participation in the conflict. German-American memoirs, historical writings, and newspapers upheld that myth with the purpose of underlining the Germans' social and political contributions to the reformation of American society. Just as the states of the former Confederacy created a cultural and historical identity through the myth of the lost cause only after their defeat, the Germans of the United States utilized their own myths to promote ethnic and historical continuity.

11. Michael Fellman, *Inside War: The Guerrilla Conflict in Missouri during the American Civil War* (New York: Oxford University Press, 1989), 39f.; translated from *Westliche Post* (St. Louis), May 8, 1861; Trefousse, *Carl Schurz,* 92.

12. William E. Parrish, *Turbulent Partnership: Missouri and the Union, 1861–1865* (Columbia: University of Missouri Press, 1963), 7; Jay Monaghan, *Civil War on the Western Border, 1854–1865* (New York: Bonanza Books, 1955), 118–28; Steven Rowan, ed., *Germans for a Free Missouri: Translations from the St. Louis Radical Press, 1857–1862* (Columbia: University of Missouri Press, 1983), 35–41; Stephen D. Engle, *Yankee Dutchman: The Life of Franz Sigel* (Fayetteville: University of Arkansas Press, 1993), 55–60. Ethnic narratives enthusiastically accepted the belief that the Germans had saved that state for the Union. Although they had indeed rescued the city of St. Louis from a material Confederate threat, the Unionist Germans always remained a minority in Missouri. The fierce guerrilla fighting that haunted the state throughout the war proved that neither North nor South had established dominance among the Missouri population. James N. Primm, "Missouri, St. Louis, and the Secession Crisis," in Rowan, *Germans for a Free Missouri,* 16–22; Frederick C. Luebke, "German Immigrants and American Politics: Problems of Leadership, Parties, and Issues," in Randall M. Miller, ed., *Germans in America* (Philadelphia: German Society of Pennsylvania, 1984), 64; Andreas Dorpalen, "The German Element and the Issues of the Civil War," *Mississippi Valley Historical Revue* 29 (June 1942) 64f.

13. Translated from *Westliche Post* (St. Louis), May 8, 1861.

14. Earl J. Hess, "Sigel's Resignation: A Study in German-Americanism and the Civil War," *Civil War History* 26, no. 1 (March 1980): 5–17; Wittke, *German-Language Press,* 150; Engle, "Raised Consciousness," 4f.; Monaghan, *Civil War on the Western Border,* 239–51.

15. McPherson, *Battle Cry,* 348f.

16. Special Orders No. 99, Hdqs. Army of the Potomac, October 12, 1861, *OR,* ser. I, vol. 51, pt. 1, 497; *OR,* ser. I, vol. 5, 716; Kaufmann, *Germans,* 104; Keller, "Germans during the Civil War," 48. In his article, Keller comprehensively outlines the difficulties in determining "ethnic" and "nonethnic" regiments.

17. Trefousse, *Carl Schurz,* 115–7; August V. Kautz, *Reminiscences of the Civil War* (typed manuscript, Manuscript Division, Library of Congress), 3.

18. Kaufmann, *Germans,* 97–9.

19. Report of Brig.-Gen. John Newton, December 6, 1861, *OR,* ser. I, vol. 5, 455; Helbich and Kamphoefner, *Deutsche,* 72, 145, 200f.

20. For discussions of the American professional military tradition, see Marcus Cunliffe, *Soldiers and Civilians: The Martial Spirit in America, 1775–1865* (Boston: Little, Brown, 1968); Edward M. Coffman, *The Old Army: A Portrait of the American Army in Peacetime, 1784–1898* (New York: Oxford University Press, 1986); Engle, *Yankee Dutchman,* 231. See also Burton, *Melting Pot Soldiers,* 85–91.

21. McPherson, *Battle Cry,* 424–7.

22. Kaufmann, *Germans,* 107; report of Maj.-Gen. John A. McClernand, April 24, 1862, *OR,* ser. I, vol. 10, pt. 1, 121; McPherson, *Battle Cry,* 407–13. Several of Buell's regiments included ethnic companies, but the Germans' role in the battle of Shiloh has not yet been adequately researched.

23. McPherson, *Battle Cry,* 425.

24. Blenker to Hon. Edwin M. Stanton, April 13, 1862, *OR,* ser. I, vol. 51, pt. 1, 572; Kaufmann, *Germans,* 167–72; report of Maj. Gen. John C. Frémont, December 30, 1865, *OR,* ser. I, vol. 15, 8. Kaufmann, in his filiopietistic style, puts all the blame for the misconduct during Blenker's march on the "Sicilian robber band of the Garibaldi Regiment." In condemning the Italian element of that multiethnic regiment, he doubtlessly wanted to exculpate its German members. Although written for a German audience, Kaufmann's argument is clearly in line with contemporary American views of southern and eastern European immigrants as inherently inferior people. Kaufmann, *Germans,* 172.

25. Frank E. Vandiver, *Mighty Stonewall* (1957; reprint, New York: 1989), 245–83.

26. Robert K. Krick, *Conquering the Valley: Stonewall Jackson at Port Republic* (New York: William Morrow, 1996), 183–209; McPherson, *Battle Cry,* 458–60; William F. Fox, *Regimental Losses in the American Civil War, 1861–1865* (Albany, NY: Albany Publishing Company, 1889), 429.

27. Kaufmann, *Germans,* 172–5; report of Capt. Michael Wiedrich, June 12, 1862, *OR,* ser. I, vol. 15, 670.

28. McPherson, *Battle Cry,* 461–71.

29. Ibid., 404f., 488f.; Engle, *Yankee Dutchman,* 105–18, 127–31, 146f.; Trefousse, *Carl Schurz,* 115–20. Sources indicate the possibility that Bohlen was actually killed by his own men of the 75th Pennsylvania in retribution for a mismanaged crossing of the Rappahannock River earlier that spring when the German division was en route to Frémont. Ignoring the dangerously swollen stream, Bohlen sent a boat that subsequently capsized, drowning seventy men. Kaufmann, *Germans,* 181, 279f.

30. General [Order] No. 21, Headquarters Army of Virginia, August 16, 1862, *OR,* ser. I, vol. 16, 135; McPherson, *Battle Cry,* 524–9.

31. Kaufmann, *Germans,* 185, 302; report of Maj.-Gen. Franz Sigel, September 16, 1862, *OR,* ser. I, vol. 16, 269; Engle, *Yankee Dutchman,* 145; McPherson, *Battle Cry,* 524–32; John J. Hennessy, *Return to Bull Run: The Campaign and Battle of Second Manassas* (New York: Simon and Schuster, 1993), 215–23, 403–6.

32. Kaufmann, *Germans,* 189, 263; Trefousse, *Carl Schurz,* 123; report of Brig.-Gen. Carl Schurz, September 2, 1862, *OR,* ser. 1, vol. 16, 302.

33. McPherson, *Battle Cry,* 532; Maj.-Gen. J. Pope to Maj.-Gen. H. W. Halleck, November 20, 1862, *OR,* ser. I, vol. 12, pt. 3, 825; Engle, *Yankee Dutchman,* 146.

34. Stephen W. Sears, *Landscape Turned Red: The Battle of Antietam* (New York: Popular Library Books, 1985), 199–328, 381–6; McPherson, *Battle Cry,* 534–45.

35. Kaufmann, *Germans,* 279, 281; report of Col. William H. Irwin, September 22, 1862, *OR,* ser. I, vol. 19, pt. 1, 412; report of Brig.-Gen. William S. Hancock, September 29, 1862, ibid., 281.

36. McPherson, *Battle Cry,* 544f., 569–74; Trefousse, *Carl Schurz,* 127.

37. Engle, *Yankee Dutchman,* 158.

38. McPherson, *Battle Cry,* 638–46; Lonn, *Foreigners,* 515f.

39. Kaufmann, *Germans,* 207; Lonn, *Foreigners,* 513–7; for detailed accounts of the battle of Chancellorsville, see Ernest B. Ferguson, *Chancellorsville: The Souls of the Brave* (New York: Alfred A. Knopf, 1993), and Stephen W. Sears, *Chancellorsville* (Boston: Houghton Mifflin, 1996).

40. Kaufmann, *Germans,* 281, 285; Maj.-Gen. O. O. Howard to Brig.-Gen. S. Williams, Assistant Adjutant-General, Army of the Potomac, May 14, 1863, *OR,* ser. I, vol. 51, pt. 1, 1041.

41. Vandiver, *Mighty Stonewall,* 478–94; Lonn, *Foreigners,* 519; Mark M. Boatner III, *The Civil War Dictionary* (New York: Vintage Books, 1991), 138–40. It has been a matter of serious discussion whether

the battle of Chancellorsville would have taken a different turn had Sigel led his old corps. In any case, the thin-skinned general resigned just at the wrong moment. After he relinquished his command in March, the Eleventh Corps was strengthened substantially under his successor Howard. Sigel's personal feud with Halleck prevented the German from reclaiming his old position. Engle, *Yankee Dutchman,* 158–60; Kaufmann, *Germans,* 262f.

42. Lonn, *Foreigners,* 512, 594f.; Trefousse, *Carl Schurz,* 132–6; McPherson, *Battle Cry,* 641–63; Levine, *Spirit of 1848,* 257; *New York Times,* May 5, 1863; *New York Herald,* May 6, 1863; Maj.-Gen. C. Schurz to E. M. Stanton, Secretary of War, May 18, 1863, *OR,* ser. 1, vol. 25, pt. 1, 658f.; Maj.-Gen. C. Schurz to Maj.-Gen. O. O. Howard, May 21, 1863, *OR,* ser. I, vol. 25, pt. 1, 659; Wittke, *German-Language Press,* 151f.

43. Herman M. Hattaway, "The Civil War Armies: Creation, Mobilization, and Development," in Stig Förster and Jörg Nagler, eds., *On the Road to Total War: The American Civil War and the German Wars of Unification* (Cambridge: Oxford University Press, 1997), 186.

CHAPTER 3

1. Victor Wolfgang von Hagen, *The Germanic People in America* (Norman: University of Oklahoma Press, 1976), 89–106; Roland Paul and Karl Scherer *Pfälzer in Amerika: Palatines in America* (Kaiserslautern Institute fur Pfalzische Geschichte und Volkskunde, Kaiserslautern, 1995), 95; Charles H. Glatfelter, *The Pennsylvania Germans: A Brief Account of Their Influence on Pennsylvania* (University Park: Pennsylvania Historical Association, 1980), 3.

2. Steven M. Nolt, *Foreigners in Their Own Land: Pennsylvania Germans in the Early Republic* (University Park: Pennsylvania State University Press, 2002), 8.

3. Don Yoder, "Palatine, Hessian, Dutchman: Three Images of the German in America," in Albert F. Buffington, Don Yoder, Walter Klinefelter, Larry M. Neff, Mary Hammond Sullivan, and Frederick S. Weiser, eds., *Ebbes fer Alles-Ebber Ebbes fer Dich: Something for Everyone—Something for You* (Breinigsville: Pennsylvania German Society, 1980), 107–8.

4. Christian B. Keller, "The Reaction of Eastern Pennsylvania's German Press to the Secession Crisis: Compromise or Conflict?" *Yearbook of German-American Studies* 34 (2000): 40–1, 53.

5. Ibid., 53.

6. Morton L. Montgomery, *Historical and Biographical Annals of Berks County, vol. 1* (Chicago: J. H. Beers, 1899), 125; John M. Lawlor, Jr., "Anti-War Sentiment of the Democratic Party in Berks County," (master's thesis, Kutztown University, 1981), 42–3; Richard E. Matthews, *Lehigh County Pennsylvania in the Civil War: An Account* (Lehighton, PA: Times News Printing, 1989) 18, 26, 31, 34, 37, n. 58.

7. Samuel P. Bates, *History of the Pennsylvania Volunteers, 1861–1865,* 5 vols. (Harrisburg: B. Singerly, State Printer, 1869–71), 1:1–8. Murphy stated, "When the chips were down and the Union at stake, Schuylkill County men forgot politics and ancestry to join in the march to the battlefields. Some military companies were composed nearly entirely of English, Welsh, Scots, Germans and Irish." When Murphy spoke of the Germans, he was referring to the Pennsylvania Dutch. Of the four companies he listed as examples, two were Pennsylvania Dutch or German. "Typical of those who left within seven days of the First Defenders: Captain James Brennan's Columbian Infantry of Glen Carbon, none less than five feet, nine inches in height, some six feet, two inches, whose 55 men included nine Brennans, four Keatings and three Lawlors. Captain H. J. Hendler's Washington Yeagers of Pottsville with such names as Schlitzer, Becker, Rassiter, Reinhardt, Foss, Dockweiler and Gluntz. Captain William H. Jennings of Jenning's Lafayette Rifles of St. Clair with Privates Morgan, Price, Jenkins, Jones, Thomas, Reese, Evans and Davis. And Captain H. H. Bechtel's Washington Light Infantry of Pine Grove with the typical names of Barr, Lookingbill, Rump, Schrope, Zimmerman, Schwartz and Spancake." Paul Murphy, "Schuylkill County in First 90 Days," in Herwood E. Hobbs et al., *Schuylkill County in the Civil War* (Pottsville, PA: Historical Society of Schuylkill County, 1961), 42. It is apparent that Bechtel's and Hendler's companies were Pennsylvania Dutch, and it is interesting to note the ethnicity identified with local communities; this is a good example of ethnic communities.

8. Throughout the Civil War, there were no federal government–related camps of instruction. Civil War soldiers received haphazard training and were often sent to the front without any formal training at all. In Pennsylvania, camps of rendezvous were established, where recruits from particular geographic regions would report. There, they would organize into companies and then into regiments. The regiment was the major building block of the Civil War army, consisting of 10 companies with 100 men per company. Once the regiments were organized, the senior officers were appointed, and the regiments were assigned state seniority numbers determined by the time of enlistment. Therefore, when discussing Pennsylvania regiments, it is important to know the regimental number, such as the 153d Pennsylvania Volunteer Infantry. Camp Curtin in Harrisburg was one of the major camps of rendezvous in Pennsylvania. For more information on Camp Curtin, see William J. Miller, *The Training of an Army: Camp Curtin and the North's Civil War* (Shippensburg, PA: White Mane Publishing Company, 1990).

9. The regiments listed had a strong Pennsylvania Dutch influence in their ranks, but because of the density of men of Pennsylvania Dutch ethnicity in the state, nearly every regiment had a few. These numbers were determined by studying all the names listed in Bates's five volumes of *History of Pennsylvania Volunteers* and by analyzing the counties from which the regiments were formed. These surnames were compared with names in the genealogical library of the Pennsylvania German Heritage Center at Kutztown University of Pennsylvania.

10. The recruitment of companies occurred at the local level and was a do-it-yourself mobilization. A person of some standing would announce that he was recruiting a company and would appeal to the men to enlist. Once a company reached the required number, the men would report to Camp Curtin or another designated camp of rendezvous. This explains the mixture of Pennsylvania Dutch companies with English companies. (A common practice among the Pennsylvania Dutch was to label anyone who did not speak the Pennsylvania Dutch dialect as "English.") For further information on the relationships between the Pennsylvania Dutch and their "English" neighbors, see Philip E. Pendleton's study *Oley Valley Heritage: The Colonial Years 1700–1775* (Birdsboro: Pennsylvania German Society, 1994), 137–40.

11. Ernest B. Furguson *Chancellorsville 1863: The Souls of the Brave* (New York: Alfred A. Knopf, 1992), 160, 173–4.

12. Bates, *History of Pennsylvania Volunteers,* 3:28–65.

13. Wilbur S. Nye, *Here Come the Rebels* (Dayton, OH: Press of Morningside Bookshop, 1998), 75–6.

14. Ibid., 76–7; U.S. War Department, *The War of the Rebellion: A Compilation of the Official Records of the Union and Confederate Armies,* 127 vols. (Washington, DC: Government Printing Office, 1880–1901), ser. I, vol. 27, pt. 2, 42, 53, 163 (hereafter cited as *OR;* unless otherwise stated, all references are to series I).

15. Nye, *Here Come the Rebels,* 120. The 67th Pennsylvania Volunteer Infantry was formed in March 1862 near Philadelphia and had companies from Carbon, Philadelphia, Pike, Monroe, Indiana, Westmoreland, Clarion, Jefferson, Northampton, and Schuylkill Counties. The highest percentage of Pennsylvania Dutch troops were found in companies H and K, recruited in Northampton and Schuylkill Counties.

16. Richard A. Sauers, *Advance the Colors: Pennsylvania Civil War Battle Flags* (Lebanon, PA: Sowers Printing Co., 1987), 184; Nye, *Here Come the Rebels,* 120.

17. *OR,* vol. 27, pt. 2, 49.

18. Ibid., 119.

19. Ibid., 197.

20. Bates, *History of Pennsylvania Volunteers,* 5:124.

21. Ibid., 223; *OR,* vol. 27, pt. 2, 79–80.

22. Bates, *History of Pennsylvania Volunteers,* 5:1222–3.

23. Samuel G. Hefelbower, *History of Gettysburg College, 1832–1932* (Gettysburg; 1932), chap. 20.

24. Nye, *Here Come the Rebels,* 271–2; Samuel W. Pennypacker, *Six Weeks in Uniform: Being the Record of a Term in the Military Service of the United States in the Gettysburg Campaign of 1863. 26th PA Emergency Infantry June 16 to August 1, 1863* (Norristown, PA: County of Montgomery, 2002), 19.

25. Pennypacker, *Six Weeks in Uniform,* 27.

26. Nye, *Here Come the Rebels,* 272–3. The route of retreat was probably over Crooked Creek Road.
27. Grant-Lee ed., *Battles and Leaders of the Civil War,* (Harrisburg: Archive Society, 1991), vol. 3, pt. 1, 289; *OR,* vol. 27, pt. 2, 344. Henry Melchoir Muhlenberg Richards was of Pennsylvania German stock. He became a noted historian of Pennsylvania Germans in the French and Indian War and the American Revolution. He eventually became president of the Pennsylvania German Society.
28. Bates, *History of Pennsylvania Volunteers,* 5:1236–8.
29. David L. Valuska, "North Musters Forces to Meet Rebel Threat to Pennsylvania," *Reading Eagle,* February 19, 1995, A19. Bates, *History of Pennsylvania Volunteers,* 5:1236–8. A check of the records in Bates shows that some companies of the 27th Pennsylvania Militia had as high as 90 percent Pennsylvania Dutch recruits, while their representation in other companies was as low as 28 percent.
30. Nye, *Here Come the Rebels,* 285; Valuska, "North Musters Forces." See also the periodicals, papers, and pamphlets in the Columbia Historic Preservation Society and York County Historical Society.
31. Bates, *History of Pennsylvania Volunteers,* 5:1231–4.
32. *OR,* vol. 27, pt. 2, 279.
33. Nye, *Here Come the Rebels,* 292–3.
34. Harriet W. Stewart, *History of Cumberland County* (n.p., n.d) 103–4; Nye, *Here Come the Rebels,* 302.

CHAPTER 4

1. There are few studies of Northern civilians during the war. Two notable exceptions are Philip Shaw Paludan, *A People's Contest: The Union and Civil War, 1861–1865* (Lawrence: University Press of Kansas, 1988, 1996 rev.), and J. Matthew Gallman, *The North Fights the Civil War: The Home Front* (Chicago: Ivan R. Dee, 1994). Neither book contains more than a brief acknowledgment that ethnic Germans lived in the North and fought in the war. By claiming that the Gettysburg campaign was the most "memorable" for the Pennsylvania Dutch, I do not imply that the burning of Chambersburg was not traumatic for the Pennsylvania Dutch of Franklin County. This chapter, however, attempts to provide a broader picture of the behavior of Pennsylvania Dutch throughout southern Pennsylvania during a military campaign that arguably affected more people and brought the war to a greater number of communities.
2. The second half of my title was derived from Mark Grimsley, *The Hard Hand of War: Union Military Policy toward Southern Civilians, 1861–1865* (New York: Cambridge University Press, 1995).
3. Mark A. Hornberger, "Germans in Pennsylvania 1800, 1850 and 1880: A Spatial Perspective," *Yearbook of German-American Studies* 24 (1989): 99.
4. Francis T. Hoover, *Enemies in the Rear: Or, A Golden Circle Squared* (Boston: Arena Publishing Company, 1895), 20–1; Christian B. Keller, "The Reaction of Eastern Pennsylvania's German Press to the Secession Crisis: Compromise or Conflict?" *Yearbook of German-American Studies* 34 (winter 1999): 5–20; Christian B. Keller, "Germans in Civil War–Era Pennsylvania: Ethnic Identity and the Problem of Americanization" (Ph.D. diss., Pennsylvania State University, 2001), 15–27, 57–93.
5. For example, Dunker Rachel Cormany lamented the plight of free blacks in Chambersburg during the Confederate invasion. "Soon [the rebs] were hunting up the contrabands and driving them off by droves. O! How it grated on our hearts to have to sit quietly & look at such brutal deeds. . . . Some of the colored people who were raised here were taken along—I sat on the front porch as they were driven by just like we would drive cattle." Rachel Cormany diary entry, June 16, 1863, reprinted in James C. Mohr, ed., *The Cormany Diaries: A Northern Family in the Civil War* (Pittsburgh: University of Pittsburgh Press, 1982), 329–30. See also James O. Lehman, "Duties of the Mennonite Citizen: Controversy in the Lancaster Press Late in the Civil War," *Pennsylvania Mennonite Heritage* 8, no. 3 (July 1984). I would like to thank Mr. Lehman, archivist emeritus of Eastern Mennonite University, Harrisonburg, VA, for allowing me to consult his unpublished manuscript about Amish and Mennonites in the Civil War: "Conscience versus Loyalty: Mennonites and Amish in the North Face the Crises of the Civil War."
6. Samuel Cormany diary entry, September 9, 1862, reprinted in Mohr, *Cormany Diaries,* 229.

7. For a good account of the federal and state governments' attempts to raise emergency troops, as well as the English-language press's outrage at Pennsylvania's lethargic response, see Edwin B. Coddington, *The Gettysburg Campaign: A Study in Command* (New York: Charles Scribner's Sons, 1968), 136–41, and the *New York Times,* June 26, 1863. According to Coddington, there was even a "German artillery company" in Johnstown that "refused to be mustered in" unless its demand never to be taken outside of Pennsylvania was granted (142).

8. In cases in which I believe that the veracity of the anecdote is questionable, I provide commentary in the notes.

9. G. Moxley Sorrel, *Recollections of a Confederate Staff Officer,* ed. by Bell Irvin Wiley (Jackson, MS: McCowat-Mercer Press, 1958), 168–70; William W. Hassler, ed., *General to His Lady: The Civil War Letters of William Dorsey Pender to Fanny Pender* (Chapel Hill: University of North Carolina Press, 1965), 254; John J. Chandler to his sister, July 17, 1863 (John J. Chandler Papers, Virginia State Library), quoted in Coddington, *Gettysburg Campaign,* 157; Hodijah Lincoln Meade to Charlotte Randolph (Meade) Lane, July 19, 1863, quoted in Reid Mitchell, *Civil War Soldiers: Their Expectations and Their Experiences* (New York: Viking Press, 1988), 150; W. P. Conrad and Ted Alexander, *When War Passed This Way* (Greencastle, PA: Beidel Printing House, 1982), 140.

10. Mitchell, *Civil War Soldiers,* 25–8; *Knoxville Tennessee Register,* June 12, 1863, article reprinted in *Philadelphia Freie Presse,* June 24, 1863. Many Southerners believed the Union army to be largely composed of foreign elements, which they derisively called "hirelings." The idea that foreign mercenaries dominated Union ranks was ubiquitous in Southern propaganda. For a basic discussion of this topic, see J. Cutler Andrews, *The South Reports the Civil War* (Princeton, NJ: Princeton University Press, 1970). In reality, German immigrants and ethnically German troops composed up to 20 percent of the Union forces, and the Irish up to 15 percent.

11. Samuel Grove Sollenberger and Grace Hege, *Jacob Grove and Elizabeth Lesher Grove Family,* quoted in Lehman, "Conscience versus Loyalty," 35; Owen quoted in Conrad and Alexander, *When War Passed This Way,* 161.

12. Harry A. Hall, *A Johnny Reb Band from Salem: The Pride of Tarheelia* (Raleigh: North Carolina Confederate Centennial Commission, 1963), 42; J. B. Polley, "Hood's Texans in Pennsylvania," *Confederate Veteran* 5, no. 4 (November 1896): 377–9; John B. Gordon, *Reminiscences of the Civil War* (New York: Charles Scribner's Sons, 1903), 141. Salem, North Carolina, was settled predominantly by Moravians who had a German-language tradition, just like Pennsylvania's Moravians and pietist sects. This unknown soldier, from a regiment largely composed of Moravians, would have had no problem conversing in German.

13. Memoir of Frederick Mason Colston, Virginia Historical Society (hereafter VHS), quoted in Mitchell, *Civil War Soldiers,* 151; Coddington, *Gettysburg Campaign,* 157–8; Conrad and Alexander, *When War Passed This Way,* 138.

14. J. G. DeRoulhac Hamilton, ed., *The Papers of Randolph Abbott Shotwell,* 3 vols. (Raleigh: North Carolina Historical Commission, 1929–36), 1:490–1.

15. Chaplain Sheeron quoted in Mitchell, *Civil War Soldiers,* 154; see Coddington, *Gettysburg Campaign,* 141–2, and Mitchell, *Civil War Soldiers,* 153–4, for these historians' arguments regarding the possible relation between Pennsylvanian apathy and "good treatment" from the Confederates.

16. Gordon, *Reminiscences,* 143.

17. Ibid., 148–9. Admittedly, Gordon is a somewhat suspect eyewitness, as his "recollections are dripping with romanticism and full of half truths," according to Peter S. Carmichael, *The Confederate General,* vol. 3, 12. It is also well known that Gordon was a lost-cause apologist who wished to paint the defunct Confederacy in a positive light. However, Gordon's accounts of possible Dutch collaboration are intriguing, even if only half true, and point to the possibility that some Pennsylvania Dutch may have welcomed the Confederates.

18. Coddington, *Gettysburg Campaign,* 140–1, 148–9; Rachel Cormany diary entries, June 15 and 16, 1863, in Mohr, *Cormany Diaries,* 328–9.

19. There were no Quakers living in Franklin County at the time. The author is certainly referring to Mennonites, Dunkers, or perhaps Amish in this excerpt. To distinguish between passivity and collaboration, a parallel can be made here between southern Pennsylvania under Confederate occupa-

tion and occupied France in World War II. Although there were many geographic, ideological, and military differences, civilians in both areas came to accept what the French called "collaboration à raison," or collaboration for the greater good. Many French civilians accepted the German occupation at first because France's military loss had to be accepted. Although they did not actively collaborate with the Germans to defeat the Allies, they saw no reason to antagonize the soldiers who controlled their towns and villages. The enemy was there to stay, and no one knew how long he might remain. One had to bow to reality, regardless of the shame of occupation. The Pennsylvania Dutch, arch-realists, had a similar reaction to the Confederate invasion. Actively resisting the enemy would result in nothing but more lost property and perhaps mortal danger. Following the rules of the occupiers, such as providing food and supplies, was the sensible way to deal with the Confederates. A passive reaction to invasion made sense as long as the Confederates remained in control. Once the Confederates were in obvious retreat, passivity yielded to more aggressive actions, a sequence not dissimilar to what happened in France. For an excellent account of the plight of civilians in occupied France and a discussion of collaboration à raison, see Ian Ousby, *Occupation: The Ordeal of France, 1940–1944* (New York: St. Martin's Press, 1997), especially 85–6, 141–2, 201–2.

20. D. Augustus Dickert, *History of Kershaw's Brigade,* quoted in Conrad and Alexander, *When War Passed This Way,* 158.

21. Rachel Cormany diary entries, June 23 and 27, 1863, quoted in Mohr, *Cormany Diaries,* 334, 337. I do not view the supplying of rebel quartermasters with extra food to be evidence of collaboration. Perhaps the farmers who did this were copperheads, as Cormany accuses, but this is impossible to corroborate, and a little extra food in the hope of good treatment hardly constitutes treason.

22. Nathan S. Wolle to "dear cousin Sylvester," June 25, 1863, in P.H.C. Correspondence, Letters from Lititz, 1832, 1853–78, 1897, Moravian Archives, Bethlehem, PA.

23. It would be incorrect to completely equate the Moravian pacifistic doctrines with those of the other three groups. Although Moravians generally shunned conflict and bloodshed, they had fought in the Revolutionary War, and several young Moravians volunteered in 1861. They were not nearly as strict in their adherence to nonviolence as were the Mennonites, Amish, and Dunkers.

24. Edward de Schweinitz to "dear brother," June 30, 1863, in P.H.C. Correspondence, Moravian Archives; *Moravian,* July 2, 1863; Richmond E. Myers, "The Moravian Church and the Civil War," *Transactions of the Moravian Historical Society* 20 (pt. 2): 226–48.

25. Hege poem translated into English from the original German in the *Gospel Witness,* a Mennonite journal, December 5, 1906. Both the Hege poem and the Strite anecdote are cited in Lehman, "Conscience versus Loyalty," chap. 6.

26. Douglas Southall Freeman, Edwin Coddington, Reid Mitchell, and a host of other historians have commented on Lee's famous order commanding his troops to behave as gentlemen and to pay for all goods taken from civilians. In the case of the Pennsylvania Dutch, it appears that the Confederates generally followed Order Number 73; the Hege and Strite anecdotes were the only instances of unprovoked Confederate attacks against Dutch civilians I found.

27. Rachel Cormany diary entry, June 23, 1863, in Mohr, *Cormany Diaries,* 334; Catherine Horst Hunsecker, "Civil War Reminiscences," *Christian Monitor* 16 (January 1924): 406–7; Henry B. Hege to Henry G. Hege, July 12, 1863, reprinted in W. P. Conrad, *Conococheague: A History of the Greencastle-Antrim Community, 1736–1971* (Greencastle, PA: Greencastle-Antrim School District, 1971). The actual financial loss to some Dutch farmers was crippling, giving credence to their complaints. Coddington gives several examples of merchants and farmers fiscally ruined by Confederate foragers. Christian Bitner of Franklin County, for instance, lost "nineteen horses, two cows, a heifer and a bull, as well as quantities of food, tens tons of straw, harnesses, and tools of all kinds." Bitner also suffered the loss of almost all his fence rails, which were used as firewood and tent poles, and 379 trees and saplings. See Coddington, *Gettysburg Campaign,* 176.

28. *Reading Adler,* June 30, 1863. Interestingly, elite white Southerners also claimed the defense of property—their slaves—as justification for secession and loyalty to the Confederacy. See James M. McPherson, *What They Fought For, 1861–1865* (New York: Anchor Books, 1994), 52–4. Appeals from Richmond for Mennonites and Dunkers in the Shenandoah Valley to actively repel the Yankee invaders also fell on deaf ears, indicating that the nonresistant religious policies of both North-

ern and Southern German pacifists outweighed geographic and political considerations. See Samuel Horst, *Mennonites in the Confederacy* (Scottdale, PA: Herald Press, 1967), and Christian B. Keller, "Pennsylvania and Virginia Germans in the Civil War: A Brief History and Comparative Analysis," *Virginia Magazine of History and Biography* 109, no. 1 (spring 2001): 37–86.

29. Provost Marshal General Patrick, Army of the Potomac, journal entry, July 5, 1863, quoted in Coddington, *Gettysburg Campaign,* 141; Conrad and Alexander, *When War Passed This Way,* 139.

30. Cormany diary, June 27 and July 3, 1863, quoted in Mohr, *Cormany Diaries,* 337, 340. For a good synopsis of anecdotes of pro-Union displays in the face of the Confederates, see Mitchell, *Civil War Soldiers,* 151–2. Again, it is unclear whether these people were Pennsylvania Dutch.

31. Shook quoted in Jacob Hoke, *The Great Invasion of 1863; or General Lee in Pennsylvania. . . . With an Appendix Containing an Account of the Burning of Chambersburg* (reprint, Dayton, OH, 1913), 502–3; Imboden quoted in Clarence Buel, ed., *Battles and Leaders of the Civil War,* 4 vols. (New York: Century Company, 1887), 3:425. For a discussion of the relative strengths of the various religious denominations in Greencastle, see Conrad and Alexander, *When War Passed This Way,* 10, 17.

32. *Pittsburgher Demokrat,* June 29, July 2, 1863.

33. *Philadelphia Freie Presse,* July 1, 1863.

34. Coddington, *Gettysburg Campaign,* 140–2; Mitchell, *Civil War Soldiers,* 152; Jim Weeks, "'A Disgrace That Can Never Be Washed Out': Gettysburg and the Lingering Stigma of 1863," in William Blair and William A. Pencak, eds., *Making and Remaking Pennsylvania's Civil War* (University Park: Pennsylvania State University Press, 2001), 190–6.

35. Samuel H. Hurst, *Journal-History of the Seventy-third Ohio Volunteer Infantry* (Chillicothe, OH, 1866), 65; Sawyer quoted in John W. Schildt, *Roads from Gettysburg* (Parsons, WV: McClain Publishers, 1979), 61; unknown soldier from the 38th quoted in Conrad and Alexander, *When War Passed This Way,* 208.

36. Colonel Robert McFarland, 151st PA, to J. Horace McFarland, n.d., 151st PA file, Gettysburg National Military Park Library, Gettysburg, PA (hereafter GNMPL). In contrast to substantial evidence to the contrary, James H. Baum of the 46th Pennsylvania, himself of Pennsylvania German descent, remembered in 1910 that his regiment had been greeted "with children in red, white and blue badges, [singing] patriotic songs and waving the good old flag." Coffee and water were free for the taking, he recalled, and one woman he met expressed deep concern for the well-being of the Union troops. Whether Baum's memory was clouded by postwar nostalgia or exaggerated by the passage of time, and regardless of the ethnicity of the unknown townspeople, his remarks indicate that there must have been at least some southern Pennsylvanians who heartily welcomed the Northern troops. See *East Liverpool Morning Tribune,* July 9, 1910, pt. 1, copy in Timothy R. Brooks Collection, U.S. Army Military History Institute, Carlisle, PA (hereafter USAMHI).

37. *Harper's Weekly,* July 11, 1863, 448; *New York Times,* July 9, 1863. The *Times* editorial also pointed out the geographic and political background of the area: "this is Adams County—a neighbor to Copperhead York, which is still nearer to the stupid and stingy Berks."

38. Conrad and Alexander, *When War Passed This Way,* 218–20; see the numerous petitions in the Claims File, #14–CF, GNMPL, especially those of Peter Frey, John Herbst, Peter Culp, and Nicholas Eckenrode.

39. *22nd Annual Proceedings of the Annual Convention of the Evangelical Lutheran Synod of Eastern Pennsylvania, Convened in Milton, Pa, Sept. 30–Oct. 6, 1863* (Philadelphia, 1863), 10–1; "One Hundred and Seventeenth Annual Session," *Acts and Proceedings of the Synod of the German Reformed Church in the United States,* Carlisle, PA, October 1863 (Chambersburg, PA: M. Kieffer and Co., 1863), 30; Stephen L. Longenecker, *Piety and Tolerance: Pennsylvania German Religion, 1700–1850* (Metuchen, NJ: Scarecrow Press, 1994), 151; Rev. S. C. Albright, *The Story of the Moravian Congregation of York, PA* (York, PA: Maple Press, n.d.), 69–72; Stephen Morgan Smith, Moravian pastor in York, to "Dear Brother Wolle" (Peter Wolle), July 20, 27, 29, 1863, in P.E.C. Correspondence, York, PA, 1857–78 box, Moravian Archives. Smith returned three separate times to care for "our North Carolina brethren" in field hospitals around Gettysburg. His letters to Wolle indicate a far greater concern for the well-being of the Southern Moravian wounded than for the Northern wounded; in fact, he asked Wolle for money to take care of their needs and showed interest in following them to various

prison camps in New York and New Jersey. It could be argued that ethnicity, as defined by religious denomination, outweighed political considerations for Wolle.

40. Fannie J. Buehler, "Recollections of the Rebel Invasion and One Woman's Experience during the Battle of Gettysburg," original pamphlet published in 1896, copy in file 8–7, GNMPL, 19, 22–3; Isaac R. Dunkleberger Recollections, 1st U.S. Cavalry, Michael Winey Collection, USAMHI. In light of the strong Dutch belief in the sanctity of private property and the actions and attitudes of the Dutch before the battle, Dunkleberger's anecdote appears somewhat fantastic. Thirty tons of hay, for instance, represented the lion's share of a large farm's hay harvest for one year.

CHAPTER 5

1. Gregory Acken, ed., *Inside the Army of the Potomac: The Civil War Experience of Captain Francis Adams Donaldson* (Mechanicsburg, PA: Stackpole Books, 1998), 264.

2. Ibid.

3. Milo Quaife, ed., *From the Cannon's Mouth: The Civil War Letters of General Alpheus S. Williams* (Detroit, MI: Wayne State University Press, 1959), 239.

4. William W. Hassler Jr., ed., *The General to His Lady: The Civil War Letters of William Dorsey Pender to Fanny Pender* (Chapel Hill: University of North Carolina Press, 1965), 253.

5. U.S. War Department, *The War of the Rebellion: A Compilation of the Official Records of the Union and Confederate Armies,* 127 vols. (Washington, DC: Government Printing Office, 1880–1901), vol. 27, pt. 1, 923 (hereafter *OR*).

6. Harry W. Pfanz, *Gettysburg: The First Day* (Chapel Hill: University of North Carolina Press, 2001), 42.

7. Charles H. Veil to D. McConaughy, April 7, 1864, in Special Collections, Gettysburg College. All strength and loss figures throughout the chapter are drawn from John Busey and David Martin, *Regimental Strengths and Losses at Gettysburg* (Hightstown, NJ: Longstreet House, 1986).

8. John T. Hubbell and James W. Geary, eds., *Biographical Dictionary of the Union: Northern Leaders of the Civil War* (Westport, CT: Greenwood Press, 1995), 458, 557. Schimmelfennig was also German-born, had significant military training and experience in Germany, and, ironically, had once been Carl Schurz's superior there. Early in the war, he was primarily responsible for raising the German 74th Pennsylvania Infantry.

9. Edwin Coddington, *The Gettysburg Campaign: A Study in Command* (New York: Charles Scribner's Sons, 1968), 283.

10. Allan Nevins, ed., *A Diary of Battle: The Personal Journals of Colonel Charles S. Wainwright, 1861–1865* (Gettysburg, PA: Stan Clark Military Books, 1962), 235.

11. *OR,* vol. 27, pt. 1, 268.

12. Louise G. Young to Major Wm. J. Baker, February 10, 1864, in Francis B. Winston Papers, North Carolina Archives.

13. *OR,* vol. 27, pt. 1, 327.

14. Pfanz, *Gettysburg: The First Day,* 236.

15. Alfred Lee, "Reminiscences of the Gettysburg Battle," *Lippincott Magazine* 6 (1883): 56.

16. Pfanz, *Gettysburg: The First Day,* 159.

17. Louise W. Hitz, ed., *The Letters of Frederick C. Winkler* (privately printed, 1963), 71.

18. Nevins, *A Diary of Battle,* 236.

19. Rufus R. Dawes, *Service with the Sixth Wisconsin Volunteers,* (Madison, WI: State Historical Society of Wisconsin, 1962), 178.

20. Harry Pfanz, *Gettysburg: The Second Day* (Chapel Hill: University of North Carolina Press, 1987), 144.

21. Gary W. Gallagher, ed., *Fighting for the Confederacy: The Personal Recollections of General Edward Porter Alexander* (Chapel Hill: University of North Carolina Press, 1989), 239.

22. Josiah M. Favill, *Diary of a Young Officer* (Chicago: R. R. Donnelly and Sons, 1909), 346.

23. John P. Nicholson, ed., *Pennsylvania at Gettysburg: Ceremonies at the Dedication of the Monuments Erected by the Commonwealth of Pennsylvania* (Harrisburg, PA: William S. Ray, 1904), 1:624.

24. J. S. McNeilly, "Barksdale's Mississippi Brigade at Gettysburg: The Most Magnificent Charge of the War," *Publications of the Mississippi Historical Society* 1914 (Jackson, MS): 241.

25. Gallagher, *Fighting for the Confederacy,* 242.

26. Pfanz, *Gettysburg: The Second Day,* 424.

27. Colonel Andrew L. Harris to John Bachelder, March 14, 1881, in David L. Ladd and Audrey J. Ladd, eds., *The Bachelder Papers* (Dayton, OH: Morningside House, 1994), 2:746.

28. Acken, *Inside the Army of the Potomac,* 307.

29. John Gibbon, "The Council of War on the Second Day," in *Battles and Leaders of the Civil War,* vol. 3 (New York: Century Magazine, reprint 1982), 314.

30. *OR,* vol. 27, pt. 2, 568.

31. "The Gettysburg Lecture," *Baltimore Telegraph,* 1879, copy in Vertical File V7-MD2Bn, Gettysburg National Military Park Library.

32. John W. Plummer (1st Minnesota) to his brother, n.d., in Brake Collection, U.S. Army Military History Insitute.

33. John Reynolds, "The Nineteenth Massachusetts at Gettysburg, July 2-3-4," in Vertical File V6-MA19, Gettysburg National Military Park Library.

34. Gallagher, *Fighting for the Confederacy,* 259.

35. James Longstreet, "Lee in Pennsylvania," in *The Annals of War* (Dayton, OH: Morningside House, 1988), 431.

36. Kathleen Georg, *Nothing but Glory: Pickett's Division at Gettysburg* (Hightstown, NJ: Longstreet House, 1987), 64.

37. Chauncey Harris to Father, July 4, 1863, in George H. Washburn, *A Complete Military History and Record of the 108th Regiment N. Y. Vols. from 1862 to 1865* (Rochester, NY: E. R. Andrews,1894), 52; "The Diary of Captain George A. Bowen, 12th New Jersey Volunteers," *Valley Forge Journal* 11, no. 1 (June 1984): 133.

38. Charles D. Page, *Fourteenth Regiment, Connecticut Volunteer Infantry* (Meridan, CT: Horton Printing Co., 1906), 152.

39. Robert G. Scott, *Fallen Leaves: The Civil War Letters of Major Henry Livermore Abbott* (Kent, OH: Kent State University Press, 1991), 188.

40. Edmund Rice, "Rebelling Lee's Last Blow at Gettysburg," in *Battles and Leaders of the Civil War,* vol. 3, (New York Century Magazine, reprint 1982), 388–9.

41. Arthur J. L. Freemantle, *Three Months in the Southern States* (Lincoln, NE: University of Nebraska Press, 1991), 269.

42. Benjamin Thompson, "Recollections of War Times" (unpublished manuscript 1910, Gettysburg National Military Park Library), 46.

43. Acken, *Inside the Army of the Potomac,* 310.

44. Henrietta S. Jaquette, *South after Gettysburg: The Letters of Cornelia Hancock, 1863–1865* (Thomas Y. Crowell, 1956), 10.

45. Georg, *Nothing but Glory,* 149.

46. William Shimp to Annie, July 9, 1863, in Archives of the U.S. Army Military History Institute, Carlisle, PA.

CHAPTER 6

1. Steven M. Nolt, *Foreigners in Their Own Land: Pennsylvania Germans in the Early Republic* (University Park: Pennsylvania State University Press, 2002), 29.

2. Ibid., 3–4.

3. Harry W. Pfanz, *Gettysburg: The First Day* (Chapel Hill: University of North Carolina Press, 2001), 21.

4. Samuel P. Bates, *History of the Pennsylvania Volunteers, 1861–1865,* 5 vols. (Harrisburg: B. Singerly, State Printer, 1869–71), 4:1001–37.

5. A majority of the Pennsylvania Dutch were either Lutheran or German Reformed; a small minority belonged to the sect groups: Mennonites, Amish, Dunkers, Brethren, Schwenkfelders, and the like.

Woomer had been raised in the Pennsylvania Dutch culture, married into that culture, and, when he entered the army, brought all his cultural background with him. Woomer enlisted at Harrisburg, Pennsylvania, and he and his fellow troopers of the 17th were assigned to Colonel Thomas C. Devin's brigade of Brigadier General John Buford's division.

6. Richard M. Shue, *Morning at Willoughby Run: The Opening Battle of Gettysburg, July 1, 1863* (Gettysburg, PA: Thomas Publications, 1998), 30.

7. The discussion between Brigadier General John Buford and Major General John Reynolds probably took place at Reynolds's headquarters at the Moritz Tavern, which still stands today. It is the large brick building at the intersection of Bull Frog Road and Emmitsburg Road.

8. Pfanz, *Gettysburg*, 39.

9. Henry P. Moyer, *History of the Seventeenth Regiment Pennsylvania Cavalry* (Lebanon, PA: Sowers Printing Co., 1911), 49.

10. Ibid., 248.

11. Shue, *Morning at Willoughby Run*, 36–7.

12. Richard Rollins and David Shultz, *Guide to Pennsylvania Troops at Gettysburg* (Redondo Beach, CA: Rank and File Publications, 1998), 4–5.

13. Shue, *Morning at Willoughby Run*, 56.

14. John P. Nicholson, *Pennsylvania at Gettysburg* (Harrisburg: William Stanley Ray, 1914), 2:884; Moyer, *History of the Seventeenth Regiment Pennsylvania Cavalry*, 61–2, 284; Shue, *Morning at Willoughby Run*, 54.

15. Pfanz, *Gettysburg*, 59–60.

16. U.S. War Department, *The War of the Rebellion: A Compilation of the Official Records of the Union and Confederate Armies*, 127 vols. (Washington, DC: Government Printing Office, 1880–1901), vol. 27, pt. 1, 927 (hereafter cited as *OR*).

17. Ibid., 927–8; Bates, *History of Pennsylvania Volunteers*, 4:1004; Rollins and Schultz, *Guide to Pennsylvania Troops*, 5.

18. Richard E. Matthews, *The 149th Pennsylvania Volunteer Infantry Unit in the Civil War* (Jefferson, NC: McFarland, 1994), 13; *Myerstown, Pennsylvania, 1768–1968* (Myerstown Bicentennial Commission, 1968), 35, 164.

19. Richard A. Sauers, *Advance the Colors: Pennsylvania Civil War Battle Flags, vol. 2* (Lebanon, PA: Sowers Printing Co., 1991), 434, 436.

20. Edward E. Quinter, "Letters Home to Myerstaun 1863–1864," *Der Reggebogge: Journal of the Pennsylvania German Society* 27 (1993): 2–3.

21. Thomas Chamberlain, *History of the One Hundred and Fiftieth Pennsylvania Volunteers* (Philadelphia: F. McManus Jr., 1905), 117.

22. Shue, *Morning at Willoughby Run*, 90.

23. Pfanz, *Gettysburg*, 123–4.

24. Bates, *History of Pennsylvania Volunteers*, 4:677, 681–97.

25. John D. Vautier, *History of the Pennsylvania Volunteers in the War for the Union, 1861–1865* (Philadelphia: J. B. Lippincott, 1894), 13–4.

26. Sauers, *Advance the Colors*, 2:307.

27. Bates, *History of Pennsylvania Volunteers*, 4:375; Sauers, *Advance the Colors*, 2:357.

28. Edwin B. Coddington, *The Gettysburg Campaign: A Study in Command* (New York: Charles Scribner's Sons, 1968), 268; Chamberlain, *History of the 150th*, 118.

29. Michael A. Dreese, *The 151st Pennsylvania Volunteers at Gettysburg: Like Ripe Apples in a Storm* (Jefferson, NC: McFarland, 2000), 38.

30. Chamberlain, *History of the 150th*, 123–4.

31. Matthews, *149th Pennsylvania*, 86–9; Chamberlain, *History of the 150th*, 122–4.

32. Matthews, *149th Pennsylvania*, 89; Pfanz, *Gettysburg*, 361–5; Bassler's Accounts, 149th Pennsylvania Volunteers Infantry, Gettysburg National Military Park Library. (hereafter GNMPL).

33. Dreese, *151st Pennsylvania*, 41.

34. *OR*, vol. 27, pt. 2, 643.

35. Dreese, *151st Pennsylvania*, 46–7.

36. By order of Major General Abner Doubleday, men of Robinson's division, primarily Paul's brigade, built breastworks in front of the seminary. This action proved beneficial to the members of the First Corps that retreated from McPherson's Ridge to the seminary.

37. Dreese, *151st Pennsylvania,* 53.

38. Ibid., 52–9.

39. Charles P. Potts, "A First Defender in Rebel Prison Pens," *Publications of the Historical Society of Schuylkill County* 4 (1914): 343.

40. Dreese, *151st Pennsylvania,* 160.

41. Ibid., 48.

42. Ibid., 49.

43. Rollins and Shultz, *Guide to Pennsylvania Troops,* 8; Dreese, *151st Pennsylvania,* 160.

44. Vautier, *History of Pennsylvania Volunteers,* 233–7.

45. Vautier, *History of Pennsylvania Volunteers,* 1–5; Pfanz, *Gettysburg,* 166.

46. From that time forward, that part of the field would be known as Iverson's Grave or Tombs.

47. Pfanz, *Gettysburg,* 171–7; Vautier, *History of Pennsylvania Volunteers,* 135–6; "Personal Experiences of Samuel G. Bone," 88th Pennsyvlania Volunteer Infantry folder, 21–2, GNMPL.

48. Coddington, *Gettysburg Campaign,* 288–9.

49. Nicholson, *Pennsylvania at Gettysburg,* 1:560–1; Pfanz, *Gettysburg,* 188–9; excerpts from the *Lebanon Courier,* 107th Pennsylvania Volunteer Infantry folder, GNMPL.

50. Rollins and Shultz, *Guide to Pennsylvania Troops,* 16–7.

51. Bates, *History of Pennsylvania Volunteers,* 4:772–94.

52. Coddington, *Gettysburg Campaign,* 288; Pfanz, *Gettysburg,* 230–1.

53. The 153d was equipped with Austrian Lorenz rifles. These rifles had been purchased abroad and were initially .54 caliber but were rebored to take standard .58-caliber ammunition.

54. Ernest B. Furgurson, *Chancellorsville 1863: The Souls of the Brave* (New York: Alfred A. Knopf, 1992), 174; W. R. Kiefer, *History of the One Hundred and Fifty-third Regiment Pennsylvania Volunteer Infantry* (Easton, PA: Chemical Publishing Co., 1909), 29; Sauers, *Advance the Colors,* 2:456; Rollins and Schultz, *Guide to Pennsylvania Troops,* 18.

55. *OR,* vol. 27, pt. 1, 727; Kiefer, *History of the 153d,* 64; Pfanz, *Gettysburg,* 216.

56. Kiefer, *History of the 153d,* 180; Pfanz, *Gettysburg,* 216, 226, 231.

57. The men of the 153d were very proud of their knapsacks. When they first enlisted, they had stenciled on their knapsacks the following words, "In Lieu of Draft," meaning that they were not draftees but had enlisted of their own free will. Kiefer, *History of the 153d,* 13.

58. Ibid., 210.

59. Ibid., 210–1.

60. Ibid., 215–6.

CHAPTER 7

1. Louis Fischer, "The 11th Corps at Gettysburg," *National Tribune,* December 12, 1869.

2. This unknown soldier was overheard by newspaper correspondent Whitelaw Reid as he arrived on the field late on July 1. Quoted in Gary W. Gallagher, ed., *Two Witnesses at Gettysburg: The Personal Accounts of Whitelaw Reid and A. J. L. Fremantle* (New York: Brandywine Press, 1994), 21. For the sake of clarity, it should be noted that the term "Dutch" or "Dutchmen," when used by Anglo-American soldiers in reference to members of the Eleventh Corps, implied German-American soldiers, not those of Pennsylvania Dutch background.

3. See David G. Martin, *Gettysburg, July 1* (Conshocken, PA: Combined Books, 1995), particularly 330–5; A. Wilson Greene, "From Chancellorsville to Cemetery Hill: O. O. Howard and Eleventh Corps Leadership," in Gary W. Gallagher, ed., *The First Day at Gettysburg: Essays on Confederate and Union Leadership* (Kent, OH: Kent State University Press, 1992), 57–91; D. Scott Hartwig, "The 11th Army Corps on July 1, 1863—The Unlucky 11th," *Gettysburg Magazine* 2 (January 1990): 33–51. Also creditable for their treatment of the Eleventh Corps on the first day are Edwin B. Coddington's masterly tome *The Gettysburg Campaign: A Study in Command* (New York: Charles

Scribner's Sons, 1968) and Warren W. Hassler Jr.'s *Crisis at the Crossroads: The First Day at Gettysburg* (University of Alabama Press, 1970). The regiments listed here were the primary Pennsylvania German-American infantry regiments. See Christian B. Keller, "Germans in Civil War–Era Pennsylvania: Ethnic Identity and the Problem of Americanization" (Ph.D. diss., Pennsylvania State University, 2001), 126–7.

4. Von Mitzel's account of his regiment's role at Gettysburg can be found in Wilhelmina von Mitzel's widow's pension file, cert. #418227, app. #367705, National Archives and Records Administration, Washington, DC (hereafter NARA).

5. For an analysis of the reactions of both the Anglo-American and the Pennsylvania German press to the battle of Chancellorsville, see Keller, "Germans in Civil War–Era Pennsylvania," 199–215.

6. Von Mitzel pension file, NARA; Caroline von Hartung's widow's pension file, app. #761758, cert. #540466, NARA; Samuel P. Bates, *History of the Pennsylvania Volunteers, 1861–1865,* 5 vols. (Harrisburg: B. Singerly, State Printer, 1869–71), 4:896; Wilhelm Roth letters, Co. K, 74th PA, Civil War Misc. Collection, U.S. Army Military History Institute, Carlisle, PA (hereafter USAMHI); John P. Nicholson, *Pennsylvania at Gettysburg* (Harrisburg: William Stanley Ray, 1914), 1:434; Fischer, "The 11th Corps at Gettysburg." The 74th was inactive on July 2 but posted sharpshooters at the edge of town on July 3, led by Major Schleiter himself. During Pickett's Charge, these men had a brisk fight of their own near the Gettysburg hotel and succeeded in capturing some of the enemy. See "A Chambersburger First: Henry Monath Tells of an Experience at Gettysburg," clipping from a Chambersburg newspaper, 74th PA Infantry file, Gettysburg National Military Park Library, Gettysburg, PA (hereafter GNMPL). Von Mitzel had already been captured at Chancellorsville and just recently exchanged.

7. *Philadelphia Freie Presse,* July 8, 1863: "Wir gingen mit 15 Offizieren und 170 Musketen in das Gefecht und brachten nur 7 Offiziere und 64 Mann, die Kampffähig waren, zurück"; U.S. War Department, *The War of the Rebellion: A Compilation of the Official Records of the Union and Confederate Armies,* 127 vols. (Washington, DC: Government Printing Office, 1880–1901), 2:I, vol. 27, 745 (hereafter *OR*); Hartwig, "The 11th Army Corps," 45; "Casualties in 75th Regiment Pennsylvania at the Battle of Gettysburg, Penna, July 1 1863," in RG 94, Misc. Regimental Unbound Papers Filed with Muster Rolls, 74th and 75th PA, Box 4382, NARA; Wickesberg quoted in James S. Pula, *The Sigel Regiment: A History of the Twenty-sixth Wisconsin Volunteer Infantry, 1862–1865* (Campbell, CA: Savas Publishing Company, 1998), 166.

8. Whether the 82d Ohio began its retreat before the 75th Pennsylvania is still a matter of debate and was a hot issue between veterans of the two organizations.

9. *OR,* ser. I, vol. 27, 745; Carl Schurz, *The Reminiscences of Carl Schurz,* 3 vols. (Garden City, NY: Doubleday, 1917), 2:12; Hermann Nachtigall, *History of the 75th Regiment, Pennsylvania Volunteers* (North Riverside, IL: W. P. Printers, 1987; trans. of *Geschichte des 75sten Regiments, Pa. Vols.* by Heinz D. Schwinge and Karl E. Sandstrom), 21; Nicholson, *Pennsylvania at Gettysburg,* 1:438.

10. *Philadelphia Freie Presse,* July 8, 1863: "Nur anderhalb Stunden waren wir im Gefecht, und doch haben wir den Verlust von 116 todten und verwundeten Offizieren und Soldaten zu beklagen. . . . Dieser, unser Verlust, ist jedoch nicht unsern Generalen oder sonstigen Commandanten zuzuschreiben, sondern blos den "edlen" Soldaten der 2. Brigade der 1. Division, die es nach der Schlacht von Chancellorsville, Va., für eine Schande hielten, noch länger neben oder mit den Dutchmen zu kämpfen. Sie rissen gleich nach dem ersten Schutz aus, und wire bekamen das ganze Feuer der Feinde, wobei auch unser geliebter Oberst Franz Mahler seinen nur zu frühen Tod fand." Importantly, the list of dead and wounded published in this issue matches almost exactly (except for three discrepancies) the list of casualties from the regiment found in the National Archives. Thus, I am apt to accept the numbers found in these sources rather than in the *OR*. There were only three men missing out of the entire regiment.

11. Bates, *History of the Pennsylvania Volunteers,* 1:390–1; Hartwig, "The 11th Army Corps," 48; Martin, *Gettysburg, July 1,* 313–4; *Philadelphia Freie Presse,* July 20, 1863; C. W. McKay, "The Eleventh Corps: What Is the Real Animus of the Attacks upon that Organization?" *National Tribune,* March 16, 1893. McKay states that Coster's three regiments stood against fourteen Confederate ones during this part of the first day's battle, which has since become known as "the brickyard fight." When forced to withdraw, the 27th's "retreat was far from being a rout, as they stopped at the kiln and

fired a few parting shots." Martin makes the mistake of confusing the 27th and 73d Pennsylvania in his account, which limits the utility of his source.

12. "The Seventy-third Regiment Pennsylvania Volunteers at Gettysburg" (pamphlet issued at the unveiling of the regimental monument, September 11, 1889), 15–7, original at Historical Society of Pennsylvania, Philadelphia; Bates, *History of Pennsylvania Volunteers,* 4:866; Andrew Deimbach, "An Incident at Cemetery Hill," *Blue and Gray* 2 (July 1893): 21–2; Wilson, Asst. Surgeon, 73d Pennsylvania, diary entry, July 2, 1863. I would like to thank Robert Keeler for kindly providing a copy of his forthcoming edited version of the diary. Wilson was an American serving in the mainly German 73d. He offered his services as surgeon after most of the Pennsylvania regiments had already formed and admitted that he had no preference regarding his assignment. The 73d needed a surgeon, and that was where Wilson reported, remaining with the regiment until the three-year volunteers mustered out in 1864.

13. *OR,* ser. I., vol. 27, 685; Major John B. Kohler's battle report, in RG 94, Regimental Order and Letter Book, 98th PA, NARA; "Wheaton's Brigade," *National Tribune,* February 11, 1909; Jacob A. Schmid, 98th PA, personal military history c.1902, in Civil War Misc. Collection, USAMHI; Nicholson, *Pennsylvania at Gettysburg,* 1:529–30.

14. One of the results of the post-Chancellorsville criticism of the German regiments of the Eleventh Corps was a War Department inquiry about the ethnic composition of Howard's command. On May 21, 1863, Howard forwarded a report that indicated eleven of his twenty-seven regiments were "all German" and another four were "of mixed nationality" but with a strong German flavor. The 29th, 41st, 45th, 54th, 58th, and 68th New York; the 27th, 74th, and 75th Pennsylvania; the 26th Wisconsin; and the 82d Illinois were classified as exclusively German, numbering 4,206 men present for duty. The 119th New York, 107th Ohio, and 73d and 153d Pennsylvania were listed as "mixed," numbering 1,930 effectives. These figures indicate that the Eleventh Corps was slightly more than half German two weeks after Chancellorsville, lending some credence to the beliefs of soldiers from other corps about the German ethnicity of the Eleventh Corps as a whole. See *OR,* ser. I, vol. 25, 660–1.

15. Colonel George von Amsberg assumed command of the First Brigade, Third Division, of the Eleventh Corps after Brigadier General Alexander Schimmelfennig became temporary commander of the Third Division earlier in the afternoon. Schimmelfennig's division was almost certainly the one most First Corps soldiers referred to in their comments. Von Amsberg's brigade was the one closest to Robinson's division, and its retreat may have indeed opened up Robinson's flank to an enfilading fire from Doles's Confederates. As A. Wilson Greene states, however, "it is difficult to determine whether von Amsberg's brigade or the right flank of the First Corps gave way first" ("From Chancellorsville to Cemetery Hill," 82). Schimmelfennig's division, however, contained seven German regiments (out of ten total), including the 74th and 75th Pennsylvania. Clearly, it was a predominantly German division.

16. James Beale, "Gettysburg: A Review of Gen. Howard's Account of the Battle," *National Tribune,* January 1, 1885; Benjamin F. Cook, *History of the Twelfth Mass. Vols. (Webster Reg't.)* (Boston: Twelfth Regiment Association, 1882), 105–6.

17. Charles E. Davis, *Three Years in the Army: The Story of the Thirteenth Massachusetts Volunteers from July 16, 1861, to August 1, 1864* (Boston: Estes and Larist, 1894), 229; Abner R. Small, *The Sixteenth Maine in the War of the Rebellion, 1861–1865* (Portland, ME: B. Thurston and Company, 1886), 116–7, 132; John D. Vautier, *History of the 88th Pennsylvania Volunteers in the War of the Union, 1861–1865* (Philadelphia: J. B. Lippincott, 1894), 126, 143. To his credit, Vautier recognized that the Eleventh Corps had been thrown into a tactically desperate situation by its commanders and that a good portion of the blame for the defeat on the first day rested with them.

18. William J. K. Beaudot and Lance J. Herdegen, *An Irishman in the Iron Brigade: The Civil War Memoirs of James P. Sullivan, Sergeant, Company K, 6th Wisconsin Volunteers* (New York: Fordham University Press, 1993), 98; unknown soldier's commentary quoted in Joseph T. Glatthaar, "The Common Soldier's Gettysburg Campaign," in Gabor S. Boritt, ed., *The Gettysburg Nobody Knows* (New York: Oxford University Press, 1997), 16.

19. The best account of the July 2 night attack on Cemetery Hill is in Harry W. Pfanz, *Gettysburg: Culp's Hill and Cemetery Hill* (Chapel Hill: University of North Carolina Press, 1993), chaps. 14 and 15.

20. Allan Nevins, ed., *A Diary of Battle: The Personal Journals of Colonel Charles S. Wainwright, 1861–1865* (New York: Harcourt, Brace and World, 1962), 245. The "Stewart" mentioned here was Lieutenant James Stewart, who commanded Battery B of the 4th U.S. Artillery under Wainwright's command.

21. Oscar D. Ladley to "Dear mother and Sisters," July 16, 1863, and "Mother C. Ladley" to Oscar D. Ladley, July 27, 1863, reprinted in Carl M. Becker and Ritchie Thomas, eds., *Hearth and Knapsack: The Ladley Letters: 1857–1880* (Athens: Ohio University Press, 1988), 146–7, 151–2. Schimmelfennig actually commanded the First Division of the Eleventh Corps for only three days, July 14–17, 1863.

22. Francis Barlow to Robert Treat Paine, August 12, 1863, quoted in Coddington, *Gettysburg Campaign,* 704. The men of the 153d Pennsylvania (a regiment recruited mainly from Northampton County's Pennsylvania Dutch residents and attached to von Gilsa's brigade under Barlow's command) keenly felt the division commander's prejudice against them, claiming that his "trifling punctiliousness" had caused widespread depression in the days before the battle. "Everyone was 'down' on the service" as a result of the "drudgery" imposed by "Dogberry" Barlow on the regiment, two soldiers asserted. See William Simmers and Paul Bachschmid, *The Volunteer's Manual, or Ten Months with the 153d Penn'a Volunteers* (Easton, PA: D. H. Neiman, 1863), 26–7.

23. Arthur T. Lee to Colonel J. B. Bachelder, February 16, 1888, reprinted in David L. Ladd and Audrey J. Ladd, eds., *The Bachelder Papers: Gettysburg in Their Own Words,* 3 vols. (Dayton, OH: Morningside House, 1995), 3:1526; Adin B. Underwood, *The Three Years' Service of the Thirty-third Mass. Infantry Regiment, 1862–1865* (Boston: A. Williams, 1881), 118.

24. Vautier, *History of the 88th Pennsylvania Volunteers,* 149, 155. Herb S. Crumb, *The Eleventh Corps Artillery at Gettysburg: The Papers of Major Thomas Ward Osborn, Chief of Artillery* (Hamilton, NY: Edmonston Publishing, 1991), is even more convinced that Dilger's performance, along with that of the other Eleventh Corps batteries, was critical in preserving the integrity of the Union corps on the first day: "The rearguard action of the four Eleventh Corps batteries . . . probably prevented the mass surrender of Schurz's two divisions" (xv).

25. For Lee's and Hill's official reports, see *OR,* ser. I, vol. 27, 704; ser. II, 317, 607; Coddington, *Gettysburg Campaign,* 295–6. In contradiction to Lee's and Hill's accounts, Private G. W. Nichols of the 61st Georgia wrote of the valor of Barlow's division of the Eleventh Corps on the first day: "We advanced with our accustomed yell, but they stood firm until we got near them. They then began to retreat in fine order, shooting at us as they retreated. They were harder to drive than we had ever known them before. . . . Their officers were cheering their men and behaving like heroes and commanders of the 'first water.'" See G. W. Nichols, *A Soldier's Story of His Regiment and Incidentally of the Lawton-Gordon-Evans Brigade, Army of Northern Virginia* (1898; reprint, Kennesaw, GA: Continental Book Company, 1961), 116. The First and Eleventh Corps retreated through Gettysburg at about the same time, but only the Eleventh Corps has traditionally received the odium for the character of that retreat. Quoting Chaplain William H. Locke of his regiment, Vautier of the 88th Pennsylvania wrote: "The Lutheran Church was crowded with our wounded. We were going in and out among these, when the broken and flying battalions of the 11th Corps came streaming in from the right. It was a sight never to be forgotten. Crowding through the streets and up the alleys and over fences, in utter ignorance of whither they were going, every moment increased their confusion and dismay. . . . But that retreat was not all confusion. The same noble corps that had maintained its ground on the left [First Corps] fell back in solid phalanx. Shoulder to shoulder they marched, rank after rank halting to fire upon the advancing foe, and then closing up again with daring coolness" (Vautier, *History of the 88th Pennsylvania Volunteers,* 148–9). The dichotomy between the two corps' retreats expressed here is quite clear, though most modern historians agree that the soldiers of the two corps generally retreated through the town simltaneously, avoiding a feeling of panic. Coddington states that "the truth is that the Yankees did not suddenly become panic-stricken"; some were even "'talking and joking'" as they worked their way through the streets of the town. The large number of Union prisoners collected by the Confederates were mainly skulkers and parts of regiments that accidentally got lost in the streets of the town, not panic-stricken troops crazed by fear (Coddington, *Gettysburg Campaign,* 295).

26. For accounts of Schimmelfennig's escapade, see Alfred C. Raphelson, "Alexander Schimmelfennig: A German-American Campaigner in the Civil War," *Pennsylvania Magazine of History and Biography*

87, no. 2 (April 1963): 176–7; "Story of a Brigadier General," *Gettysburg Compiler,* August 9, 1905, copy in GNMPL; Martin, *Gettysburg, July 1,* 330–1; Schurz, *Reminiscences,* 3:11–2.

27. Frank A. Haskell, *The Battle of Gettysburg* (Boston: Massachusetts Commandery, Military Order of the Loyal Legion, 1908), 9–10.

28. Abner Doubleday, *Chancellorsville and Gettysburg* (New York: Scribners, 1882; reprint, New York: DeCapoPress, 1994), 150; Bruce Catton, *Never Call Retreat,* Centennial History of the Civil War, vol. 3 (Garden City, NY: Doubleday, 1965), 182; James M. McPherson, *Battle Cry of Freedom* (New York: Oxford University Press, 1988), 654. Interestingly, another modern historian who bought into the erroneous perceptions was Mark M. Boatner III, author of the famous *Civil War Dictionary.* Under the heading "Gettysburg," Boatner states that "Reynold's I Corps and Howard's XI ('German') Corps rushed up" on the first day to relieve Buford's dismounted cavalry troopers. See Boatner, *The Civil War Dictionary,* rev. ed. (New York: Vintage Books, 1991), 334. By pointing out the stereotype of the cowardly Dutchmen at Gettysburg, I am not attempting to reduce the significance of the sacrifices of the First Corps on the first day. Indeed, Reynolds's veterans fought a bloodier, tougher, and longer fight than did their comrades in the Eleventh Corps. That does not, however, excuse the persistence of the erroneous images of the German-Americans and the Eleventh Corps as a whole.

29. David G. Martin, *Carl Bornemann's Regiment: The Forty-first New York Infantry (DeKalb Regt.) in the Civil War* (Hightstown, NJ: Longstreet House, 1987), 170–2; Raphelson, "Alexander Schimmelfennig," 177. Martin insinuates that von Gilsa may have either asked to leave or been ordered away as a result of the accusations against the Eleventh Corps at Gettysburg.

30. *OR,* ser. I, vol. 27, pt. 3, 778–9.

31. Ibid., pt. 1, 105; James S. Pula, *For Liberty and Justice: The Life of Vladimir Krzyzanowski* (Chicago, IL: The Polish-American Charitable Foundation, 1978), 119–21. Why the War Department rejected Meade's proposal is unknown, but it may have had something to do with the significant political clout of the Northern German-American community.

32. Pula, *For Liberty and Justice,* 122–3; Jonathan M. Berkey, "The Foundations of Transformation? The Experiences of Hooker's Command during the Chattanooga Campaign" (master's thesis, Pennsylvania State University, 1994), 6–7.

33. *Baltimore American,* July 2, 1863.

34. *Washington Daily National Intelligencer,* July 3, 1863; *Pittsburgh Post,* July 4, 1863.

35. *Chicago Tribune,* July 4, 1863; *Weekly Pittsburgh Gazette,* July 4, 1863.

36. *Cincinnati Daily Gazette,* July 8, 1863; *New York Evening Post,* July 6, 1863. For total losses suffered by the Eleventh Corps, including captured (reported at 1,510), see *OR,* ser. I, vol. 27, 183.

37. *Philadelphia Inquirer,* July 3, 1863; *Cleveland Plain Dealer,* July 3, 1863; *New York Times,* July 4, 1863.

38. *New York Herald,* July 3, 1863. Vosberg inaccurately implied that the 74th Pennsylvania was part of Krzyzanowski's brigade; in fact, the 74th was part of von Amsberg's brigade.

39. Ibid. The *Philadelphia Public Ledger* of July 4 reprinted portions of Vosberg's account. According to John W. Busey and David G. Martin, *Regimental Strengths and Losses at Gettysburg* (Hightstown, NJ: Longstreet House, 1994), 254, the 74th lost 110 of 333 men present for duty throughout the three-day battle. This figure is deceptive when examining the losses of the regiment on the first day, however. According to Lieutenant Colonel Alexander von Mitzel, approximately half of the regiment's men were detailed to various guard duties before the rest of the regiment was sent into battle. Hence, the regiment numbered only 134 men when it took up its position in von Amsberg's line on July 1, and Vosberg's numbers do not appear so disproportionate. See von Mitzel's account of the battle in Wilhelmina von Mitzel's pension file, NARA, as well as Bates, *History of the Pennsylvania Volunteers,* 4:896, and Nicholson, *Pennsylvania at Gettysburg,* 1:434.

40. *Philadelphia Freie Presse,* July 4, 1863; *Pittsburgh Freiheitsfreund und Courier,* July 7, 1863. Notice the editor's use of the possessive "our" when prefacing his sentence about the losses of the Eleventh Corps. The immigrant Germans of the North—at least those in Philadelphia—still perceived the Eleventh Corps as "their" corps, filled with "their" soldiers.

41. Ibid.

42. *Pittsburgher Demokrat,* July 6 and 7, 1863; *Allentown Unabhängige Republikaner,* July 13, 1863.

43. *Pittsburgh Freiheitsfreund und Courier,* July 12 and 17, 1863. Although he was not specifically named, the comments of one non-German general in particular were a close match to those of Francis Barlow.

44. See the *Philadelphia Freie Presse,* July 9, 15, 21, and 25, 1863; *Pittsburgher Demokrat,* July 14–16, 19, and 20, 1863; *Pittsburgh Freiheitsfreund und Courier,* July 12, 1863. Earlier in the war, casualties from non-German regiments were frequently printed alongside those of the German regiments. After Gettysburg, this practice mysteriously declined. The German-American papers did not, however, completely neglect other war news in the weeks after Gettysburg. The New York City draft riots received special attention in several papers. The *Freie Presse* severely criticized the Irish involved in the New York City riots, relieved that the New York Germans "had the good sense. . . not to be misled by the crazy band of fools, firebrands, and murderers" (July 15). It is conceivable that the absence of public nativism against the Germans after Gettysburg may have been due in part to the riots, for which the Irish were widely blamed. With the attention of the Anglo-American press thus riveted on another ethnic group, the German-Americans may have escaped the scrutiny they normally received. For an excellent study of the riots, see Iver Bernstein, *The New York City Draft Riots: Their Significance for American Society and Politics in the Age of the Civil War* (New York: Oxford University Press, 1990).
45. *Philadelphia Freie Presse,* July 9, 1863; *Pittsburgh Freiheitsfreund und Courier,* July 12, 1863.

CHAPTER 8

1. Harry W. Pfanz, *Gettysburg: The First Day* (Chapel Hill: University of North Carolina Press, 2000), 6.
2. U.S. War Department, *The War of the Rebellion: A Compilation of the Official Records of the Union and Confederate Armies,* 127 vols. (Washington, DC: Government Printing Office, 1880–1901), ser. I, vol. 27, pt. 1, 252, 290, 322, 730 (hereafter *OR;* unless otherwise stated, all references are to series I); Pfanz, *Gettysburg: The First Day,* 332–3.
3. The 99th had portions of Companies B and D from Lancaster and Schuylkill Counties. Those numbers were so small that Bates did not include them in his original count. See Samuel P. Bates's history of the 99th in *History of the Pennsylvania Volunteers, 1861–1865,* 5 vols. (Harrisburg: B. Singerly, State Printer, 1869–71), vol. 3; Richard A. Sauers, *Advance the Colors: Pennsylvania Civil War Battle Flags* (Lebanon, PA: Sowers, 1991), 2:333.
4. Sauers, *Advance the Colors,* 2:333.
5. Harry F. Pfanz, *Gettysburg: The Second Day* (Chapel Hill: University of North Carolina Press, 1987), 268.
6. J. W. Muffly, *The History of the 148th Pennsylvania Volunteers* (Des Moines, IA: Kenyon Printing and Mfg. Co., 1904), 494.
7. Bates, *History of Pennsylvania Volunteers,* 4:583–6.
8. Muffly, *History of the 148th,* 497–8.
9. Sauers, *Advance the Colors,* 2:443.
10. Muffly, *History of the 148th,* 455
11. Bates, *History of the Pennsylvania Volunteers,* 4:578.
12. At the battle of Gettysburg, Colonel Edward E. Cross commanded the First Brigade, First Division, Second Corps, Army of the Potomac.
13. Muffly, *History of the 148th,* 716.
14. Ibid., 461.
15. Ibid., 603.
16. A. M. Gambone, *The Life of General Samuel K. Zook: Another Forgotten Union Hero* (Baltimore: Butter Nut and Blue, 1996), 46–53.
17. Ibid., 11–24.
18. Pfanz, *Gettysburg: The Second Day,* 284–6.
19. Richard Rollins and David Schultz, *Guide to Pennsylvania Troops at Gettysburg* (Redondo Beach, CA: Rank and File Publications, 1998), 30.
20. At the outbreak of the Civil War in April 1861, Governor Andrew Curtin put out a call for volunteers, and in the early rush of recruitment, there were more volunteers than needed. Also, Secretary of War Simon Cameron, a political foe of Governor Curtin, refused to take them into Federal service. Curtin was reluctant to let these volunteers go, so he formed the Pennsylvania Reserves. Thir-

teen infantry regiments of Pennsylvania volunteers were kept on duty at state expense. They were initially referred to as the 1st through the 13th Pennsylvania Reserves, but they later became the 30th through 42nd Pennsylvania Volunteers. The thirteen regiments were grouped into three brigades to constitute a division of Pennsylvania Reserves. Mark M. Boatner, *The Civil War Dictionary* (New York: David McKay, 1959), 634–5.

21. Bates, *History of the Pennsylvania Volunteers,* 2:545–75.
22. H. N. Minnigh, *History of Company K 1st Inf Penn'a Reserves* (Gettysburg: Thomas Publications, 1998), 49–50.
23. Pfanz, *Gettysburg: The Second Day,* 391–5.
24. Minnigh, *History of Company K,* 28.
25. Pfanz, *Gettysburg: The Second Day,* 397–8; Minnigh, *History of Company K,* 61; Rollins and Schultz, *Guide to Pennsylvania Troops,* 37.
26. Penrose G. Mark, *Red, White, and Blue Badge: A History of the 93d Regiment Pennsylvania Volunteers* (Harrisburg: Aughinbaugh Press, 1911), 219; Rollins and Schulz, *Guide to Pennsylvania Troops,* 42.
27. Minnigh, *History of Company K,* 52.
28. W. R. Kiefer, *History of the One Hundred and Fifty-third Regiment Pennsylvania Volunteer Infantry* (Easton, PA: Chemical Publishing Co., 1909), 86–7.
29. Bates, *History of Pennsylvania Volunteers,* vol. 3.
30. *OR,* vol. 27, pt. 1, 803.
31. Rollins and Schultz, *Guide to Pennsylvania Troops,* 83.
32. M. S. Schroyer, "Company G History" *Snyder County Historical Society* 2, no. 2 (1939): 338.
33. Ibid., 344.
34. Powwowing, or *brauche,* in the Pennsylvania Dutch dialect, is a magicoreligious practice, grounded in Christian belief, whose chief purpose is the healing of physical ailments in humans and animals. However, it has other aims as well, such as conferring protection from physical or spiritual harm, bringing good luck, and revealing hidden information. It may involve the use of incantations (in many cases, mouthed or whispered), gestures, and material components. In the past, many powwowers used "charm books," published in German and sometimes English, which consisted of incantations and recipes to accomplish their purpose. Perhaps the best known of these is John George Hohman's *Der lang verborgene Schatz und Haus Freund* (1971), published originally in Reading in 1820 and known popularly as *The Long Lost Friend* (more correctly, *The Long Hidden Friend*). Other well-known manuals include *Albertus Magnus Egyptian Secrets* and the *Sixth and Seventh Books of Moses.* The latter, however, has often been shunned as a "hex book," since it contains formulas for conjuring demons" David W. Kriebel, "Powwowing: A Persistent Healing Tradition," *Pennsylvania German Review* (fall 2001): 14.
35. Schroyer, "Company G History," 346.
36. Ibid., 357–8.
37. Ibid., 359–60.
38. *OR,* vol. 27, pt. 1, 845–6; Rollins and Schulz, *Guide to Pennsylvania Troops,* 74–5, 87.
39. Sauers, *Advance the Colors,* 1:257.
40. Rollins and Schultz, *Guide to Pennsylvania Troops,* 96.
41. Michael A. Dreese, *The 151st Pennsylvania Volunteers at Gettysburg: Like Ripe Apples in the Storm* (Jefferson, NC: McFarland, 2000), 78; Rollins and Schulz, *Guide to Pennsylvania Troops,* 88–9.
42. Rollins and Schultz, *Guide to Pennsylvania Troops,* 95.
43. *OR,* vol. 27, pt. 1, 432; Rollins and Schultz, *Guide to Pennsylvania Troops,* 89–90.
44. Schroyer, "Company G History," 361.

EPILOGUE

1. *Philadelphia Freie Presse,* October 13, 1863; *Allentown Unabhängige Republikaner,* October 13, 1863; *Reading Banner von Berks,* December 1, 1865; *Pittsburgh Abend-Zeitung,* November 6, 1864; William A. Helffrich, *Lebensbild aus dem Pennsylvanisch-Deutschen Predigerstand: Oder Wahrheit in Licht und Schatten,* ed. N. W. A. Helffrich and W. U. Helffrich (Allentown, PA, 1906), 301; B. R. Ulrich to

"Dear Brother," September 29, 1864, original in possession of Mr. Steven Zerbe, Cherry Hill, NJ. Mark A. Hornberger, "Germans in Pennsylvania 1800, 1850, and 1860: A Spatial Perspective," *Yearbook of German-American Studies* 24 (1989): 97–104. I would like to thank Zerbe for his kindness in sharing his family's Civil War letters with me. A comparison of voting statistics for the 1864 presidential election and Hornberger's map showing the concentrations of German speakers in 1850 Pennsylvania is intriguing. In only four of the predominantly "German" counties—Dauphin, Franklin, Lancaster, and Lebanon—did the Republicans win the majority of votes. The defeats in these counties (particularly Lancaster and Franklin) could be attributed to a stronger concentration of Republican-voting pacifist sectarians in the townships and to a higher percentage of Anglo-Americans versus Pennsylvania Dutch. In some of the strongest Dutch counties, such as Berks, Lehigh, and Northampton, Lincoln was outvoted almost two to one. See the Reading *Banner von Berks,* December 1, 1865, for statewide election results.

2. *Reading Banner von Berks,* December 1, 1865.
3. J. Hoke, August 10, 1864, letter to the *Religious Telescope* (German Baptist Brethren newspaper), reprinted in Rev. B. S. Schneck, *The Burning of Chambersburg, Pennsylvania, by Rev. B. S. Schneck, D.D., an Eyewitness and a Sufferer, with Corroborative Statements from Rev. J. Clark, Hon. A. K. McClure, J. Hoke, Esq., et al.,* 4th ed. (Philadelphia: Lindsay and Blakiston, 1865), 13, 46–8. Schneck was a pastor in a Chambersburg German Reformed church. Hoke wrote extensively about his experiences during the war, and his other accounts of the burning of the town are riveting. See *The Great Invasion of 1863; or General Lee in Pennsylvania . . . with an Appendix Containing an Account of the Burning of Chambersburg, Pennsylvania* (reprint; Dayton, OH, 1913), and *Historical Reminiscences of the War; or Incidents which Transpired in and about Chambersburg during the War of the Rebellion* (Chambersburg, PA, 1884).
4. Article by John K. Shryock in the *Philadelphia Lutheran and Missionary,* August 11, 1864.
5. Rachel Cormany diary entry, August 6, 1864, in James C. Mohr, ed., *The Cormany Diaries: A Northern Family in the Civil War* (Pittsburgh: University of Pittsburgh Press, 1982), 446; Schneck, *Burning of Chambersburg,* 74–5; *German-Reformed Messenger,* September 7, 1864. The newspaper relocated to Philadelphia immediately after the fire and was publishing again in just over a month.
6. Samuel P. Bates, *History of the Pennsylvania Volunteers, 1861–1865,* 5 vols. (1869–71; reprint, Wilmington, NC: Broadfoot Publishing Company, 1993), 2:392–3, 867–8, 920–1; Hermann Nachtigall, *History of the 75th Regiment, PA. Vols.,* 18–20.
7. Bates, *History of Pennsylvania Volunteers,* 4:897, 5:466–9.
8. Don Yoder, "The Reformed Church and Pennsylvania German Identity," *Yearbook of German-American Studies* 18 (1983): 63–82.
9. Kathleen Neils Conzen, "German-Americans and the Invention of Ethnicity," in Frank Trommler and Joseph McVeigh, eds., *America and the Germans: An Assessment of a Three-Hundred Year History,* 2 vols. (Philadelphia: University of Pennsylvania Press, 1985), 1:139–41.
10. Stephen D. Engle, "A Raised Consciousness: Franz Sigel and German Ethnic Identity in the Civil War," *Yearbook of German-American Studies* 34 (1999): 1–17.
11. For analytical treatments of this movement, see Yoder, "The Reformed Church and Pennsylvania German Identity;" William W. Donner, "Abraham Reeser Horne: To the Manor Born," *Der Reggeboge* 33, nos. 1 and 2 (1999): 3–17, and "'We Are What We Make of Ourselves': Abraham Reeser Horne and the Education of Pennsylvania Germans," *Pennsylvania Magazine of History and Biography* 124, no. 4 (October 2000): 522–46.

INDEX